By the author of
A History of Valois Burgundy
in four volumes:

1. *Philip the Bold.*
The Formation of the Burgundian State,
1962

2. *John the Fearless.*
The Growth of Burgundian Power,
1966

3. *Philip the Good.*
The Apogee of Burgundy,
1970

4. *Charles the Bold.*
The Last Valois Duke of Burgundy,
1973

Richard Vaughan

Valois Burgundy

Archon Books

Copyright © Richard Vaughan 1975

First published 1975 by
Allen Lane, Penguin Books Ltd.
London SW1, England
and in the United States of America
as an ARCHON BOOK, an imprint of
The Shoe String Press, Inc.,
Hamden, Connecticut 06514

LIBRARY OF CONGRESS CATALOGING IN PUBLICATION DATA

Vaughan, Richard, 1927–
    Valois Burgundy.

    Bibliography: p.
    Includes index.
    1.   Burgundy – History.   I. Title.
DC611.B78V357   1975   944'.4   74–34019
ISBN 0–208–01511–6

Printed in Great Britain

Contents

Maps and Genealogical Tables

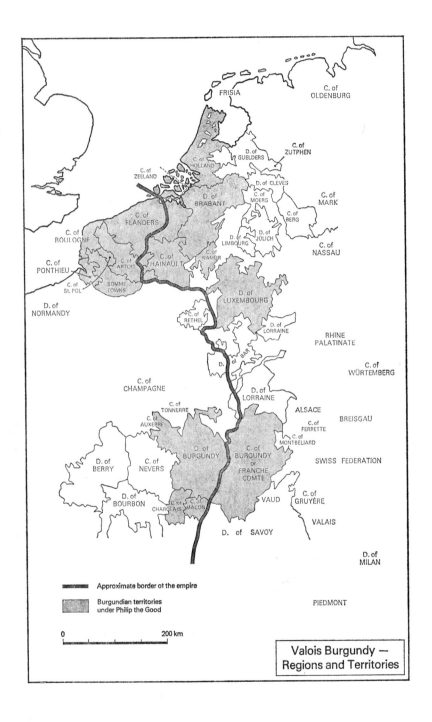

FRISIA

C. of
OLDENBURG

D. of
GUELDERS

C. of
ZUTPHEN

C. of
HOLLAND

C. of
ZEELAND

D. of CLEVES

C. of
MOERS

C. of
MARK

D. of
BRABANT

C. of
FLANDERS

C. of
BERG

C. of
BOULOGNE

D. of
LIMBOURG

D. of
JÜLICH

C. of
NASSAU

C. of
PONTHIEU

C. of
ARTOIS

C. of
HAINAULT

C. of
NAMUR

C. of
St. POL

SOMME
TOWNS

D. of
LUXEMBOURG

D. of
NORMANDY

C. of
RETHEL

D. of
LORRAINE

RHINE
PALATINATE

D. of BAR

C. of
WÜRTEMBERG

C. of
CHAMPAGNE

D. of
LORRAINE

C. of
TONNERRE

ALSACE

BREISGAU

C. of
AUXERRE

C. of
FERRETTE

C. of
MONTBÉLIARD

D. of
BURGUNDY

C. of
BURGUNDY
or
FRANCHE
COMTÉ

SWISS FEDERATION

D. of
BERRY

C. of
NEVERS

VAUD

C. of
GRUYÈRE

D. of
BOURBON

C. of
CHAROLAIS

C. of
MACON

VALAIS

D. of SAVOY

D. of
MILAN

Approximate border of the empire

Burgundian territories
under Philip the Good

PIEDMONT

0   200 km

Valois Burgundy —
Regions and Territories

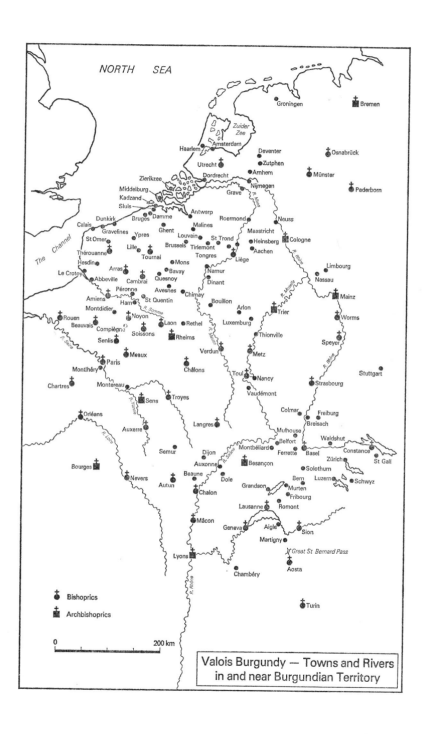

NORTH SEA

The Channel

Groningen · Bremen ✠

Zuider Zee

Amsterdam
Haarlem ✠
Utrecht ✠
Deventer
Zutphen · Osnabrück ✠
Arnhem
Dordrecht ✠ Münster ✠
Zierikzee Nijmegen Paderborn ✠
Middelburg Grave
Kadzand
Sluis
Antwerp
Calais Dunkirk Bruges · Damme Roermond · Neuss ✠
Gravelines · Malines Maastricht
Ypres Ghent St Trond Cologne ✠
St Omer Louvain Heinsberg
Lille Brussels Tirlemont Aachen
Thérouanne Tournai Tongres
Hesdin Mons Liège Limbourg
Arras Bavay · Namur Nassau
Le Crotoy Cambrai Quesnoy Dinant
Abbeville Péronne Avesnes Bouillon Mainz ✠
Amiens Ham · St Quentin Chimay Arlon Worms
Montdidier Trier ✠
Rouen Noyon Laon Rethel Luxemburg
Beauvais Compiègne Soissons Thionville Speyer
Senlis Rheims ✠ Verdun
Meaux Metz Stuttgart
Paris Châlons Nancy Strasbourg ✠
Montlhéry Toul Vaudémont
Chartres Montereau Troyes Colmar Freiburg
Sens ✠ Breisach
Orléans Auxerre Langres Mulhouse Waldshut
Semur Dijon Belfort Basel Constance
Bourges ✠ Montbéliard Zürich St Gall
Nevers Auxonne Ferrette
Autun Beaune Besançon Solothurn
Chalon Dole Luzern Schwyz
Mâcon Grandson Bern
Geneva Murten
Lausanne Fribourg
Lyons ✠ Aigle Romont
Martigny Sion
Chambéry Great St Bernard Pass
Aosta
Turin ✠

R. Meuse · R. Rhine · R. Moselle · R. Somme · R. Seine · R. Meuse · R. Yonne · R. Loire · R. Saône · R. Rhône · R. Rhine

✠ Bishoprics

✠ Archbishoprics

0   200 km

Valois Burgundy — Towns and Rivers
in and near Burgundian Territory

Preface

My four-volume *History of Valois Burgundy* was not conceived as a series of biographies but rather as a descriptive history of the polity which, for want of a better name, one has to call 'the Burgundian state'. It was divided into four volumes coinciding with the four ducal reigns of Philip the Bold, John the Fearless, Philip the Good and Charles the Bold. These four dukes are called Valois because they were descended from the second king of France of the house of Valois, John the Good (1350–64). Their predecessors in the duchy of Burgundy, like the earlier kings of France, belonged to the house of Capet, and are known as the Capetian dukes of Burgundy. This division of the larger work into four volumes, one for each duke, was partly for convenience, but also because of the differing personalities, interests, attitudes and, less often, policies, of the four dukes. Each, in fact, made his distinctive mark on history. But this division of the work made it difficult to draw sufficient attention to the long-term developments and also led to the repetition of discussion of certain topics at different periods. The aim of this single-volume history of Valois Burgundy is to gather some of the material and all the more important arguments and conclusions of the larger work into a form convenient for the general reader and the student, neither of whom may wish to work through the separate four volumes, still less purchase them. Emphasis, throughout the larger work, was on the duke, the court, the central administration and whatever could be defined as general and Burgundian, rather than on what was particular and regional. This emphasis has been retained, even strengthened, here: we set out to describe a political organization, not to write the history of territories, regions, areas.

The scope of this book includes an explanation of how the so-called Burgundian state came into being, an examination of its nature and identity, and a description of how it was ruled in terms of the personalities of the dukes and their officials, and in terms of institutions. An attempt is made to analyse the role and efficacy of Burgundian military power and to examine Burgundian cultural developments. Something is said, too, about the sources of information available for Burgundian history, which is based on my inaugural lecture on this subject. Finally, the reasons for the collapse of Burgundian power in 1477 are considered. At the end, a brief and very selective list seeks to inform the reader, subject by subject in so far as this is possible, of some of the most important books and articles on the Valois dukes of Burgundy. This is followed by a supplementary bibliography, arranged duke by duke, listing those books and papers which have appeared since the publication of the individual volumes of the larger history.

From the friends of my student days in Cambridge twenty-five years ago onwards to my present colleagues and students, very many people have helped, directly or indirectly, in the writing of this book and the larger work on which it is based. It is impossible to thank them all by name, but I take this opportunity of thanking each and every one of them from my heart. As to the present work, I have to thank in particular my colleague Mr Peter Heath, who has been kind enough to read through the typescript, thereby helping me to remove many errors and imperfections; Professor Cedric Pickford for help with Chapter 8; and Dr Leslie Price.

Richard Vaughan
February 1974

CHAPTER ONE

The European Context

The history of Valois Burgundy was played out between 1360 and 1480; more exactly, between the grant of the duchy of Burgundy to Philip the Bold in 1363 and the death of his great-grandson Charles the Bold in the battle of Nancy on 5 January 1477. This century-long time-span of the four great dukes began in the world of the Black Death and the Peasants' Revolt, of Sir John Froissart and heroes of the Hundred Years War like the Black Prince and Bertrand du Guesclin, and of Petrarch and the Avignon papacy. It ended in a very different world: the era of printing and of new continents, of Botticelli, Leonardo da Vinci and the Italian Renaissance, of powerful new monarchies in England, France and Spain. But the proudly self-conscious *literati* of Renaissance Italy went too far in their vision of change. Excusably, they exaggerated the novelty of their own times and the modernity of their own attitudes; inexcusably, historians have retained their myth of a middle ages giving way to modern times in the very period when the political and cultural life of much of western Europe was dictated or at least influenced by the Valois dukes of Burgundy. Avoiding such farfetched and unrealistic or even misleading concepts, it is still useful and legitimate to try to pinpoint the dynamic elements in the Europe of those days. For changes there undoubtedly were, uneven and unpredictable but often of sufficient importance to make the political, social and cultural context of Valois Burgundy seem thoroughly unstable.

The history of Burgundy itself, and above all the behaviour and ambitions of the last Valois duke, Charles the Bold, exemplifies very well the portentous and nearly ubiquitous increase in the authority of central governments that took place during the fifteenth century. The acquisition of more power by princes, the emergence of larger polities, the growing arbitrariness of governments; these changes, which took place at the expense of the nobles, of local autonomies, of local privilege, were often connected with the rise to power of a single remark-

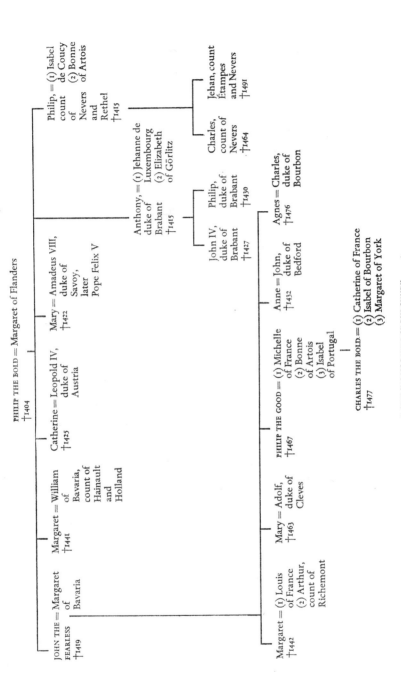

I. THE VALOIS DUKES OF BURGUNDY

able, and usually purposeful, ruler. These men were tyrants, dynasts, egoists. First, Italy produced a string of ruthless and often supremely successful despots of this type, from Ezzelino da Romano in the thirteenth century to Ludovico Sforza in the fifteenth. Then they sprouted at large in Europe and transformed their respective political organizations. It is unfashionable now to call them 'New Monarchs', but new in many ways they certainly were.

In England, between 1461 and 1483, King Edward IV, whom some mistakenly thought of as a mere jovial philanderer, fought and killed his opponents, dispensed with Parliament, forced the London merchants to lend him their money and their wives, and laid the foundations of subsequent Tudor despotism. In Scandinavia a petty German count, Christian of Oldenburg, became in 1448 king of Denmark and Norway, held Sweden also for a time, and annexed Schleswig-Holstein in 1460. His ambitions extended to the imperial crown of Germany; in 1474 he visited Italy and was entertained by the most famous *condottiere* of the day, Bartolomeo Colleoni, at his spendid castle of Malpaga. He founded the University of Copenhagen in 1479 and his descendants ruled Denmark after him for four hundred years. In Spain King John II of Aragon, though he lost Roussillon to France, smashed the Catalan opposition to him after a long struggle, thereby much enhancing the monarch's power. By marrying his son Ferdinand to Isabella of Castile he was also the indirect and unwitting architect of subsequent Spanish unity. Among other European rulers of this period and type were Frederick III of the house of Habsburg, Ivan III the grand duke of Moscow, George Podiebrad and Matthias Corvinus of Bohemia and Hungary respectively, Charles the Bold himself and, most important of all perhaps, King Louis XI of France.

In spite of his somewhat puerile impulsiveness, his overt superstitions, his epilepsy, his piles and his other medical adventures or fears, Louis XI contrived to make an extraordinarily decisive impact on the evolution of France. It was not just the benign and efficient way in which he presided over the recovery of France after the Hundred Years War; not just his military and diplomatic restraint; nor even his creation of the Poste and his encouragement of trade, that made him important. Rather it was the ruthless and arbitrary manner in which he crushed opposition, cheated rivals out of inheritances and cut off the heads of his enemies. Moreover, he was the first of several

French rulers or statesmen who have imposed themselves successfully on their fellow men in the guise of the spirit of France. He still stalks, impossibly larger than life, through the pages of our history books. But all the same, myths apart, Louis XI was surely the most remarkable of all fifteenth-century rulers. There are twelve printed volumes of his correspondence to prove the point.

If the rising power of princes was the single most significant change in Europe during the 'century of Burgundy', perhaps the next most important was the collapse of the unitary church system and of the papacy as a universal institution. These wide-ranging developments closely coincided with the emergence of Valois Burgundy. It was in 1378 that the Great Schism bisected and disastrously damaged the papacy. Already that institution had been vigorously and profoundly attacked by some of the greatest thinkers of the day, Marsilio of Padua, William of Ockham and John Wycliffe among them. Already, long before 1400, dissent was spreading inside the frontiers of Christendom. Throughout the fifteenth century the spontaneous piety of the New Devotion, spreading particularly in Burgundian territories, reflected religious interests turning away from the pope and the religious establishment. The foundation, in bloodshed and turmoil, of the Hussite Church in Bohemia, constituted a sort of prototype Protestant Reformation. In the second half of the fifteenth century the papacy was just one of several rival Italian principalities with little European influence or prestige. Instead of excommunicating emperors and intervening in affairs at large, the popes turned to collecting books and coins and defending themselves against their local enemies. That they were still proud of these more limited achievements is shown by the death-bed boast of Nicholas V in 1455: 'I found the church in a state of civil war and crippled with debts. I have ended the schism, reconquered St Peter's Patrimony, paid the debts, raised solid fortresses for the defence of the Holy See, built beautiful palaces, collected a treasure of jewels and tapestries, caused a large number of books to be copied and I have collected together and supported the greatest scholars of my time.'

Apart from the emergence of Valois Burgundy itself, several other changes affected what was later to be called the balance of power in fifteenth-century Europe. In the West, the old and well-established kingdoms of England, France and Aragon all under-went and survived severe internal crises. Between 1380 and 1422, in the reign of the mad king Charles VI, France suffered rebellion and the civil wars of Armagnacs and Burgundians, quite apart from the disastrous depredations of the English from 1415 onwards. After 1422 England had a mad king too, Henry VI, founder of Eton College; she experienced her own civil wars, the Wars of the Roses, in the middle years of the fifteenth century. Aragon's worst trial came in 1461–72 with the already mentioned Catalan revolt against John II. The general situation of these three kingdoms was radically changed between 1360 and 1480. As a result of France's eventual victory in the Hundred Years War, England's continental possessions were reduced to the mere toehold of Calais; the French monarchy was immeasurably strengthened, above all by Louis XI after 1461; and of course Aragon was united with Castile in 1479 to create the entirely new perspective of a single Spanish monarchy. The Moorish kingdom of Granada fell to this new power in 1491, but diminutive Portugal survived, leading the rest of Europe in the exploration and exploitation of the African continent and later taking her share of America.

In northern Europe the lifetime of Valois Burgundy saw the attempted merging of the northern monarchies in 1397 in the Union of Kalmar, but while the union of Denmark and Norway persisted through much of the fifteenth century, the Swedes fought successfully for a separate monarch of their own. In the Baltic the period witnessed the rise, and then the fall, of the German Hanseatic League which reached its apogee in 1370. Its fifteenth-century decline was caused by internal disputes, inadequate organization, warfare and trade rivalry with England and Holland, and other developments. The other great fourteenth-century power in the Baltic, likewise German, was the Order of Teutonic Knights, which possessed and governed a territorial state of its own creation in what is now Estonia, Latvia, Lithuania and northern Poland. Its apogee was reached at the same time as that of the Hanse; its rapid decline in the fifteenth century was associated with the conversion of Lithuania to Christianity when that principality was united with Poland in 1386. This weakened what was almost the *raison d'être* of the Teutonic Knights – the annual summer crusade against their pagan neighbours in Lithuania. Furthermore, these neighbours henceforth enjoyed the protection of the powerful Polish monarchy. At the battle of Tannenburg in 1410, which makes Agincourt look like a skirmish, the massed armies of Poland

and Lithuania overran the German knights. Thereafter the Order suffered very serious losses of territory to the Poles. Other important changes occurred at this time in the east. While Poland went from strength to strength, Hungary lost ground to the Turks and, obscurely but effectively, the grand dukes of Moscow laid the foundations of a Russian empire.

The Italian political scene was as kaleidoscopic at this time as ever. Its main feature, in the second half of the fourteenth and the early fifteenth centuries, was the replacement of numerous small city-states by five major powers, each occupying a large block of territory. While Naples and the Papal States divided between them the southern half of the peninsula, in the north Milan first, then Venice and Florence, transformed themselves from cities into empires by swallowing up their unfortunate neighbours. The French and Germans, in these years, were kept out of Italy, more or less; but the Spanish presence was substantially reinforced in 1442 when Alfonso of Aragon conquered the kingdom of Naples from its French-speaking rulers of the house of Anjou.

Apart from the rise of the Swiss Federation, which had come into existence in the first half of the fourteenth century and continued to consolidate its power through the fifteenth, political changes inside the boundaries of the Holy Roman Empire were mostly of limited importance. The kingdom of Bohemia remained the largest single political unit and became in the fifteenth century the home of the first more or less national and more or less Protestant church. Imperial authority still made fitful appearances on the stage of history. It was the Emperor Sigmund who called the Council of Constance into being in 1414, and imperial armies were still occasionally assembled, against the Hussites in the 1420s, against Charles the Bold of Burgundy in 1475. But creative political activity in the Empire was engaged in much more effectively by the princes, who vied with one another in constructing territorial states. Prominent among them were Frederick the Victorious, elector-palatine of the Rhine, and Albert Achilles, elector of Brandenburg, both of whom perhaps deserve to be ranked among the so-called New Monarchs mentioned above. But the efforts of these princes were often vitiated by partible inheritance or family disputes, so that the Habsburg territories, the Wittelsbach lands in Bavaria and almost all the other German territories were in fact ruled by and shared between two or more relatives. Burgundy, a large part of which lay within the Empire, was a notable exception to this phenomenon of territorial disintegration. At any one time there were invariably at least two or three princes using the title and calling themselves 'duke of Austria' or 'duke of Bavaria' or whatever, but nobody else except the single legitimate duke ever dared use the title 'duke of Burgundy'.

This multiple use of identical titles was a characteristic symptom of political organization in the fifteenth century. Europe was by no means divided then, as it was to be later, into mutually exclusive and independent polities, each comprising a single absolutely powerful government ruling over subjects of more or less equal status. In the fifteenth century no ruler or state was completely independent, nobody wielded absolute power, even though some rulers appeared to be groping towards it. Instead, every territory was riddled with enclaves of privilege and immunity; even the rulers of large-scale monarchies like France and England were hampered by contractual obligations towards their subjects; indeed power was everywhere shared, everywhere scattered and diffuse. Spain did not exist; France was a sort of organization; Germany merely a concept.

Against this background of complex, sophisticated, ever-changing political arrangements and rivalries, the monolithic, dynamic empire of the Ottoman Turks stood out in increasingly stark contrast. Gallipoli was seized in 1354; then a long process was begun of engulfing the Christian kingdoms of the Balkans, obliterating the ancient Greek empire of Byzantium, and disrupting the arteries of east–west trade. The fall of Constantinople in 1453 was only one event in the Ottoman expansion into Europe which the Burgundian-led crusade of Nicopolis had failed to halt in 1396. It continued into the seventeenth century. Already by the end of the fifteenth century, however, the entire Balkan Peninsula south of the Danube and the Save was in Turkish hands.

The political transformations undergone by Europe in the fourteenth and fifteenth centuries were accompanied by other upheavals of no less moment. Some among these came too late to make any real impact on the world of the Valois dukes of Burgundy. The art of printing was perfected only around 1450, and the earliest books published in the Burgundian Netherlands appeared in 1473, at Utrecht in Holland and at Alost in Flanders. As for the new geographical discoveries, although the Atlantic

Islands were being explored from the beginning of the fifteenth century, the Portuguese only began serious investigation of the West African coast in the 1430s, and America was not discovered until fifteen years after Charles the Bold's death.

On the other hand, the Italian Renaissance was in full swing at just the time when Burgundian power and prestige reached their apogee in the middle years of the fifteenth century during the long ducal reign of Philip the Good. Petrarch and Boccaccio had died in the 1370s, a decade before Philip the Bold became count of Flanders, Artois and Burgundy; Erasmus was born in 1467, the year Philip the Good died. Between these dates the youthful, short-lived genius of Masaccio had added a new dimension to painting; Brunelleschi had revolutionized architecture, completing the dome of Florence cathedral and the Pazzi chapel before his death in 1446; Lorenzo Valla had founded what has been called bibliographical humanism and exposed the Donation of Constantine as a forgery; the Platonic Academy had been established in Florence; a new humanist or italic script had been evolved; and Italian ambassadors were transforming international relations into a fine art. The famous contest for the carved bronze doors of the Baptistry at Florence, competed for by the two greatest Italian sculptors of the age, Donatello and Ghiberti, was held in 1402. At that very date the greatest sculptor outside Italy, the Dutchman Claus Sluter, was at work at Dijon on a series of monumental carvings for the duke of Burgundy. Burgundian culture was, and remained, essentially northern or Netherlandish. While the popes had summoned Italian artists to Avignon in the fourteenth century the dukes of Burgundy in the fifteenth century drew their artists from Holland, from Flanders, from Brabant. Only in the last decade of the history of Valois Burgundy, in the reign of Charles the Bold, was there an important Italianate element at the Burgundian court. Even so, Charles the Bold was hardly a Renaissance prince.

Historians warmly dispute the economic state of Europe in the Burgundian period, but none has denied the importance of the evolution of capitalism at this time. The course of political events had been dictated by the power of money, the availability of funds, ever since Tuscan bankers had advanced to the pope and to Charles of Anjou the necessary cash for Charles's conquest of Naples in 1265–8. Philip the Bold rose to power on the broad financial shoulders of a financier from Lucca who had taken up residence in Bruges, Dino Rapondi. In the 1450s it was Jaques Cœur's wealth which enabled the French to expel the English from Normandy and thus bring the Hundred Years War to a victorious conclusion. There was no more striking example of capitalism in the fifteenth century than the Medici bank at Florence, which became fully fledged under the care of Cosimo de' Medici, a contemporary of Philip the Good, who ruled Florence from 1434 to 1464. Branches were set up at Lyons, Bruges, London and elsewhere, and it seemed as if the accumulated wealth of the Medicis was paying for the Florentine Renaissance; indeed more than anything else making Florence the centre of the Italian Renaissance.

The rise of capitalism was one of the salient features of the economic and social life of Europe in the later middle ages. Another was the appearance and spread of 'class' warfare. The spectre of violent revolution had been absent from most of Europe for many centuries before the outbreaks of social turbulence which occurred from the mid-thirteenth century onwards. They culminated in the savage uprising of Flemish peasants in 1323. Some revolts which followed, the Jacquerie in France in 1358 and the Peasants' Revolt in England, were predominantly rural but others, including the revolt of Ghent in 1379 and the revolt of the *Ciompi* or cloth-workers in Florence in 1378, were urban, Indeed from 1378 onwards a series of violent attempts to subvert and overthrow existing régimes took place in many of Europe's leading towns. All four Valois dukes of Burgundy were involved in these urban revolts. Naturally, they consistently supported those in power against the revolutionaries, notably at Ghent and at Liège.

Economic and social patterns were changing in many other ways in the age of Valois Burgundy. Parts of Europe had suffered severe regression in the course of the fourteenth century as a result of famine, plague, poor harvest. In France devastation due directly or indirectly to the Hundred Years War was widespread in the first half of the fifteenth century. While some areas experienced economic and perhaps even demographic decline, others enjoyed increased prosperity. The rise of Burgundy was only possible because of an economic upsurge in the Low Countries in the late fourteenth and early fifteenth centuries. If some cities, like Ypres, declined at this time, others, like Bruges, Brussels and Antwerp developed and expanded. In the fifteenth century Italy continued wealthy while the Baltic experienced economic stagnation or decline. These changing patterns were linked to changes in commerce and agriculture which affected virtually the whole of Europe, for it was at this time that increasing crop specialization led to the development of stock raising in some areas at the expense of other forms of agriculture; to the concentration of wine production in Europe's now traditional vinelands; and to the large-scale cultivation of cereal crops in parts of northern Europe and the Mediterranean.

This review of some of the dynamic elements in fifteenth-century Europe ought not to be concluded without at least a mention of some of its traditional, more or less static, features. Most notable among these were the towns, the parliaments, and the universities. The towns had grown and evolved spontaneously from the eleventh and twelfth centuries onwards in all parts of Europe, but they were most numerous and most powerful in the Low Countries, along the Rhine and in North Italy. In these favoured areas, as well as to a lesser extent elsewhere, they had become strong enough to gain virtual autonomy. Important places like Strasbourg, Ghent or Florence had become empires in themselves. They fielded armies, defied princes, squabbled among each other, bullied and conquered their smaller neighbours, and formed defensive or commercial leagues. All through Burgundian history they were a force to be reckoned with: at the end Strasbourg, Basel and Bern were the architects of Charles the Bold's destruction.

In the fifteenth century representative institutions of one kind or another were convened, consulted and cajoled into voting taxes by the princes. In times of crisis they could exercise a decisive influence on the course of events. Often it was they who effectively chose a new ruler. Throughout most of continental Europe every single territory had its Estates; in Burgundy the dukes created a States General for their Low Countries territories which later acquired European renown. In Germany especially the Estates clashed with the princes and, particularly after 1378, caused havoc by conducting savage civil wars against each other. Spain had its Cortes, England its Parliament: these were mere local variations of a universal theme.

While the parliaments of today are utterly different from their fifteenth-century counterparts in composition, powers and even purpose, Europe's universities have changed little – too little – in the last five hundred years. In the fourteenth and fifteenth centuries they trained civil servants and churchmen, collected privileges and defended them assiduously against rulers and the rest of the community, and even on occasion meddled in politics. Though the first universities boasted no founders, rulers soon found it convenient and prestigious to have their own. A famous princely foundation, a state university in embryo, was established at Prague in 1348 by the Emperor Charles IV. One of the Burgundian universities, Louvain, was inaugurated by the duke of Brabant in 1425; the other, at Dole in Franche-Comté, which traces its history from 1422, was founded by Philip the Good.

How exactly did Burgundy fit into this European context? And how did her situation change between 1360 and 1480? These questions can only be answered intelligibly after the emergence of Valois Burgundy has been explained and her constituent elements defined.

CHAPTER TWO

The Origins and
Identity of Valois Burgundy

Valois Burgundy came into being through a series of historical accidents and through the agency of far-reaching socio-economic and political forces; but partly it was created by the will of men intent on establishing for themselves and their descendants a place in the sun, a power, a lordship; intent, too, on doing what they conceived to be their duty to God and to the people He was supposed to have appointed them to rule over. These elements in the emergence of Valois Burgundy will be apparent in what follows.

Some contemporary observers noted with astonishment that a fourteen-year-old boy stood by the king of France John the Good (who was actually among the worst of medieval French kings) on the battlefield of Poitiers even though he was too young effectively to carry arms. He was the king's youngest son, Philip of Valois; his elder brothers had been withdrawn out of harm's way. This battle, fought on 19 September 1356, was arguably the most decisive and significant defeat suffered by the French at the hands of the English in the entire Hundred Years War. John the Good and his son Philip were both taken to England as prisoners-of-war and remained there until the French had accepted the humiliating peace settlement of Brétigny in 1360 and promised to pay an enormous ransom for their release. While France suffered, Philip's heroic behaviour at Poitiers had brought him important advantages: the nickname Bold was probably given him at this time, and his grateful father granted him the duchy of Touraine. But a greater opportunity for his youngest son's advancement soon presented itself to John the Good. Philip of Rouvres, the last Capetian duke of Burgundy, died on 21 November 1361, and the vacant duchy fell to the French crown. King John lost little time in arranging for Philip the Bold to exchange Touraine for the much larger and more important duchy of Burgundy, and Philip was confirmed as duke of Burgundy when his brother Charles V succeeded his father John II as king of France in 1364.

Through much of European history marriage has been a ruler's most fruitful means of political advancement. When Philip of Rouvres died he was only seventeen, and a promising political and dynastic future had seemed ahead of him through his marriage to Margaret of Flanders, who was the only child and heiress of the count of Flanders Louis of Male. Not unnaturally, the hand of this dynastically desirable young lady, aged eleven when widowed in 1361, was sought in marriage by Philip of Rouvres' successor in the duchy, Philip the Bold, and eventually, in 1369, it was successfully obtained, against English competition. Thus, from 1369, Philip was, through his wife, in line of succession as the next count of Flanders after Louis of Male. Moreover, Philip had secretly promised his father-in-law that he and his successors as counts of Flanders would retain the important French towns and territories of Lille, Douai and Orchies which King Charles V had ceded to Louis of Male to induce him to agree to his daughter's marriage to Philip the Bold. This was in spite of the fact that he had also promised his brother King Charles that he would hand them back to the crown of France on his father-in-law's death. Besides becoming prospective ruler of a Flanders enlarged by these territories, which lay next to it and which naturally he never did hand back to France, Philip the Bold also became in 1369, again through his wife, prospective count of Artois and Burgundy, territories then ruled by Louis's mother Margaret of Artois, and prospective count of Rethel and Nevers, not to mention prospective ruler of the towns of Malines and Antwerp and the barony of Donzy.

Such were the scintillating perspectives of dynastic aggrandizement secured by Philip the Bold in 1369 at the age of twenty-seven. But he was perhaps not too confident about these attractive possibilities for, though Philip's mother-in-law Margaret of Brabant was forty-six, his father-in-law Louis of Male was only thirty-nine at the time of his nineteen-year-old daughter's marriage. Philip's succession to all these rich and extensive lands was not quite assured.

For ten years, from 1369 to 1379, Duke Philip of Burgundy bided his time, devoting himself, as a loyal French prince, to helping his brother King Charles V fight and negotiate with the English, but not forgetting at least an annual visit to Flanders. Then, in the first days of September 1379, the weavers and other artisans of Ghent rose in arms, assassinated the count's bailiff, burnt down his castle of Wondelgem on the outskirts of the town, and led and organized the revolt of a large section of the Flemish populace against his authority and against the ruling classes of Flanders. In these critical circumstances Louis of Male appealed for help to the king of France and to his son-in-law Philip, who promptly sent a detachment of Burgundian soldiers to fight the Flemish rebels. In 1382 he went much further and brought a French army into Flanders with the new king of France, his nephew Charles VI, at its head. Although on 27 November 1382 the Flemish were decisively beaten by this army on the field of Roosebeke, Ghent continued the revolt on her own and, in 1383, obtained important military assistance from England. The war dragged on until the end of 1385, but Louis of Male had died on 30 January 1384, two years after his mother Margaret of Artois. From that date on Philip the Bold was the proud ruler of five counties, Flanders, Burgundy, Artois, Rethel and Nevers, besides his duchy of Burgundy.

Philip the Bold's first task as ruler of these territories was the pacification of Flanders, and this was eventually achieved on 18 December 1385, when rebellious Ghent accepted the peace settlement of Tournai. It was in 1385, too, that Philip created the nucleus of a genuine central government for his scattered lands by appointing the Frenchman Jehan Canard as 'chancellor of my lord the duke of Burgundy' with the function of presiding over his entire administration. The chanceries of Burgundy and Flanders were allowed to lapse. Soon afterwards, in 1386–7, Philip the Bold undertook a thorough overhaul of the administrative machinery of his various lands which virtually amounted to the establishment of a new, unified administration. One or two treasurers and a single receiver-general of all finances were to control the whole of the financial administration. Then, in ordinances of February and July 1386, the duke reorganized his regional administrations in the two main groups of territories so that henceforth a single combined council and accounting office at Dijon was responsible for the government of the southern territories, while a similar institution at Lille was responsible for Flanders, Artois, Rethel and the other northern lands. It could perhaps be said without exaggeration that a single new polity, a Burgundian state, was created in this way by Philip the Bold out of the amalgam of territories he and his wife had brought together as a result of their marriage.

It was a fortunate historical accident for Philip the Bold, which he successfully exploited, that at just the time of the genesis of this new polity the established powers in the West were being crippled by internal crises and ineffective monarchs. In England the heroic days of continental conquest under Edward III and the Black Prince gave way, in 1377, to the feebler, uncertain rule of the youthful Richard II, which was severely shaken in 1381 by the Peasants' Revolt. In the Holy Roman Empire, the reign of the bibulous Wenzel or Wenceslas, who was deposed by some of the imperial electors in 1400, began in 1378 amid scenes of turmoil and civil strife. More favourable still for the rise of Burgundian power were contemporary circumstances in France. Here, in 1380, Philip the Bold's statesmanlike elder brother Charles V gave place to his nephew Charles VI, who had scarcely come of age when, in 1392, he went mad.

From the very moment of Louis of Male's death at the beginning of 1384, Philip the Bold showed by his actions that the power-base he envisaged for himself and his family extended far beyond the boundaries of the lands he had so far acquired. His father-in-law had staked a claim to the duchy of Brabant through his wife Margaret of Brabant, and in March 1384, before he had even taken formal possession of his newly inherited county of Flanders, Philip the Bold was in Brussels, the capital of Brabant, haggling with that duchy's ruler his aunt Joan of Brabant, who was childless and likely to remain so, being then over sixty. It took Philip six years to persuade and bully Joan into secretly making the duchy over to him and his wife Margaret and their heirs, but Joan still retained possession of it for the rest of her life. This arrangement was made in September 1390 but already, three years before, Philip had harassed Joan into ceding to him rights in some isolated territories beyond the River Meuse and outside the boundaries of Brabant, the most important of which was the duchy of Limbourg, finally ceded to Philip in full ownership in 1396.

As to the duchy of Brabant, the succession could by no means merely be settled by a private arrangement between princes, for the Estates of Brabant had a right to be consulted. In this instance they refused to permit Brabant to be incorporated into Philip the Bold's new Burgundian state. Instead he was only able to obtain their agreement, given eventually in 1401, that the aged Joan – she died in December 1406 when over eighty – would be succeeded as ruler of their duchy by Duke Philip's younger son

Anthony. Moreover, as a price for this agreement, Philip had to promise to return Limbourg, which he had acquired in 1396, and Antwerp, which his father-in-law had annexed to Flanders in 1357, to Brabant.

Of Philip the Bold's other territorial acquisitions, the only one of any importance was the county of Charolais, a territory bordering on the duchy of Burgundy which Philip bought from one of his vassals in 1390. This addition to the southern group of territories was somewhat comparable in importance to the purchase of the county of Namur by Philip the Good in 1421, which bordered on Brabant and formed a useful addition to the northern territories.

Philip the Bold's various schemes for the succession of his children to his territories show that he never envisaged the separation of the northern from the southern lands, for in every one of his suggested settlements the eldest son John was to inherit both Flanders and the duchy of Burgundy. Nor, after Philip the Bold's death in 1404, did the partitioning of his territories between his sons seriously undermine their essential unity. John the Fearless became ruler of the duchy and county of Burgundy, with Charolais, as well as of Flanders and Artois in the north; Anthony became duke of Brabant in 1406; and Philip was given the relatively small and insignificant counties of Nevers and Rethel. Although he did not in his short ducal reign (1404–19) acquire much reputation as an empire-builder, John the Fearless was careful to maintain the Burgundian state in being, and indeed by acquiring the French territories of Boulogne, Péronne, Roye and Montdidier in the north and Tonnerre and Mâcon in the south he virtually made up for the loss of Rethel and Nevers to a junior branch of his dynasty.

The son and successor of John the Fearless, Philip the Good (1419–67), added so many territories to the Burgundian state that he has often been regarded as its founder. However, the way towards the acquisition of these lands had in every single case been prepared by his grandfather. In 1385 Philip the Bold had arranged a marriage alliance between his own children and those of Albert of Bavaria, ruler of Hainault and Holland, which established a Burgundian claim to those more or less united counties. He had laboured for years to obtain the duchy of Brabant and at last succeeded in bringing it into the Burgundian orbit. And in 1401 he had obtained control for a time of the duchy of Luxembourg. These were the very lands which his grandson

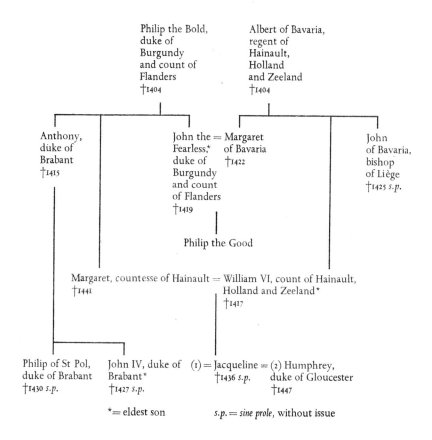

Philip the Bold, duke of Burgundy and count of Flanders †1404

Albert of Bavaria, regent of Hainault, Holland and Zeeland †1404

Anthony, duke of Brabant †1415

John the Fearless,* duke of Burgundy and count of Flanders †1419 = Margaret of Bavaria †1422

John of Bavaria, bishop of Liège †1425 s.p.

Philip the Good

Margaret, countesse of Hainault †1441 = William VI, count of Hainault, Holland and Zeeland* †1417

Philip of St Pol, duke of Brabant †1430 s.p.

John IV, duke of Brabant* †1427 s.p.

(1) = Jacqueline †1436 s.p. = (2) Humphrey, duke of Gloucester †1447

*= eldest son   s.p. = *sine prole*, without issue

2. THE SUCCESSION TO BRABANT AND TO HAINAULT, HOLLAND AND ZEELAND

added to the Burgundian state: Holland and Hainault, with Zeeland, in 1428–33; Brabant, with Limbourg, in 1430; Luxembourg in 1443. Thus Philip the Good only had to complete, in 1425–43, the structure half-built by his grandfather in 1363–87.

When William of Bavaria died in 1417 he left an only child, the sixteen-year-old Jacqueline of Bavaria, to succeed him in his lands of Hainault, Holland and Zeeland. At once she and her territories became the centre of attention of neighbouring dynasts. The duke of Burgundy, John the Fearless, succeeded in arranging her marriage to his nephew John who had succeeded John the Fearless's brother Anthony as duke of Brabant when Anthony was killed at the battle of Agincourt in 1415. The wedding took place at Easter 1418 and it seemed likely that Brabant might now be united with Hainault, Holland and Zeeland under a junior branch of the ducal family of Burgundy. However, by 1420 another prince, the brother of the deceased ruler of Holland, Jacqueline's father William of Bavaria, had succeeded in wresting from her and her husband a good part of the counties of Holland and Zeeland. This was John of Bavaria, who had resigned his bishopric of Liège in order to pursue these territorial ambitions in Holland at the expense of his nearly defenceless niece Jacqueline.

A complex situation thus confronted Philip the Good when he became duke of Burgundy in 1419, and it soon became more complex. On 11 April 1420 Jacqueline ran away from her husband, who appears to have subjected her to a petty domestic tyranny; in 1421 she fled to England; and in 1422 she married Duke Humphrey of Gloucester, one of the several sons of King Henry IV who formed a council of regency after Henry V's death in 1422 on behalf of that king's child son Henry VI. No doubts apparently troubled her and Duke Humphrey's consciences as to the validity or propriety of this marriage. While the pope at Rome, Martin V, dithered and appointed a commission of cardinals to investigate and decide on the validity of her first marriage to Duke John IV of Brabant, Jacqueline applied to Martin's rival, Benedict XIII, who continued to regard himself as the one and only true successor of St Peter even though he had been exiled to the rocky retreat of Peñiscola on the coast of Aragon, and even though he had been abandoned by the whole of Christendom. This obstinate old man was happy to do what his rival Martin had refused to do, and the wedding of Duke Humphrey and Jacqueline thus received the seal of his approval.

Humphrey of Gloucester was an ambitious and aggressive adventurer. Optimistically styling himself count of Hainault, Holland and Zeeland, in the autumn of 1424 he crossed to Calais with his wife Jacqueline and marched into Hainault with a contingent of English troops. They were opposed there by Philip the Good, who challenged Duke Humphrey to a single combat and even went into training for it in the grounds of his castle at Hesdin in Artois. In the event, Jacqueline fell into his hands, but in September 1425 she escaped from his custody at Ghent disguised as a man and once more fled to England. The struggle for the succession of Hainault, Holland and Zeeland continued, for Jacqueline obtained further help from England, from substantial elements of the Dutch populace, and from the neighbouring bishop of Utrecht. Her uncle, John of Bavaria, had died in January 1425, leaving the field clearer for Burgundian intervention. This had been persistent since 1417; it was now greatly intensified. Nonetheless, though he enjoyed support there, especially in the towns, Philip the Good had to conquer Holland by force of arms, and four large-scale campaigns between 1425 and 1428 were necessary to achieve this. In the end Jacqueline was forced to submit and make over her lands and all her claims to them to the duke of Burgundy, who finally took them over in 1433. Jacqueline had been abandoned by Duke Humphrey, who married his mistress Eleanor Cobham soon after Pope Martin V, in January 1428, had pronounced that his marriage to Jacqueline was invalid. She died in 1436.

The acquisition of the duchy of Brabant by the Valois house of Burgundy was a much more straightforward affair. The younger branch of the family, which Philip the Bold had contrived to install in Brabant, came to an end in August 1430 on the unexpected death of Philip of St Pol, younger brother and successor of Duke John IV, who had ended a brief, totally ineffective and more or less disastrous reign as duke of Brabant by dying in 1427. Philip the Good had already taken the precaution of persuading Philip of St Pol to recognize him as his heir if he died without children; he now entered into negotiations with the Estates of Brabant and triumphed over his rival claimants to the duchy by persuading the Estates to accept him. On 8 October 1430 he made his 'joyous entry' into the city which he was to transform into the capital of the Burgundian state.

The last substantial territory which was incorporated on a permanent basis into the Burgundian state by Philip the Good was the duchy of Luxembourg. Before he had become its temporary ruler in 1401, Philip the Bold had made numerous other interventions in this duchy. His successor John the Fearless pursued a similar policy and, mainly as a result of his efforts, his younger brother Duke Anthony of Brabant was effective ruler of Luxembourg between 1409 and his death at Agincourt in 1415. Naturally Philip the Good continued these Burgundian initiatives towards Luxembourg. This time the role of unfortunate heiress, victim of Burgundian aggrandizement – the role which had been played by Joan of Brabant and by Jacqueline of Bavaria – was taken over by Elizabeth of Görlitz, a granddaughter of the Emperor Charles IV. By 1440 this duchess of Luxembourg was an elderly widow, encumbered with debts. Everyone of any account with even the remotest claims had their eyes on her extensive and strategically important territories, but it was to her nephew Philip the Good that she eventually made them over, in 1441. Once again, Burgundian military power had to be called on, and the town and duchy of Luxembourg were conquered from one of the other claimants, Duke William of Saxony, in autumn 1443, after that ruler had rejected another of Philip the Good's flamboyant challenges to single combat. From 1443 on the duchy of Luxembourg formed part of the Burgundian state, though several other European princes besides the duke of Burgundy regarded themselves as its rightful duke.

The Burgundian state, then, was put together between 1363, when Philip the Bold became duke of Burgundy, and 1443, when his grandson became ruler of Luxembourg. Subsequent additions of territory can only be regarded as temporary or superficial; in any event they were made too late to contribute to the emergence of the Burgundian state. The so-called Somme towns – a slab of territory on the River Somme which included Amiens, Abbeville and the county of Ponthieu – came nearest of these additional lands to being genuinely incorporated into the Burgundian state. Charles VII mortgaged them to Philip the Good in 1435, but his successor Louis XI redeemed the mortgage in 1463 and restored them to France. Admittedly, Charles the Bold forced Louis XI to return the Somme towns to Burgundy in 1465, but subsequent history showed that the crown of France would never be content until it had regained possession of them. As to Charles the Bold, his territorial acquisitions were short-lived, and the only one that might be considered an addition to the Burgundian state was the duchy of Guelders. Administratively, this was indeed integrated fully into the rest of Burgundy, but it was only acquired in 1473 and then only at the cost of imprisoning the lawful ruler Adolf of Egmond. Further south, Lorraine was conquered by Charles the Bold, but in 1475 only, and he held it for scarcely a year; and the rights and lands acquired in mortgage by Duke Charles in 1469 in Upper Alsace were forcefully taken from him by the inhabitants five years later. It seems unwise, therefore, to regard any of these territories as belonging effectively to the Burgundian state.

It is not easy for us now to picture Valois Burgundy in the mind's eye or relate it on the map to the other European powers of the fifteenth century. From Holland in the extreme north to the south of Franche-Comté in the neighbourhood of the Lake of Geneva is about 500 miles. At its widest point on this north–south axis, in the Low Countries, Valois Burgundy extended some 250 miles from the Somme to the Zuiderzee (now the Ijsselmeer). In the south, the two Burgundies were about 125 miles long from north to south and some 155 miles across from west to east. But the north–south axis, even after Charles the Bold's conquest of Lorraine in 1475, was incomplete. There was still a thirty-mile gap between the northern and southern group of territories. For thirty years before that, since Philip the Good's conquest of Luxembourg in 1443, the gap was 125 miles wide, and during the first half of the history of Valois Burgundy, from 1384 to 1443, it extended for some 185 miles as the crow flies, between southern Artois and the northern frontier of the duchy of Burgundy. Two map features meandered north–south more or less through the centre of Valois Burgundy along its north–south axis – the frontier between France and the Empire, and the Rivers Meuse and Saône.

In area, Valois Burgundy was comparable in size to the kingdom of England (with Wales), or Portugal, or Aragon, or Naples (with Sicily and Sardinia); but it was not as large as Castile or France. If size, wealth, population and natural re-sources be taken together it was a lesser power than France but greater than Savoy or any of the German or north Italian states. The scatter of its territories must have caused administrative delay: it took anything from one to four days to deliver a letter within either group of territories, and a week to communicate between Brussels and Dijon (250 miles apart as the crow flies). But this scatter also conferred on Valois Burgundy a remarkable variety of resources. In the south, besides wine and salt, were boundless deciduous forests, parts of which still survive, affording abundant supplies of timber and game. In the northern territories, where the rolling chalklands of Artois contrasted with the lush water-meadows of Flanders and Holland and the afforested hills of Luxembourg, was the greatest centre of urban development in medieval Europe: Antwerp, Amsterdam, Ghent and Bruges were all inside the frontiers of Valois Burgundy.

What individual lands together made up this Burgundian state in its prime, that is between 1443 and 1465? Geographically, these lands formed a northern group in the Low Countries and a southern in Burgundy. The two groups were separated by the county of Champagne, which was part of the kingdom of France, and the duchy of Lorraine, which belonged to the Empire. Neither group of territories had a name. When the duke was in the north he referred to the Netherlandish territories as 'our lands round here', and the two Burgundies as 'our lands over there'. When he was in Dijon he reversed this somewhat inadequate terminology and 'the lands round here' became the two Burgundies, that is, the duchy and county of Burgundy. But the territories which made up the Burgundian state were not only divided geographically in this way, they were also politically divided, for they lay on the border-line between France and the Empire. The duchy of Burgundy was in France, but the county was in the Empire. In the north, nearly all the county of Flanders was a French royal fief, so was the county of Artois; but Brabant, Holland and the rest were in the Empire. The dukes of Burgundy owed homage to the king of France for their French territories; they were supposed to be imperial vassals for their imperial lands. Linguistically, too, the Burgundian state was split in two, if not three, parts. French was the language of the two Burgundies, Artois and Hainault, but Netherlandish (Dutch or Flemish) was spoken in Flanders, most of Brabant and Holland, and in the eastern half of Luxembourg the language was German. These three dichotomies, one geographical, one political, the third linguistic, were part of the very nature of the Burgundian state.

The duchy and county of Burgundy lay side by side on either bank of the River Saône. Towns in this agricultural region were small and scattered, but Dijon with its 10,000 or so inhabitants had already become the natural capital of the duchy as well as the seat of its administration. Beaune, Autun, Semur, Montbard were smaller, indeed probably considerably less than half that size. In the county of Burgundy, which acquired during the fifteenth century the name Franche-Comté, the principal town was Besançon, but this was really an enclave in Burgundian territory, for the count had to share control of it with the archbishop, the civic authorities and others. It was proud of its status as an imperial free city and not particularly Burgundian in its loyalties. Auxonne and Dole were the next most important places in the county: the counts had a mint at Auxonne, and Philip the Good established a Burgundian university at Dole. In the duchy, commercial and agricultural activity already centred on the export of fine wines, especially to Paris and the Low Countries. As the mayor and corporation of Dijon reported in 1452, 'this town is based on the culture of vines and wine is its chief merchandise'. If the calculations of a modern historian can be relied on, wine consumption in the rural France of those days was somewhat higher than it is now: at Auxonne the mean annual consumption per head is supposed to have approached 300 litres. In the county of Burgundy salt took the place of wine as the main commercial commodity. It was extracted at Salins from several brine springs or wells.

Salt and wine gave the two Burgundies a significant economic role in the Burgundian state, but their importance administratively and militarily far outshone this commercial activity. Right up till the beginning of Charles the Bold's reign the armies of Burgundy were based on the military service of the nobility of the two Burgundies, and even after he had reorganized the ducal forces, the élite contingents and some of the most famous captains were from the duchy and county. As to the administration, the duchy in particular, but also the county, continued to supply personnel for the central administration of the Burgundian state right till the end. When the Parlement of Malines was set up in 1473, at least twenty-one of the forty-five persons given posts in it were Burgundians. Thus, in spite of the increasing and natural tendency for the centre of gravity of the Burgundian state to shift from the southern to the northern territories as more lands were added in the north, the two Burgundies never ceased to be an essential part of it.

Among the northern territories, the county of Artois, with its administrative capital and largest town of Arras, was the most similar in general character to the two Burgundies. It too provided captains for the Burgundian armies. It was visited relatively often by the dukes because one of their most famous and elaborate residences, the castle of Hesdin, was situated in it. The county of Flanders, lying next to it, was the wealthiest of the ducal territories and the most urbanized. In Bruges, it could boast Europe's busiest port; in Ghent, one of her largest industrial towns, concentrating on the manufacture of cloth. Ypres was declining at this time, but Lille, which had been annexed to Flanders by Philip the Bold, expanded and flourished in the fifteenth century. It was the seat of the financial administration of Artois and Flanders and it had developed a tapestry industry of sufficient importance to receive export orders from England and Italy. Along the coast of Flanders the herring industry was of growing significance.

South of Flanders lay the rather small French-speaking county of Hainault with its chief towns of Mons and Valenciennes. Although it had been joined for a time under the same ruler as Holland and Zeeland, the connection was not maintained by the Burgundian dukes, who treated it administratively as a separate territory. The duchy of Brabant was roughly equal in size to Flanders. Its largest town, Brussels, was beginning to emerge in the fifteenth century as one of Europe's great cities; it became a favourite place of residence of Duke Philip the Good, and a centre for the manufacture of jewellery, metalwork, arms and armour, and other goods. To the north the counties of Holland and Zeeland, treated as a single unit under the dukes of Burgundy, were rapidly increasing in commercial importance, and in Holland the city of Amsterdam was on its way to pre-eminence.

Even if we were to include the duchy of Guelders, we can hardly regard the Burgundian state as embracing the whole of the Low Countries; still less attempt to see it as a geographical precursor of Benelux. Tournai and the immediate environs, enclaved in Burgundian territory and wedged between Hainault and southern Flanders, were French. Cambrai was an episcopal principality; so were Liège and Utrecht. Moreover, in spite of attempts against Frisia, the Burgundian dukes never managed to extend their northern boundary in the Low Countries beyond Enkhuizen and Zutphen.

How far is it legitimate and realistic to consider these various territories as forming a single whole? Was there really such a thing as a Burgundian state? Or is the phrase a mere terminological convenience? We can go some way towards answering these questions, firstly by identifying the integrative elements, the forces which made for unity, in the polity of the Valois dukes; and secondly by examining (in so far as this is possible) the motives and attitudes of the dukes and their advisers.

The most immediately apparent of the forces making for some sort of Burgundian unity is perhaps the very conspicuous tendency towards the combination of smaller political units into larger ones by a process, usually, of dynastic union under a single ruler. This process had gone far and was in full swing by the mid-fourteenth century, so that the unification of the Low Countries under the Burgundian dukes, as well as that of the two Burgundies, look very much like the natural outcome of earlier developments. Thus the Capetian dukes of Burgundy had acquired the county of Burgundy in 1330 after a long series of interventions there, and by the mid-fourteenth century they had established the tradition or principle of the indivisibility of the ducal domain. In the Low Countries, Hainault and Holland were united in 1299; Artois had been joined to the county of Burgundy in the fourteenth century; Limbourg had been incorporated into Brabant. In Flanders, Philip the Bold could not have failed to take a leaf or two out of his father-in-law's notebook, for Louis of Male was one of the most ambitious and successful rulers of the age. We should note, in particular, the immediate relevance to the history of the Valois dukes of Burgundy in the Low Countries of Louis of Male's attack on Brabant in 1356, his annexation of two of that duchy's most flourishing cities, Antwerp and Malines, his acquisition of the right to call himself duke of Brabant, and his recognition as prospective ruler there. Thus the Valois dukes of Burgundy followed their Burgundian and Netherlandish predecessors' footsteps in putting smaller political units together to make larger ones. They were surely being impelled by an enduring historical force. It was not as if they just happened to find themselves, more or less accidentally, ruling a haphazard hotch-potch of different territories.

Important integrative forces can be discerned at work within the territories of the Valois dukes of Burgundy, some of which were the product of specific ducal initiatives, others not. The central government probably conferred a higher degree of unity on the whole structure than was provided by the person of the duke and his court, important though these naturally were. There was a single chancellor and chancery, a single council or supreme law court, a single financial organization, for all these territories. Moreover, since they were all ultimately based on the same French models, the regional or provincial administrative institutions, although inescapably separate, were extremely similar to each other. Uniformity is not unity, but it can be a step towards it. A single Burgundian Order of Chivalry, the Toison d'Or or Golden Fleece, included among its members noblemen from virtually all the duke's territories, as well as from other countries. The church too, was important in fostering some sort of unity because promotion in its upper echelons was more or less in the hands of the dukes and was used by them to provide for their leading officials irrespective of their land of origin. It should be pointed out that in the central government, in the Golden Fleece and in the church, Burgundians, that is people from the southern territories, tended to do better and to be more numerous than northerners. This was very largely because the language of the dukes, of the court and of the central administration was French.

Whether Duke Philip the Good had any notion of bringing his different lands together when he founded the Order of the Golden Fleece at the end of 1430 is a moot point. In the case of two other initiatives which promoted unification in the northern lands he surely had not. These were the issue in 1433-4 of a single gold and silver currency for Flanders, Brabant, Holland, Zeeland and Hainault, and the encouragement, if not the creation, of the States General of the Burgundian Netherlands, which emerged fully fledged as it were in 1464. Possibly more important than anything so far mentioned was warfare. The war against Ghent in 1453 and the war of the League of the Public Weal in 1465 were the first campaigns in which troops from all the Burgundian territories took part, but many if not most earlier wars at least brought together men from several different territories in a common enterprise. Other integrative or unifying forces will come to light in the pages that follow.

What did the Valois dukes of Burgundy and their councillors think about their own state? Usually, their motives for political and administrative moves of one kind or another are quite unknown to us. Doubt surrounds, for example, one matter of supreme importance. Both Philip the Good and Charles the Bold wanted to enhance their status as rulers by acquiring a crown; did they hope that this would promote the unity of their lands? The possibility was suggested in 1444 and again near the end of his reign, that Philip the Good should be elected king of the Romans or, what this title really meant, of Germany. Alternatively he might be appointed regent, or imperial vicar, for his own and other imperial territories – perhaps all the imperial territories on the left bank of the Rhine. A similar ambition was entertained by Charles the Bold; according to King Louis XI he was already trying to have himself appointed an imperial vicar before his father's death in June 1467. By 1469 there was a widespread feeling, actively promoted at the Burgundian court, that Duke Charles the Bold should and would very shortly be elected king of the Romans, and that he would succeed the then emperor Frederick III on that ruler's death or retirement. At the end of 1472 Duke Charles sent an ambassador with detailed instructions to this effect to Frederick III's cousin Duke Sigmund of Austria-Tirol.

Although notorious for his lethargy, Frederick III was decidedly unwilling to share power with Charles the Bold, still less to abdicate for his benefit. This recalcitrance may explain the modification in Duke Charles's plans which became evident in 1473, when he appeared to be willing, at least momentarily, to accept a territorial kingdom for himself instead of imperial advancement. This kingdom was to comprise all the Burgundian lands within the Empire, the ecclesiastical principalities which were enclaves in them, Utrecht, Liège and the rest, and the duchies of Cleves, Lorraine and Savoy. The price offered Frederick III in return for the crown Charles wanted was the hand of his heiress Mary of Burgundy in marriage to Frederick's son Maximilian. The project suffered from serious limitations. In the first place it was extremely difficult to find a suitable name for the new kingdom. Philip the Good had suggested in 1447-8 that he might become king of Frisia or Brabant. In 1473 the alternatives seem to have been either a kingdom of Frisia or a kingdom of Burgundy. A second difficulty which vitiated all these schemes was that the duke of Burgundy could never seriously hope to be king in his French territories. After all, Flanders, Artois and the duchy of Burgundy were all of them indubitably and inseparably part of the kingdom of France. Nonetheless, it seems possible that behind these royal ambitions lay, among other attractions, the hope that the royal title and status would help to consolidate the Burgundian territories and increase the power of the dukes. Burgundy might become one of the great monarchies of the West, alongside England and France.

If the last two Valois dukes' desire for a crown be dismissed as mere personal ambition, other evidence does throw some light on the dukes' attitudes towards their own political organization. The notion of Burgundy as a quite distinct power was well expressed in a speech which may have been approved, if not drawn up, by Philip the Bold himself. It was delivered in 1398 in Brussels before the Estates of Brabant and was meant to persuade them to accept Philip as their ruler. The Estates were told that Duke Philip and his successors would be exceptionally well placed to defend and administer their duchy since he already possessed Flanders and his son-in-law William of Bavaria was likely to become count of Hainault, Holland and Zeeland. If Brabant became theirs, Philip and his sons 'would be as powerful as France or England'. Interesting too is a memorandum submitted by John the Fearless's chancellor Jehan de Saulx in 1413 in response to the duchess's request for advice concerning whether or not a ducal Parlement, or law court, should be established in Besançon. Even though this would in itself be of limited importance, argued the chancellor, it could still be advantageous. Great powers have been built up step by step with a series of such small moves. Witness Philip the Bold's establishment of a council in Flanders. Moreover, that duke had only agreed to act as guardian or protector of Besançon in 1386 in the hopes that some greater advantage would follow that small one.

On the whole, the dukes and their advisers do seem to have had some idea of the nature of their own political prospects and ambitions. It looks as though they made purposeful and determined efforts at aggrandizement. They strove consistently to increase their own power, which however was thought of as something essentially personal. One fifteenth-century ducal councillor, Hue de Lannoy, advising his duke, Philip the Good, on how to become a rich and powerful prince, reminds him of the need to win the loyalty and support of his subjects. This way of regarding a state, as comprising a ruler and his subjects, is in a sense modern and in another sense medieval; but at least it emphasizes an essential element of unity in it. We are reminded of Charles the Bold's assertion in the preamble to his famous ordinance of Thionville (1473) setting up the Parlement at Malines, that God has 'instituted and ordained princes to rule principalities and lordships so that the regions, provinces and peoples are joined together and organized in union, concord and loyal discipline'. By that time a distinctive Burgundian loyalty or sentiment had emerged to support and consolidate the dukes' admittedly somewhat incoherent attempts to unify their lands. It even survived the collapse of the Burgundian state in 1477.

CHAPTER THREE

Sources of Information

How can the historian obtain information about the history of Valois Burgundy? And what sort of information will he find? These questions need to be answered because every history is inevitably conditioned by and dependent on its source material, even when, as is the case with Valois Burgundy, that material is of extraordinary richness.

The chronicles and memoirs dealing with the four Valois dukes of Burgundy are so well known that they scarcely require more than a passing mention. In general, one can say that the first three dukes appear in their pages in a very favourable light, for many of these chroniclers were Burgundian in sympathy, and some in origin too. But Charles the Bold was much less fortunate. He figures very largely in the mendacious and partisan pages of that arch-liar Philippe de Commynes, who deserted Charles's service for that of Louis XI, and there are extremely unflattering accounts of him in the German chronicles. The *Memoirs* of Philippe de Commynes contain no significant information from before 1464; the chronicle of John Froissart ends at 1400. These are the two best-known historical writers of the age and their works have been translated more than once into English, as has the chronicle of Enguerrand de Monstrelet, which continues Froissart to 1444. Other famous chroniclers, who wrote between Froissart and de Commynes, were George Chastellain and Olivier de la Marche, both of whom were Burgundian in every possible respect. The interests of these men, all of them noble, revolved round warfare, chivalry and the life of the court. Monstrelet speaks for them all when he says that he wrote

for the instruction and information of those who in a just cause may be desirous of honourably exercising their prowess in arms; and also to celebrate the glory and renown of those who by strength and bodily vigour have gallantly distinguished themselves, as well in sudden rencounters as in pitched battles, armies against armies, as valiant men ought to do . . .

Some of these men wrote poetry as well as history. Some of them tempered their interest in deeds of arms with a certain amount of hero-worship for their ruler, with an interest in politics, or with a measure of curiosity about other matters. One of them, George Chastellain, was the first official chronicler at the Burgundian court. He was paid by Philip the Good the salary of £657 16s. of Tours, a salary equal to that of the Duke's best-paid and most senior officials and councillors. Chastellain's task was 'to put into writing novel and rightful happenings which he knows about and is expert in. Also to record in the form of a chronicle notable deeds, worthy of remembrance, which have occurred in the past, which are still occurring, and which will often occur in the future.'

Besides these and other aristocrats of fifteenth-century historiography there are plenty of others, some similar, some quite different in character and outlook, whose works remain invaluable to the historian of the dukes of Burgundy even if they have entirely escaped the attention of the reading public of the twentieth century: the ducal secretary Edmond de Dynter, for instance, who copied innumerable documents into his accurate and informative Latin chronicle, and who was often consulted by Philip the Good on matters of state; the ecclesiastic, Thomas Basin, who became bishop of Lisieux in 1447 at the age of thirty-five, and who also wrote in Latin; and the official French 'historiographer' Jehan Chartier, brother of the celebrated poet Alain Chartier. Nor must we omit civic chroniclers like the anonymous burgess of Paris and Jehan Denis, burgess of Mâcon in the extreme south of Burgundy, of whose *Journal* unfortunately only a fragment, extending from 1430 to 1438, survives. In this category must be included the local chronicles of Tournai, of Liège and of Speyer, to name but a few, as well as the magistrate of Ypres Oliver van Dixmude's interesting and detailed but little-known book entitled *Remarkable events, especially in Flanders and Brabant*, which might more modestly and accurately have been called *Remarkable events, mostly in Ypres*. Another chronicle, the so-called *Dagboek* or diary of Ghent, beginning in the middle of the fifteenth century almost exactly where van Dixmude leaves off, deserves mention. Both the Ypres and the Ghent chronicles are written in Flemish.

The subject of civic chronicles can hardly be passed by without some mention of two of the most remarkable pieces of historical writing of the fifteenth century, both of which are of prime importance for the last Valois duke of Burgundy, Charles the Bold. One, the Latin diary of the chaplain of Basel, Johann

Knebel, is civic in outlook and interest though clerical in authorship and inspiration. It contains every kind of report and rumour, every scrap of news, every document the writer could lay hands on. Knebel was in close touch with the civic, university and ecclesiastical authorities of Basel. He was a friend of the Swiss and a bitter enemy of the duke of Burgundy. The surviving sections of his diary cover the years 1473–9 and describe in brilliantly spontaneous detail but with all kinds of error and falsification the campaigns of Charles the Bold against the Swiss and the antics of Peter von Hagenbach, the unpopular, indeed in Knebel's pages positively satanic, Burgundian bailiff of Alsace.

The other civic chronicler of outstanding relevance for Burgundian history was Diebold Schilling, originally of Solothurn, a clerk of the court and town councillor at Bern, who was commissioned in 1474 to write the official chronicle of Bern in German. His three massive and superbly illustrated volumes are still to be seen in the Burgerbibliothek there. They constitute an absolutely invaluable source for the reign of Charles the Bold from 1468 onwards, even though Schilling is often unreliable or downright erroneous. Part of his passion derives from his firm belief that warfare was profitable and that God was fighting for the Swiss against the French-speaking foreigners or Burgundians. He makes no effort to tell the truth but he tries hard and with success to tell a marvellous story supremely well. It is this that makes him one of the greatest of all chroniclers. Today he would be a journalist, and a good one.

Chroniclers describe contemporary events, often in valuable detail. Obviously they are a vitally useful source of information; but they tend to concentrate unduly on a handful of topics: either on the life of the court, on embassies, on military matters, on the actions of the rulers; or else, in the case of civic chroniclers, on the affairs of their own town or region. The court chroniclers may copy out treaties and challenges but they throw little light on economic matters, on administration or on institutions. They tell us about wars rather than about armies; about the costly manifestations of courtly life and luxury organized by the dukes, but not about their revenues; they describe the revolts of urban artisans but do not explain them. For information on these and many other points ignored by the chroniclers we must turn to the records.

It is sometimes thought that records surviving from the middle ages are so scanty that they have to be searched for. The historian is envisaged actually hunting for documents in libraries and muniment rooms, if not in cellars and attics. This may be true of the early middle ages but, for the period after about 1200, abundant material has survived in an accessible form. Indeed, quantities of medieval documents have still not even been looked at, let alone calendared or inventoried. At Genoa over 50,000 notarial contracts have survived for each year during the thirteenth century, illustrating the commerce, and the history in general, of a single Italian city. In the case of Burgundy, the eighteenth-century monk Urbain Plancher, in his four enormous folio volumes, printed the full texts of nearly 600 documents relating to the reigns of the four Valois dukes of Burgundy which he had found in the archives at Dijon. But this hardly scratched the surface. In fact, it was only a kind of distillation from over one hundred manuscript volumes of transcripts of Dijon documents used by Plancher in the preparation of his history of Burgundy. Because of their accessibility and the careful arrangement of their contents these volumes, forming the famous *Collection de Bourgogne* in the Bibliothèque Nationale at Paris, have been more often used by historians of Burgundy than their documentary exemplars in the archives at Dijon.

The official documents, the records of government, of the Valois dukes of Burgundy have for the most part remained in the towns where they were originally made, that is, in the administrative centres of the Burgundian state; at Lille, seat of the ducal accounting office or *chambre des comptes* for Flanders and other northern lands; at Brussels, capital of Brabant; and, in the south, at Dijon. Only a few have been moved elsewhere. The archives, as well as the treasure, of the Golden Fleece, the Burgundian Order of Chivalry, were evacuated from Brussels in 1794 when the French revolutionary armies invaded the Low Countries. They have remained in Vienna ever since, in spite of Belgian attempts to recover them from Austria by diplomatic pressure after the First World War, and in spite of the hopes of some Belgians after the Second World War.

The most abundant, the most valuable to the historian, and rightly the most famous of the Burgundian governmental records are the remarkable series of accounts which survive nearly complete for the period of the Valois dukes. These bulky imperial-size quarto parchment books occupy shelf after shelf in the archives at Dijon, Lille, Brussels and The Hague. First and foremost among them is the series of so-called central accounts, those of the receiver-general of all finances. Over eighty of these annual volumes survive for the period between their start around 1380 and the death of the last Valois duke of Burgundy in 1477. Next come the several series of regional accounts. Those of the receipt-general of the duchy and county of Burgundy are nearly complete up to the end of the reign of the third duke, Philip the Good; that is to say, again, over eighty annual volumes survive. From the receipt-general of Flanders and Artois in this period thirty-two volumes survive, while the accounts of the separate territories added by Philip the Good to the Burgundian state are for the most part tolerably complete: those of the county of Hainault at Lille, those of Brabant and Luxembourg at Brussels, those of Holland at The Hague.

Besides these nearly complete series of central and regional accounts, the accounts of local receivers in the different territories survive literally in thousands. Take the local receivers' accounts in the county of Artois which, in the fifteenth century, was divided for purposes of administration into bailiwicks and castellanies. In each bailiwick or castellany a local receiver submitted his accounts annually to the ducal accounting office for Flanders and Artois at Lille. For the ducal period we possess 'runs' of accounts from nearly all these administrative divisions in Artois, and some of them are continuous over many years. The accounts of the castellany of Bapaume, for instance, are unbroken between 1422 and 1428 and between 1442 and 1468, and those of the ducal domain at Hesdin form an almost continuous series from before Artois came into the hands of the dukes in 1384 until a few years before Charles the Bold's death in 1477, with only four breaks of less than five years each.

What exactly can be discovered, in quantitative or financial terms, from these Burgundian ducal accounts? And what are the limitations of this source of information? To see how the accounts are actually arranged or set out, we have to look at the different headings or rubrics which occur in them and under which the various items are grouped. Let us take a fairly typical series of regional accounts, those of the receipt-general of the duchy and county of Burgundy. First come receipts. The revenues of the main administrative divisions of the duchy, called bailiwicks, are followed by the revenues from each castellany, and by those from the ducal rights over waters and forests, those from the ducal salt monopoly, and those from the county of Burgundy. Sometimes receipts from loans, and revenues from mints, are entered. Finally, a number of small, miscellaneous receipts are grouped under the title *recepte commune*.

What were the main headings of expenses in the accounts of the regional receiver-general of Burgundy? First come moneys paid to other ducal accounting officers, mostly to the receiver-general of all finances and to the officials responsible for court expenses, who had no territorial or domanial revenues of their own, but who relied on payments from the regional and local receivers. Sometimes, after this, follow payments for buildings and repayments of loans, but these sections are small and of irregular occurrence. Next come a whole series of payments to ducal officials: pensions or annual salaries, daily wages for councillors away from home on special missions, payments for ambassadors and messengers, and gifts and compensations to officials, for instance of money for robes or for the loss of a horse on ducal service. At the end of the account expenses for war materials and for troops sometimes occur, miscellaneous minor expenses are grouped under the heading *despense commune*, and the book closes with the sum totals of all expenses and of all receipts. The balance is then drawn up and a statement made of what was owed to or by the accounting officer concerned.

This last point illustrates one of the difficulties facing the historian using these Burgundian accounts. They are not, like modern accounts, designed to throw light on the financial situation of the accounting organization. Far from it. Their primary purpose was to make it difficult or impossible for the duke's financial officers to embezzle the funds which they had to be permitted to handle on his behalf.

It will be noted that the headings of receipts and expenses just mentioned are by no means particularly suited for the extraction from these accounts of useful or interesting quantitative information. We cannot use them directly, or at all easily, to ascertain what the duke spent say, on war or books, or what he borrowed in the course of an average year. There is no heading or classification which reveals how much was spent on administration, how much on food, how much on court festivities. The expenses are not classified in this way. And even when there is such a heading, as in the case of wages of councillors, or money spent on jewellery and plate, it only covers the expenses on those items of one receiver. Suppose, for example, that we wish to discover what the duke spent on clothes. If we consult the relevant sections among the expenses recorded in the accounts of the receiver-general of all finances, headed 'Purchases of cloth of gold and of silk' and 'Purchases of woollen cloths, furs, etc.', we shall find set out in detail, and totalled, the moneys spent on these things by the receiver-general of all finances. But almost every other receiver, both regional and local, may have spent something on the ducal wardrobe, so we cannot hazard even an estimate of the total ducal expenditure on clothes until all the accounts for the period concerned have been searched.

The same goes for receipts. Just as the Burgundian accounting officers made no attempt anywhere to centralize and total all the expenditure on one particular group of objects or services, so, likewise, there is no attempt to centralize or total the receipts coming from the individual ducal territories. Exactly the same problems face the historian trying to ascertain whence the dukes obtained their revenues as face him when he tries to analyse their expenditure. The moneys from one particular territory are partly recorded in the accounts of the local receivers of bailiwicks and castellanies, partly in those of the regional receivers, and only a kind of arbitrary contribution, rather than a surplus, appears in the accounts of the receiver-general of all finances.

The fact that many of the Burgundian accounts were submitted and made up at irregular intervals, and that there was no such thing, in fifteenth-century Burgundy, as a uniform financial year, is a minor snag compared to the task of rendering the sums recorded in them into a common money of account. Even the officials themselves often did not trouble to add together the sums recorded in groats, crowns, nobles, francs, pounds of Paris and pounds of Tours. They simply totalled each currency separately at the end of their account and left it at that. But even this difficulty is surmountable: the current exchange rates are often given in the accounts. A more serious obstacle to using these accounts in a straightforward manner is the fact that they are not purely cash accounts. That is to say, the transactions recorded in them are often only accounting transactions. When the Burgundian receiver-general records a sum of 50,000 francs paid to the duke of Burgundy by the king of France, this may have been handed over in cash, or in the shape of a promissory note, in which some royal accounting official is instructed to pay over 50,000 francs on demand to the bearer. Similarly we find recorded among the receipts of the receiver-general of all finances payments which had in fact been assigned by him to some junior colleague, and which are therefore also recorded by the junior colleague in his accounts, but this time among the expenses. This is the system of assignments, which was apparently designed to minimize the need for transporting coin.

The main lesson of all this is one of caution. It is simply irrelevant and uninformative to compile statistics based on the analysis of one series of accounts only. Yet this is exactly what has been done by historians, who have tried, and still try from time to time, to derive an idea of the total ducal income and expenditure from the accounts of the receiver-general of all finances alone, as if all receipts and payments were centralized by him. The fact is that the Burgundian accounts are extremely difficult to use quantitatively, partly because of their internal arrangement and partly because of the complexity of the relationship of the different series of accounts to one another. On the other hand, from the qualitative point of view they abound in information of all kinds, some of it of the utmost value to the historian, some of it trivial in the extreme. Almost every historian of the Valois dukes of Burgundy has drawn on these accounts, using them as a sort of mine of information covering all aspects of ducal life and government.

The accounts record in detail payments to artists and writers, to jewellers and goldsmiths, to shopkeepers and publicans, to ambassadors and secretaries. What happened at Dijon in 1410 when the duke decided to muster his army? An entry in the accounts tells us that a group of clerks were paid for hastily writing 633 letters close on paper, four copies of each letter, for dispatch to the nobles, and also to some captains and burgesses, of Burgundy, summoning them all to be ready to serve the duke in arms on 8 August. What happened when a new cannon was made at St Omer? It is the accounts that tell us that it was set up outside the walls of the town and tried out in the presence of Duke John himself. A cover had been made for it in case of rain; the stone which it fired into the fields was carefully retrieved; and the cannon was afterwards moved elsewhere by three men and two horses. What happened when Duke Philip the Good acquired a manuscript for his library? An illuminator was paid to erase the coats-of-arms of the former owner, painted into it, and to insert those of Philip and his wife in their place. From the accounts too, we learn that Philip the Good was interested in war materials as well as illuminated manuscripts: he rented a garden in Brussels in 1448–50 not for recreation or horticulture, but in order to store in it a prefabricated wooden bridge designed to enable his army to cross rivers and moats.

The accounts of the ducal household or court, in which a special official, called the *maître de la chambre aux deniers*, recorded the day-to-day expenses of the duke's court, are of special interest. They were entered daily and totalled monthly. The importance of these accounts for the historian lies not only in the accurate information they provide about the expenditure of the court, but also in the fact that they establish firmly the duke's itinerary. That is to say, they tell us exactly where the duke of Burgundy dined and slept on any particular day and night. Unfortunately the destructive fervour of the French revolutionaries was directed against these monuments of aristocratic indulgence and few of them avoided the fate of conversion into glue, cartridges or some other mundane commodity. It should not be thought, however, that with them we have lost all record of Burgundian court extravagance. Not at all. For the *chambre aux deniers* was only responsible for the day-to-day expenditure on food and drink, while the numerous payments for tapestries, jewels, plate, lions and other animals for the duke's menagerie, paintings and so on are recorded in the account of the receiver-general of all finances, and scattered entries of this kind are also to be found in almost every other series of accounts.

It sometimes happens that an apparently quite insignificant series of accounts proves on investigation to be of exceptional interest. Take the case of the surviving records of the council of Flanders, one of the main governmental institutions in the Burgundian Netherlands. No record of the proceedings of this council has come down to us, but we do have the accounts of the judicial fines it levied in the course of its work as a law court. They form a continuous series, without a single gap or interruption, from before the first establishment of the council at Ghent in 1407 until after the death of Charles the Bold in 1477. They are important, not for the details of the fines levied which are recorded in them, but because the clerk who received and accounted for the money they realized was instructed to spend it too and, among other things, he spent it on messengers sent by the council. Moreover, being a meticulous civil servant, he recorded the date the message was sent, the name of the messenger, and details of the message itself, or an analysis of the letter if it took the form of a letter. Thus, from these apparently trivial documents we can re-create in all its detail and variety the administrative history and much of the general history of fifteenth-century Flanders.

So far, few historians have used these accounts. They contain a great deal of information about the coastal defences of Flanders, about English pirates and raids, and about Anglo-Flemish relations in general. For instance, on 4 May 1418 a messenger was hurriedly dispatched by the council on a hired horse to warn the magistrates of the Flemish coastal towns that the English had threatened or boasted that they were about to raid the Flemish coast with a large fleet, having refused to renew the truces. Earlier, in 1406, this same source records the dispatch of a messenger to the duke of Burgundy in Paris to inform him that the English had actually landed at Ostend; but this expedition consisted only of twelve men and a dog. On the relations between the ducal administration and the Flemish towns, too, these accounts have much to say. At Ghent for example, riots occurred one Tuesday night in June 1406 which had been provoked by the duke's enemies there; at Ypres the councillors reported to their duke on 18 April 1407 that six malefactors had conspired to kill the ducal bailiff and the magistrates. Trouble arose again in December 1416 when the duke was trying to raise a subsidy of 60,000 double crowns from the Flemings: one of the magistrates of Ghent received an anonymous letter threatening to burn down all his houses and granges outside the town if he and his colleagues agreed to this tax.

Informative as they are, the accounts alone provide a somewhat one-sided view of the Burgundian state and its administration and of the activities of the dukes. Also, much of the information in them is banal in the extreme. Do we really require a detailed description of every pair of shoes worn by the duke? Do we really want to know which of the household officers could beat the duke at tennis? Or the cost of making a leather cover for the portable washbasin Philip the Bold carried about with him? A high proportion of the factual material in the ducal accounts is made up of this sort of information.

Fortunately there are plenty of other documents, besides the accounts, for the historian to turn to. At Lille, for instance, he will find the *Registres des chartes*, a series of registers in which were transcribed numerous documents issued by the ducal chancery of which copies were needed in the accounting office for purposes of financial administration. These documents include ducal letters granting pardons, legitimations and privileges of all kinds, letters containing instructions for the accounting officials, and the letters of appointment of ducal officials. They concern all the northern territories of the Burgundian state. They touch on negotiations and treaties, the court and family of the duke, the privileges and possessions of the towns, the clergy and religious foundations, seigneurial rights and commercial activity. Fifteen large folio volumes of stout paper cover the period of the Valois dukes. There are seventy-nine of these registers in all, containing over 25,000 acts, from the years 1386 to 1667. Some examples will serve to illustrate the variety and scope of the information to be obtained from them. We learn that a ducal accounting officer who either omitted something from his account, or entered too much, was to be fined twice the offending sum. We learn, too, that if by chance the same vacancy was filled twice, priority was to be given to the candidate appointed first; that ducal officials were not permitted to keep public houses; that their illegitimate children were frequently legitimized by the duke; and that they enjoyed gifts of land and rents from him to supplement their salaries.

Thus far on the ducal administration and administrative personnel. But the scope of these registers is by no means purely administrative. They include copies of treaties with England. They include disciplinary ordinances which, among other things, prohibit the nobles from distributing liveries and badges and forbid them to hold assemblies or reviews. We find here, too, the record of homages done to the dukes of Burgundy in return for money fiefs by minor German and Low Countries lords whom the dukes wished to win over to their interests. We find documents about fortifications, for instance one recording that the moats of the duke's castle at Ruppelmonde in Flanders had to be cleaned out every seven years by the local inhabitants. We find documents about urban taxation and about the sea defences along the Flemish coast. But, above all, these registers abound in information about commerce and industry. They contain copies of letters concerning commercial negotiations with the Hanseatic League and copies of trading privileges granted by the dukes to different groups of merchants resorting to Flanders, for example those from Scotland, Portugal, Newcastle and Norwich. They include, too, numerous ducal regulations concerning the Flemish cloth industry and the growing herring fishery of the Flemish ports. On 27 October 1395 Duke Philip the Bold prohibited the use of fine mesh nets between Gravelines and Sluis in order to stop the killing of young fish, and he appointed a commission to look into the whole question of the mesh of fishing nets. We also learn from these registers of the damage done by his rabbits in the coastal warrens both to the sea defences and to crops. In 1398 the inhabitants were permitted by the duke to stop up their holes.

The Burgundian councillors and financial officials did not content themselves with compiling registers of documents which they needed for administrative purposes. They also recorded the minutes of their own proceedings. For example the combined accounting office and council at Dijon, which administered the southern territories, kept two registers for this purpose: the *Livre des mémoriaux* or *mémoires* and the *Journal des causes*. The former comprises the minutes of the ordinary sessions; the latter records the legal cases held and judged by the council. For the general historian, the *Livre des mémoriaux* is by far the more interesting. From it we can learn a great deal about the structure and personnel of the ducal administration in Burgundy; about the additional taxes or *aides* levied there by the dukes; about the ducal archives, domains, buildings, artillery and so on. This source invariably gives the names of the councillors attending each session; an analysis of the contents of important letters received from the duke and others and demanding action by the council or accounting office; and details of the oaths on taking office of newly appointed officials. The frequent changes in handwriting show that it is a strictly contemporary record, written up after each meeting of the council.

Similar in interest and scope are the *Memoriaal boeken* of Philip the Good's council of Holland at The Hague, in which numerous documents are transcribed. Indeed these registers are the most important single source of information for fifteenth-century Dutch history.

The accounts, the *Registres des chartes*, the minute-books so far described are all of them books kept by ducal officials for record purposes. But the Burgundian officials also carefully filed away and preserved all the letters they received from whatever source, together, in many cases, with drafts or copies of the letters they sent. The abundant original correspondence of the accounting office at Lille is still for the most part preserved there, though some of it is now at Brussels. These letters have been neither used nor indeed even fully inspected by historians. There are thousands of them, still uncatalogued, but filed roughly in chronological order, with one bundle for each year. On the back of every incoming letter is recorded the name of the messenger who brought it, the date it arrived at Lille and the name of the sender. Since the accounting office was concerned primarily with the administration of the ducal finances, much of this correspondence is from, or addressed to, the ducal financial officers. A receiver-general of Flanders writes to invite the accounting officials to his daughter's wedding. Another explains that he cannot come to Lille on the day fixed because he has caught a cold. A bailiff has a more elaborate excuse for not bringing his accounts for audit on the appointed day. Just as he was all ready to set out with his accounts, a suspected murderer was brought in. Tortured, he confessed and accused his accomplices, and the bailiff felt it his duty to go after them then and there. Another bailiff writes asking the accounting officials to recommend him for promotion; a ducal secretary writes with important news from Paris. Above all, this correspondence throws light on the day-to-day working of the ducal administration in the northern territories, on the administrative personnel, and on the activities of the accounting office itself.

The correspondence of the Lille accounting office is only a small part of the enormous quantity of original material in the Burgundian archives. There are thousands upon thousands of the actual documents issued or received by the dukes of Burgundy and their officers, including treaties, ordinances, letters patent and receipts, to name a few categories only. Their quantity is often unnerving. Well over 800 original letters and other documents concerning Anglo-Flemish relations in John the Fearless's time as duke, that is the fifteen years between 1404 and 1419, survive at Lille. They are arranged roughly in chronological order and some are mentioned in the printed inventory of the Lille archives. But this is not true of the thousands of unsorted documents in the series called *Acquits de Lille* at Brussels. These are stored in boxes and folders, the contents of which may or may not correspond with the all too brief description in the typescript inventory at the archives. Other series of original documents in the Archives Générales du Royaume at Brussels are filed in chronological order, but are still undescribed in print. This applies, for example, to the two series called *Trésor des chartes de Flandre*, which include several thousand documents from the ducal Burgundian period.

Many of these documents are unsorted simply because they are undated or even undatable, and their value to the historian is thus in any case severely restricted. Such a document is the paper roll at Lille, containing instructions for the ducal council at Ghent, but without date. According to this document, the president of the council must always take the chair at meetings. He must respect the decision of the majority of councillors. If a councillor is late, or misbehaves in any way, the president is empowered to fine him a day's wages. The councillors are not permitted to read, write, chat or otherwise divert themselves while their president is talking. The document ends by stating that the duke is not going to give his councillors a rise even though things cost more now than they ever did before.

So much, then, for the official governmental archives of the Burgundian state. What with the hundreds of volumes of accounts of all kinds, the registers in which letters, ordinances, records of judicial proceedings and the like are copied or calendared and, finally, the actual documents themselves, the historian of Valois Burgundy cannot conceivably be short of material. Indeed, it is surely true to say that no one scholar could possibly survey, still less master, all the official documentary sources of information at his disposal. Moreover, quite apart from this specifically Burgundian material, the archives of almost every European power, especially the towns, contain documents relating to Burgundy. The town archives contain minutes of the meetings of town councils, incoming correspondence and accounts of income and expenditure, and they survive in quantity in most of the towns which particularly concerned the dukes of Burgundy. The minute-books of the town councils often contain analyses of letters and documents received by the municipality, as well as records of its deliberations and decisions, and mentions of important events. Their value is illustrated by the fact that many of them have found their way into print: for instance those of Geneva, Cologne, Troyes and Tournai. A great deal of information about the dukes is to be found here. Naturally the as yet unprinted record of the deliberations of the magistrates or councillors of the dukes' capital in Burgundy, Dijon, called the *Papier du Secret*, is of special importance for the history of Valois Burgundy. Thirty-five of these paper volumes cover the ducal period and they may be supplemented by the files of correspondence of the municipality, where some 370 letters from the Valois period will be found. With this wealth of material from Dijon available, the historian may not think it necessary to examine the magnificent series of town accounts. If he does, he will discover, among many other things, the actual addresses of the ducal officials resident in Dijon.

The correspondence that passed between towns, especially between the south German and Swiss towns, and especially in Charles the Bold's reign as duke, would provide a mass of information about Burgundy if some enterprising scholar could find time to search the present-day town archives. Already, however, much has been done by way of printing, or at least calendaring, the correspondence between the Swiss towns relating to Charles the Bold's campaigns there. Besides this inter-town correspondence, there are many letters from individuals, captains in the field writing home, and so on. Such a one is the still unprinted letter which a certain Jorg Hochmut, chaplain of Nördlingen in Bavaria then living at Zürich, sent to his home town with a very full account of Duke Charles's defeat by the Swiss at the battle Grandson on 2 March 1476 and the events leading to it.

An unusual document of a quite different kind is the earliest chapter book of the Order of the Golden Fleece, now at Vienna. It contains a full account of each meeting or chapter of the Order made by its clerk, who often took the trouble to record the duke's speeches verbatim. It is particularly valuable for Duke Charles the Bold and is perhaps the most important single source of information for Valois Burgundy still unprinted. Parts of it were however summarized by the nineteenth-century historian of the Order, the baron de Reiffenberg.

Last but by no means least, a quite new historical source only begins to shed light on affairs in the course of the fifteenth century: the dispatches of ambassadors. More or less permanent ambassadors first appear at European courts in the second half of the fifteenth century. They spread from Renaissance Italy, and the first ambassadors at the French and Burgundian courts were Italians. These men were well educated and highly trained spies. They wrote an impeccable italic hand. Sometimes they wrote in code. They spied on each other as well as on the governments they were accredited to, and they intercepted and deciphered each other's dispatches. Most important for Burgundian history are the dispatches in the Italian state archives at Milan which were sent to Duke Galeazzo Maria Sforza of Milan by his ambassador at Charles the Bold's court in 1475-6, Johanne Petro Panigarola. Two volumes of printed texts were published as long ago as 1858, but these were sadly incomplete, many dispatches being abridged or omitted altogether. It is to be hoped that the American scholars now engaged on editing the earlier dispatches will soon make good this deficiency and print all Panigarola's dispatches in full. The Venetian ambassador at Charles the Bold's court, Bernardo Bembo, was instructed to send a dispatch every day, but nearly all of them have perished.

How do the sources of information available for Burgundian history compare with those for other fifteenth-century states? As far as records go, the papacy and England are probably better documented than Burgundy; France less well. A few fifteenth-century states have lost virtually all their archive material: in September 1943 the German authorities removed and deliberately destroyed the rich archives of medieval Naples. On the whole, Burgundy has thus fared well. The documentary material is there and the historian's main difficulties lie in using it: he may be hampered by its very abundance, its division among many different archive repositories, and the fact that it is written in Latin, French, Netherlandish, German and Italian. As to chronicles, here Valois Burgundy is unchallenged. Almost all the finest historical writers of the age wrote about Burgundy. Who else is there besides Froissart, Monstrelet, Chastellain, de la Marche, de Commynes, not to mention Knebel and Schilling?

CHAPTER FOUR

Burgundy and her Neighbours

Valois Burgundy can only be understood in relation to the other European powers. Naturally, she had a special relationship with the French monarchy, whose offspring in a sense she was. Naturally, she was a cog in the wheels of the Hundred Years War, endlessly interlocked in confrontations and connections with England and Brittany as well as the French monarchy. Naturally, too, she had a distinct relationship with the emperors, whose territories she had annexed. Broadly speaking, both the kings of France and the emperors resented and feared the political upstart which had arisen through combining together a number of different territories in that no-man's-land of assorted polities which lay between them. Broadly speaking, the dukes of Burgundy were able to reduce the precariousness of this situation and even extend their power by means of a system of allies and clients. More often than not, they were in alliance with England; consistently they maintained good relations with the popes. To enhance their influence they made contacts of many kinds at one time or another with almost every European power from Portugal to Poland. But what was far more essential to their political survival was the structure of connections with small powers which they put together and carefully maintained both inside France and inside the Empire, and especially along the frontier between them. These relationships, between Burgundy and her neighbours large and small, form the subject-matter of this chapter.

The Valois dukes of Burgundy originated in the royal family of France. They spoke French. The territories which formed the nucleus of their state, put together under Philip the Bold, were mostly fiefs of the French crown. Their administration was modelled on that of France, their intellectual and cultural interests were French; they were, after all, French princes. But, while Philip the Bold planned in 1386 to make war against England arm-in-arm with France, Charles the Bold hoped in 1475 to make war against France arm-in-arm with England.

While Philip the Bold spent more than half his time in France, Charles the Bold only visited that country at the head of an army. Thus the relationship of the Valois dukes to the French crown was transformed from intimacy to open hostility. But since all the time the dukes were vassals of the kings, the French connection inescapably persisted.

When Philip the Bold lay dying in the Stag Inn at Hal near Brussels in April 1404 he insisted that his sons John and Anthony should swear loyalty and obedience to King Charles VI of France. Such an allegiance must have seemed essential, as well as natural, to Philip the Bold. After all, he had served his brother King Charles V as a royal lieutenant and in other capacities, in the 1370s. He had acted virtually as regent for his youthful nephew Charles VI in the 1380s and again after that monarch went mad in 1392. Paris was his favourite and habitual place of residence in the last ten years of his life. His own personal and dynastic interests may have seemed to him identical to those of France and he may well have sincerely believed, for example, that it was in the interests of the French crown for the towns and territories of Lille, Douai and Orchies to be transferred to him and to Burgundy. Nevertheless, Philip the Bold certainly appears in the perspective of history as a ruthlessly successful dynast who more or less unscrupulously manipulated the French connection for the benefit of Burgundy. He seems no different in these respects from his brothers Louis of Anjou and John of Berry, nor from his rival for power in France, Charles VI's brother Louis of Orleans; except that he was spectacularly successful in exploiting French resources in his own interests while they were not.

Valois Burgundy was really carried into history on the broad shoulders of France. France provided the title and the territories to set Philip the Bold up as a European prince in the first place. When his accession to power in Flanders seemed blocked by the revolutionaries of Ghent, the French king and army were brought to his aid; not once only, but on three separate occasions, in 1382, 1383 and 1385. When he needed experienced officials for the administration of his lands, France supplied them. The treasurer of France was placed at the head of the Burgundian financial administration. A French royal official was on several occasions temporarily seconded to Burgundy to preside over the duke's Parlement or law court at Beaune. When Philip the Bold needed consorts for his descendants these were found in France: in May 1403 no fewer than four children of King Charles VI were promised in marriage to four of Philip the Bold's grandchildren. Finally, and most blatantly of all, Philip dipped into the French royal treasury to fill his own Burgundian coffers. Perhaps here too he managed to convince himself he was acting in the best interests of France. In 1384 he persuaded Charles VI to make him a free gift of 100,000 francs. In 1386 a further payment of 120,000 francs was described as compensation for the expenses Philip had incurred in defending and pacifying Flanders on behalf of the French crown. In December 1402 Philip had the effrontery to help himself to a New Year's gift of 10,000 francs from the king, on the grounds that he had given the king the usual gift on 1 January 1401, but the king had omitted to return the compliment! By this time Duke Philip was receiving annually an average of something like 235,000 francs from the French royal treasury, amounting to nearly half of his total annual revenue from all sources.

It will be understood that this massive French contribution to the rise of Burgundy was by no means an act of independent French royal policy. On the contrary, the king and the royal government were in Philip the Bold's pocket. From 1392 onwards he was in control of French affairs and of the French royal administration while the unfortunate king, during his protracted fits of madness, capered about the corridors of the royal palace howling like a wolf; or else, believing he was made of glass, proceeded with the utmost caution, for fear of breaking himself.

This was the background to Duke Philip's deathbed adjuration to his sons, mentioned above. But John the Fearless found it quite impossible to maintain himself in Paris as master of royal France as his father had done. He was vigorously opposed there by Louis, duke of Orleans, who evidently had more right to act as regent in his brother's 'absences' (as they were euphemistically called) than had Duke John, who was only a cousin of the insane king. It soon became clear that Burgundian influence in France could be maintained only by violence and force of arms: even Philip the Bold had had to deploy Burgundian troops in the streets of Paris in 1401. John the Fearless, who found the flood of French royal finance reduced to the merest trickle because most of it was now diverted to Louis of Orleans, hired a group of thugs and contrived to have Louis assassinated in a Paris street on the evening of 23 November 1407. Thereafter, opposition to John the Fearless in France was coloured by hatred and heightened by thoughts of revenge. Although John returned to Paris in 1408, a league of French princes was formed against him in 1410 headed by the count of Armagnac, Bernard VII, who gave his name to his party. Intermittent civil war between Armagnacs and Burgundians now intervened. The duke of Burgundy was at times little more than the leader of a faction but, imperceptibly, he tightened his control of the French government. In 1410 he managed to obtain some 165,500 francs from the French treasury. But that was his best year. In 1413, after a popular uprising in Paris, he was expelled from the capital and only succeeded in returning there, at the head of an army, in 1418. A year later, on 10 September 1419, he was murdered by his political opponents according to a carefully prearranged plan on the bridge at Montereau during what was supposed to have been a diplomatic parley.

John the Fearless had devoted nearly all his time and energy during his brief reign as duke to trying to keep control of the French government. His excuse for this preoccupation was expressed in one of his ordinances of 1408, in which he explained that he had to be in France 'because of the important affairs of the king, whom we wish to support with all our power, as we are bound to do by virtue both of lineage and homage'. His son Philip the Good was faced with a difficult situation in the autumn of 1419 when he succeeded John the Fearless as duke. France was divided into three parts. In the north was Lancastrian France, including Normandy, recently conquered and now ruled by King Henry V of England, who had won the battle of Agincourt on 25 October 1415 partly because of the absence from the French army on that occasion of John the Fearless and his eldest son Philip, who had been prohibited by his father from joining the French army, and of several other French princes. South of the Loire was Dauphinist France, the inhabitants of which had transferred their allegiance from the mad King Charles VI to his eldest son, the sixteen-year-old Dauphin Charles, who had certainly been involved in the assassination of John the Fearless. In the north-east was Burgundian France, which was being ruled by John the Fearless. He had set up a sort of court and government at Troyes, where he had installed King Charles VI and his queen Isabel. After much deliberation of councillors the new duke Philip the Good determined in 1419 to withdraw from the exposed, dangerous and no longer profitable position which his father had tried to maintain for himself in France. His signature of the treaty of Troyes, on 21 May 1420, which made King Henry V of England, now married to Catherine of France, regent of France and successor to the French crown after Charles VI, thus disinheriting the Dauphin Charles, marks a turning-point in Burgundian history and in Burgundian policy towards France. For throughout his long reign (1419–67) Philip the Good's back was turned to France and his attention held elsewhere. Burgundian history was no longer to be made in Paris, but in the Low Countries and towards the Rhine.

Philip the Good's alliance with England of 1420 was followed by some half-hearted displays of Burgundian military co-operation with the invading and occupying English. But after Henry VI's death in 1422 these minor Burgundian attacks on Dauphinist France were interrupted by negotiations; even before then they had been carefully restricted by local truces. Philip the Good was soon charging the English for the cost of the limited military assistance he was grudgingly prepared to give them. His alliance with England was of limited scope in any case because, while he co-operated with one English prince, John, duke of Bedford, in France, he was fighting wars against another, Bedford's brother Humphrey, duke of Gloucester, in defence of Burgundian territorial claims in the Netherlands. By the time Joan of Arc appeared on the scene in 1429 to galvanize the dauphin into having himself crowned king of France at Rheims (his father had died in 1422) and to lead French troops to victory against the English, Philip the Good was preparing for a settlement with Charles VII. This came as a result of the Congress of Arras in 1435, Europe's first large-scale international peace conference.

In spite of the apparent diplomatic revolution at Arras – the creation of a Franco-Burgundian alignment and the dislocation of the Anglo-Burgundian connection of 1420 – the general relationship of France, Burgundy and England was not greatly changed. No general peace settlement could conceivably have come about because the English and French were engaged at that very moment in warfare for control of Paris, which the invading English had held since 1420. The English and French delegations at Arras would not even attend divine service together, let alone meet in the same room. Naturally, England and Burgundy were estranged by the Arras negotiations between France and Burgundy. Indeed they fought a rather absurd little war in 1436; Philip the Good tried to lay siege to Calais, but his fleet was delayed and his army mutinied and decamped at the end of July, and Duke Humphrey of Gloucester led a retaliatory raid into Flanders in August. But this was a mere interlude. Anglo-Burgundian relations very soon settled down again and they remained friendly during the remainder of Philip's reign. As to the Franco-Burgundian alliance of Arras, this was an alliance in name only. It was dominated by growing suspicion and distrust between Charles VII and his councillors on the one hand and Duke Philip the Good on the other. Through the 1440s indeed, French policy towards Burgundy became more and more threatening. And it stayed that way, especially after the withdrawal of the English from Normandy in the 1450s and the flight of the Dauphin Louis, in dispute with his father Charles VII, to the Burgundian court in 1456. For Philip the Good flatly refused the king's requests for Louis's extradition. A well-informed though admittedly biased chronicler, the bishop of Lisieux Thomas Basin, pictures the house of Burgundy at this time as a massive and ancient tree, and Charles VII as the forester intent on removing it. He digs a deep trench all round it in order to sever the roots one by one.

Duke Philip the Good thought of himself as a French prince and nourished a naïve belief that only a handful of hostile French royal councillors prevented the permanent solution of all outstanding problems between France and Burgundy. Joyfully he attended Louis XI's coronation in Rheims cathedral on 14 August 1461, probably hoping that the prince he had protected and entertained as a refugee from his father's anger would now be his grateful friend, so that a new era of Franco-Burgundian amity could begin. In 1463 he further demonstrated his faith in French goodwill by returning the Somme towns to Louis XI – against the wishes of his son and heir Charles the Bold. Charles's attitude was very different and, from the autumn of 1464, when Charles succeeded in gaining power at the Burgundian court after a long and bitter quarrel with his father, Burgundian policy towards France became at once positive and aggressive.

When Charles the Bold, then only count of Charolais, joined Louis XI's brother and other French princes in an armed revolt against the French crown in 1465, his aim was to force King Louis to return the Somme towns and at the same time to recover Péronne, Roye and Montdidier which his father had ceded to

Jehan, count of Nevers and Étampes. In this aim he was completely successful, but the war of the League of Public Weal,
as it is pretentiously called, only exacerbated the hostility
between France and Burgundy. As duke, Charles the Bold was
constantly on the brink of war with France, but the two
campaigns that were fought in January 1471 and summer 1472
were inconclusive. The episode at Péronne in 1468, when Charles
held Louis prisoner for a time and extracted an impossibly
favourable treaty from him, had not helped to dispel the suspicion and antipathy between the two rulers. Louis thought
Charles was mad and was fond of imitating his alleged maniacal
gestures. Charles regarded Louis as a menace and kept dreaming
of the total destruction of French royal power. But each was
deflected by other interests so that no head-on collision ever
occurred. Louis was preoccupied with establishing his own
authority within France against the power of the princes; with
France's old enemy England; and with Aragon. Charles was
diverted by possibilities of conquest and expansion in the area
of the Rhine. When, in 1474, he drew up a master-plan for the
dismemberment of France by means of simultaneous attacks by
himself, King Edward IV of England and John II, king of Aragon,
the scheme collapsed because Charles was more concerned
with Burgundian expansion in the Empire, which included
Lorraine, than with attacking France. Recent historical scholar-
ship has shown that Charles's downfall at the hands of the
Swiss and their allies was by no means engineered by Louis XI.
True, that king launched an all-out military offensive against
Charles the Bold's northern and southern territories in the
summer of 1475, but after the treaty of Soleuvre in the autumn
of that year Louis punctiliously observed the truces between
himself and Charles.

Other aspects of this rather complex Franco-Burgundian
relationship may be noticed in passing. Although Philip the
Bold and John the Fearless both married non-French wives,
Margaret of Flanders and Margaret of Bavaria respectively, the
last two Valois dukes, who each married three times, each chose
French princesses for their first two wives. Thus Philip the Good
married Michelle of France and Bonne of Artois before marrying
Isabel of Portugal; and Charles the Bold married Catherine of
France and Isabel of Bourbon before Margaret of York. Burgundian dependence on France is also apparent in adminis-
trative affairs, especially in the duchy of Burgundy. When, in

1438, the ducal accounting officials at Dijon decided to cease working on Saturday afternoons their excuse was that the officials of the Paris *chambre des comptes* did not do so. In 1441 the Dijon officials sought advice from their Paris colleagues. Other examples could be given of close administrative connections between France and Burgundy persisting right through the period of the Valois dukes.

In general terms it may be said that the French crown was of use to Burgundy under Philip the Bold; it was a preoccupation for John the Fearless; and under the last two Valois dukes it was a source of increasing hostility. England, naturally, was a valuable counterweight for Burgundy against French royal power, but it was not merely the growing tension between Burgundy and France which produced a more or less permanent Anglo-Burgundian alliance. More important were the close economic ties between England and the Burgundian Netherlands, especially between England and Flanders, which made good political relations nearly essential. The dukes were well aware of the catastrophic effects which might ensue from an English commercial blockade of Bruges and their other Low Countries ports, and of English naval attacks on their shipping. This explains why, in spite of an occasional hostile interlude, as in 1386 when Philip the Bold planned a French invasion of England, or in 1436 when his grandson attacked Calais, Anglo-Burgundian relations were normally friendly. The alliance culminated in Charles the Bold's marriage to Edward IV's sister Margaret of York in 1468. It found characteristic expression at that time in the person of William Caxton, a merchant who was one of the officials concerned with English trade relations with Flanders. He set up his first printing press at Bruges in Flanders in 1473.

The ancient monarchies of England and France, though seeming at times in the fourteenth and fifteenth centuries in danger of disintegration from within, were rock-solid compared to the frail, faltering and indeed largely hypothetical political organization which went under the name of Holy Roman Empire. But Burgundian relations with the emperors were of some importance, not just because of the crown which the last two Valois dukes hoped to obtain, and the schemes they both conjured up of themselves becoming emperors or vice-emperors, but because many of the territories they might hope to lay their hands on were inside the frontiers of the Empire.

Philip the Bold's repeated and partly successful moves towards the annexation of Brabant and Luxembourg, both of them imperial territories, could have aroused no serious counter-measures from King Wenzel, the ruler of the Empire at that time. A series of domestic political upheavals forced him from time to time to interrupt one or other of his favourite pursuits, which were hunting, drinking and philandering; but he was quite powerless to defend his far-flung frontiers, and utterly uninterested in trying to do so. His brother Sigmund became undisputed ruler of the Empire in 1411, was eventually crowned emperor in 1433, and died in 1437; he was made of sterner stuff. Though he lacked any real political power, Sigmund repeatedly tried to restore the dying fortunes of the once great Empire, but his grandiose ideas and somewhat outlandish projects ended in failure or farce. He won a certain renown in some quarters by summoning the Council of Constance but, partly by permitting the learned fathers of the church gathered there to burn John Hus, the holder of his safe-conduct, as a heretic, he brought about an armed confrontation between himself and the Hussites which led him into repeated military disaster. His stature was similarly diminished by his anti-Burgundian posturings and their very meagre results. In 1414 he signed an alliance with John the Fearless's enemies in France, the Armagnacs, and put forward the rather unrealistic proposal of a partition of Valois Burgundy, once it had been conquered, between England, France and himself. These plans were easily circumvented by John the Fearless, who became a dutiful vassal of Sigmund in 1416 by doing homage to him for his imperial territories.

Not until 1430 was Sigmund in a position to reopen his diplomatic campaign against Burgundy. In that year he protested against Duke Philip the Good's acquisition of Brabant, and in 1434 he signed an offensive treaty against Philip with King Charles VII of France and went so far as to actually declare war on Burgundy though, being without an army or any support in the Empire for his bellicose plans, he was in no position to wage it. The most he contrived was a ridiculous little invasion of the duchy of Limbourg in 1437 by a contingent of German knights, who were promptly chased away by the local inhabitants. A few months later Sigmund was dead. Most of the Low Countries had passed into Burgundian hands without any effective opposition from their imperial owners.

No serious efforts to assert imperial rights against Burgundy were made by the Emperor Frederick III of Habsburg. He met Philip the Good at Besançon in the first year of his reign, 1442, but nobody has ever discovered what passed between them. Twelve years later, when Philip travelled to Regensburg to attend the imperial diet there in 1454, Frederick was careful to avoid another personal meeting. He dodged or ignored Burgundian requests for a crown even when, after 1467, these were intensified by Charles the Bold; and even when, in the autumn of 1473, he met Charles at Trier with the express intention of having him crowned. In 1474 Charles the Bold invaded imperial territory and laid siege to the imperial city of Neuss on the Rhine opposite Düsseldorf, in support of his ally Archbishop Ruprecht of Cologne who was at war with his rebellious subjects. Frederick responded to this overt act of aggression by somehow collecting together an army and marching to attack the Burgundians, but peace was made before any real fighting took place. During the rest of Duke Charles's brief reign Frederick was his ally, and he was able to attack various other parts of the Empire, notably Lorraine and the Swiss, with complete impunity.

Relations between Burgundy and her neighbours on either side, France and the Empire, were necessarily bitter-sweet. In some sense Burgundy was to them a rival, an upstart, who had usurped their territory to construct her own power. Thus friendly moves were as often as not countered by innate hostility. Yet, as we have seen, the state of affairs between all three powers was normally pacific. With that other power of those days, the papacy, the Valois Burgundian dukes successfully cultivated a lasting and mutually profitable friendship.

The Burgundian lands were brought together in the first place with papal permission, for the wedding of Philip the Bold and Margaret of Flanders in 1369 was made possible only by means of a papal dispensation issued by Urban V. In 1371 Philip the Bold travelled to Avignon on a personal visit to Pope Gregory XI. From 1372 onwards the dukes of Burgundy maintained at least one resident agent at the papal court to look after their interests there, and gifts of wine, tapestries and so on were intermittently dispatched to Rome. The advantages for the Burgundian dukes of good relations with the popes were partly diplomatic and political. Philip the Good was able to enlist the backing of Pope Martin V in the struggle for the succession to Holland. Eugenius IV confirmed him as legitimate ruler of all his lands. In the 1470s several diplomatic initiatives were made by the popes on Charles the Bold's behalf and papal legates negotiated for him with the emperor in 1475 and with the Swiss in 1476. Other advantages bestowed by the popes were financial: in 1441 Eugenius IV allowed Duke Philip the Good to levy a tax of ten per cent on all clerical incomes in his lands. But the prime objective of the papal connection concerned appointments to church benefices: it was indeed the control of ecclesiastical preferment.

Why should the dukes of Burgundy want to appoint people to ecclesiastical office? Firstly, although their officials – secretaries, legists, financial experts and the like – were all of them salaried, these salaries could usefully be supplemented and the exertions and loyalty of the civil servants abundantly rewarded, at no cost to the dukes, by the revenues from ecclesiastical office. Secondly, if the abbacies and bishoprics and other important benefices in the duke's lands were occupied by his employees, friends and relatives, the disputes and disagreements which constantly arose in those days between secular and spiritual authorities might be minimized. And then again, some of the bishops and archbishops in and near the Burgundian territories wielded such political power that it was essential that as many as possible of them should be duke's men. We might categorize these three uses of ecclesiastical appointment as administrative, juridical and political, though without wishing to differentiate too clearly between them.

It was mainly with a view to providing for his civil servants that Philip the Bold took care to obtain from Pope Clement VII power to appoint to one benefice in each of the collegiate churches in Flanders and to 120 other benefices both in and outside France. In October 1428 a document was drawn up on Philip the Good's instructions 'in order to provide chiefly for the clerics of his court, but also for other servants and friends, and for his principal officials'. It reserved the first vacant prebend in the duke's gift at Courtrai and the first at Mons in Hainault for the chancellor's two sons; the first chaplaincy at Alost for the senior chamberlain's chaplain; the second vacancy at the Bruges Beguinage for the governor-general of the duke's finances; and so on. Hundreds of benefices were disposed of in this way by the duke. His most senior officials could hope to obtain cardinal's hats for themselves or their relatives; Jehan Rolin, son of the chancellor Nicolas Rolin, got one in 1448.

In the case of the Burgundian bishoprics of Autun and

Chalon, the archbishopric of Besançon, and the bishoprics of Thérouanne, Tournai and Arras, it was mainly in order to avoid juridical disputes and other friction that the dukes took such trouble to fill them with their own candidates. At Tournai Louis de la Trémoille (1388–1410) was followed by the Burgundian chancellor Jehan de Thoisy (1410–33). At Thérouanne in Artois, a diocese extending over much of Flanders, Philip the Good persuaded the dean and chapter in 1451 to accept his bastard son David; his bastard brother Jehan had become bishop of Cambrai in 1439. In 1439 too, Duke Philip persuaded the pope to transfer one of his councillors, Quentin Menart, from the see of Arras to that of Besançon, so that another councillor could become bishop of Arras. Every bishop of Chalon in the Valois Burgundian period was a Burgundian ducal protégé or nominee.

The political importance of certain bishoprics near the duke's lands was mainly due to the enormous size of their dependent territories, which made them into principalities as large as some of the duke's individual territories. The lands of the bishopric of Utrecht were as extensive as the neighbouring county of Holland; the episcopal principality of Liège was as big as Hainault. No wonder Philip the Good used his papal connection in 1455–6 to place his bastard son David on the episcopal throne of Utrecht and his nephew Louis de Bourbon on that of Liège. Earlier, Pope Eugenius IV had gone a little too far on the duke of Burgundy's behalf when in 1446 he deposed the archbishops of Cologne and Trier and appointed in their place Philip's nephew Adolf of Cleves and his bastard brother Jehan de Bourgogne. The incumbents, Dietrich von Moers and Jacob von Sierck, simply refused to budge.

The placing of Burgundian supporters and relatives, particularly Philip the Good's bastards and nephews, in neighbouring bishoprics was part of the widespread and effective system of Burgundian alliances and connections. This strong ecclesiastical element in the system penetrated into France to embrace the sees of Tournai, Auxerre, Soissons and Lyons, as well as into the Empire at Utrecht, Toul and Liège. It was supported by numerous treaties and connections between the dukes of Burgundy and the lesser secular princes near and on either side of their territories.

In France Burgundian allies were readily available among the leading princely houses. Though few or none of the connections formed with them endured continuously from generation to generation, as a whole they probably acted as a reasonably effective check on French royal aggression against Burgundy. They were normally maintained either by means of marriage alliances or by mere common political interests sealed with a formal agreement. In 1467 Charles the Bold signed a treaty with Charles of France, Francis II, duke of Brittany, and John, duke of Alençon, so that they could help each other 'to obviate and resist more effectively the sudden swift and devious enterprises which my lord the king may contrive'. Some French princes were attached to the Burgundian interest by being maintained at court and paid annual allowances. Jaques de Bourbon was receiving £2,400 annually from Philip the Good towards the end of that duke's reign. Membership of the Order of the Golden Fleece was also used to win the support of French princes, notably in the case of the brothers Charles and Jehan de Bourgogne, who successively ruled the counties of Nevers and Rethel (1415–91). They belonged to the junior branch of the Valois ducal family. As well as relatives, they were loyal supporters, until Jehan decamped to the French court in 1463. But they were of little importance compared to the two main allies of Burgundy in France, Brittany and Bourbon.

Just as Duke John IV of Brittany was a loyal ally of Philip the Bold, so John V (1399–1442) was a more or less consistent ally of John the Fearless and Philip the Good. For one year during John V's minority Philip the Bold even acted as regent of Brittany. In 1423 John V's brother Arthur, count of Richemont, married Duke Philip the Good's sister Margaret. But the connection was dismantled by Duke Francis I, who even refused in 1445 to accept membership of the Order of the Golden Fleece which his father John V had accepted five years before. Under Francis II (1458–88) the alliance was re-formed, and this duke joined the coalition of princes which fought the war of the League of the Public Weal against Louis XI in 1465, though he took care to see that his troops were not actually engaged in battle. He and Charles the Bold were supposed to be military allies in further confrontations with the French crown which took place in 1467–72, but in fact the two dukes repeatedly left each other in the lurch. They were too distant geographically; nor was their common interest against Louis XI strong enough to hold them effectively together. Nonetheless, by and large, for the hundred years or more of the Valois Burgundian period Brittany was Burgundy's most important ally in France.

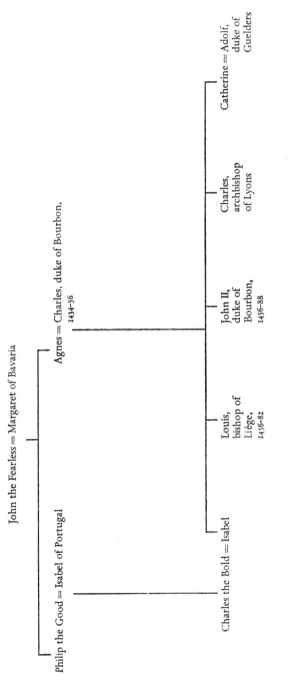

John the Fearless = Margaret of Bavaria

Philip the Good = Isabel of Portugal

Agnes = Charles, duke of Bourbon, 1434-56

Charles the Bold = Isabel

Louis, bishop of Liège, 1456-82

John II, duke of Bourbon, 1456-88

Charles, archbishop of Lyons

Catherine = Adolf, duke of Guelders

3. BURGUNDY AND BOURBON

The house of Bourbon, too, was normally closely linked with Valois Burgundy; after all the two were territorial neighbours along the southern borders of the duchy of Burgundy. In the years after Agincourt, while Duke John of Bourbon was a prisoner in England and Duke John of Burgundy was struggling for the mastery of Paris, their wives, Mary of Berry and Margaret of Bavaria, grass widows, energetically looked after their respective lands and established friendly relations which matured in 1422 into an elaborate treaty designed to avoid military encounters and to promote trade between the two countries. A marriage alliance was also signed in 1422; Duke Charles of Bourbon (1434–56) married Philip the Good's sister Agnes. Subsequently the link was reinforced when Charles the Bold, while still only count of Charolais, married their daughter Isabel in 1454. Though she died in 1465, before he became duke of Burgundy, this Bourbon connection was a source of potential support for Charles the Bold. Isabel's brothers were influential people: Louis was bishop of Liège from 1456 to 1482; John was duke of Bourbon from 1456 to 1488; and Charles became archbishop of Lyons.

Other French connections of the Burgundian dukes were more transient than their links with the houses of Brittany and Bourbon. The dauphins of France, equivalents of the princes of Wales across the Channel, were sometimes Burgundian allies, even in opposition to their fathers. John the Fearless married his eldest daughter Margaret to the Dauphin Louis, duke of Guienne, in 1404, when she was ten and he was seven; and he was able to keep Louis in his pocket for several years. During the last five years of his father's reign (1456–61), Louis XI lived at the Burgundian court under Philip the Good's protection. Brothers of French kings were made use of in the same way: Louis XI's younger brother Charles, duke of Berry, was an ally of Charles the Bold. On the other hand Louis, duke of Orleans, younger brother of King Charles VI, was the rival and, in 1407, the victim of John the Fearless. But Philip the Good befriended his son Duke Charles of Orleans, bailing him out of the Tower of London in 1440, where he had been held since Agincourt as a prisoner-of-war, and making him a Knight of the Golden Fleece. Of intermittent value to Burgundy was the connection with the house of Anjou. René of Anjou, duke of Lorraine and titular king of Sicily, probably never forgave Philip the Good for keeping him a prisoner-of-war for six years at Dijon and for demanding an exorbitant ransom for his release. Yet King René's son John and his grandson Nicolas fought with Charles the Bold in 1465 and 1472 respectively against King Louis XI of France.

In France, the dukes of Burgundy were French princes with a natural role to play in affairs of state. Inevitably, they built up connections there which became important whenever Franco-Burgundian relations became important. But the French sector of the ducal system of alliances was more limited in scope and of lesser value to the dukes than the imperial sector. Again here, the dukes of Burgundy had an internal role to play, in German affairs as imperial princes. But here was also their one real hope of territorial expansion, of obtaining a crown, of aggrandizement of any kind. So, the system of alliances on the imperial side of the border assumed greater importance than the French connections so far described. It should be noted, incidentally, that the Franco-imperial border did not separate the French from the German-speaking world, for the linguistic frontier was a good deal to the east of the political frontier. Thus a string of six territories of major importance were French-speaking but within the Empire. From north to south these were Hainault, Luxembourg, Lorraine, Franche-Comté or the Free County of Burgundy, Savoy and Provence. Three of these territories became Burgundian; Charles the Bold tried hard to lay his hands on the other three or to incorporate them into his proposed kingdom. The county of Provence belonged to the house of Anjou already mentioned; Lorraine and Savoy were two of the Burgundian dukes' most valuable and loyal allies in the Empire.

On the imperial side, as in France, the Burgundian system of connections was maintained by marriage alliances. The tone was set by Philip the Bold. He married his children to the Habsburgs, the counts of Savoy, the ruling house of Hainault-Holland, and the house of Luxembourg. More important in the Empire than in France was the payment of pensions or annual allowances in return for promises of support or military assistance, which sometimes took the form of fief-rents, that is, involved the recipient in doing homage for his annual grant. In 1457–61 we find the Burgundian treasury paying out such pensions to Adolf of Cleves and to Count Eberhard of Württemberg, as well as to the French prince Jaques de Bourbon. Other ways and means of holding together the dukes' imperial allies were invitations to court or offers of membership of the Golden

Fleece. The dukes of Savoy, Cleves, Guelders and others visited the Burgundian court, and princes of these and other imperial houses spent protracted periods there; just as French princes did. As to membership of the Golden Fleece, the first twenty-four knights were from the duke's own territories, but between 1431 and 1473 at least seven representatives of imperial princely families were elected. Treaties of alliance, too, were a favourite method of fostering connections within the Empire, as also in France. John the Fearless signed such treaties with Duke Frederick of Austria and Dietrich von Moers, archbishop of Cologne; Philip the Good with Duke Adolf of Jülich-Berg and Duke Ludwig VIII of Bavaria-Ingolstadt. An element of military obligation was incorporated into most of these arrangements. In 1455 Philip the Good gave military aid to his imperial ally Ludwig of Zweibrücken; eighty years previously, in 1377, Philip the Bold had assisted the duke of Lorraine in a war against the archbishop of Trier. And Burgundy's imperial allies naturally returned the compliment: contingents from Cleves must have fought in nearly every Burgundian army. It was in these ways and with such mutually satisfactory arrangements that the Burgundian system of alliances within the Empire was held together.

The Burgundian connection with Lorraine, which was established under Philip the Bold, was further developed by John the Fearless in 1408 when Duke Charles of Lorraine (1390–1431) accepted a Burgundian fief-rent. That is, he did homage and promised to perform military service in return for an annual Burgundian pension or allowance of 2,000 francs. He also earned a reputation as a 'perfect Burgundian' by prohibiting his daughter from marrying a French subject. But Isabel de Lorraine married the French prince René of Anjou who has been mentioned already in connection with France. René's succession to the duchy of Lorraine was blocked for a long time by Count Anthony of Vaudémont, who was supported by Philip the Good, but at the end of Philip the Good's reign and early in Charles the Bold's good relations between Burgundy and the Angevin house of Lorraine were fully restored. When Anthony's grandson Count René of Vaudémont became duke of Lorraine in 1473 he signed a treaty with Charles the Bold giving Burgundian troops rights of passage through Lorraine.

Like Lorraine, Savoy was a territorial neighbour of Burgundy. Its rulers were already allies of at least ten years' standing when,

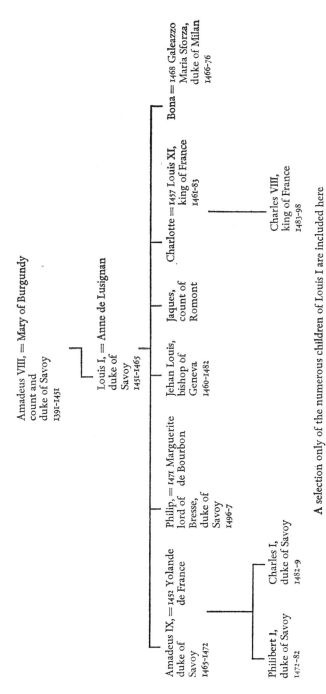

Amadeus VIII, = Mary of Burgundy
count and
duke of Savoy
1391-1451

Louis I, = Anne de Lusignan
duke of
Savoy
1451-1465

Amadeus IX, = 1452 Yolande
duke of   de France
Savoy
1465-1472

Philip, = 1471 Marguerite
lord of   de Bourbon
Bresse,
duke of
Savoy
1496-7

Jehan Louis,
bishop of
Geneva
1460-1482

Jaques,
count of
Romont

Charlotte = 1457 Louis XI,
                king of France
                1461-83

Bona = 1468 Galeazzo
              Maria Sforza,
              duke of Milan
              1466-76

Philibert I,
duke of Savoy
1472-82

Charles I,
duke of Savoy
1482-9

Charles VIII,
king of France
1483-98

A selection only of the numerous children of Louis I are included here

4. BURGUNDY AND SAVOY

in 1379, Philip the Bold signed a mutual defence pact with Count Amadeus VI. In 1393 Philip's daughter Mary was married to Amadeus VIII of Savoy. Since Amadeus was only ten years old and his father had died in 1391, Philip the Bold was able to take over the regency of Savoy on his son-in-law's behalf. Unlike Cleves, Savoy was not an active military ally of Burgundy. But, although Amadeus VIII did not send troops to help John the Fearless in France, he did permit the duke of Burgundy to recruit mercenaries in his lands. From the start of Charles the Bold's reign the Savoy connection was a vital part of the Burgundian political system. In 1468 Duke Amadeus IX and his wife Duchess Yolande and three of Amadeus's brothers were all Charles's allies. And if one of the brothers, Philip, lord of Bresse, went over to Louis XI, another, Jaques, count of Romont, remained a faithful and extremely valuable Burgundian ally: from 1473 to 1475 he was Charles the Bold's lieutenant-general in all the Burgundian Low Countries.

After 1473 Burgundian relations with both Lorraine and Savoy were transformed by the somewhat brutal ambitions of Charles the Bold. In the autumn of 1475 he conquered Lorraine and contrived to occupy it militarily for a year. In 1476 he tried to gain control of Savoy by arresting the Duchess Yolande and incarcerating her at Rouvres near Dijon. But these events are significant only in terms of the collapse of Burgundian power.

Besides the neighbouring French-speaking countries of Lorraine and Savoy, the Burgundian imperial system included important links with a group of territories in north-west Germany. Cleves became virtually a Burgundian client state after the marriage in 1406 of Philip the Good's sister Mary to Duke Adolf of Cleves (1394–1448). That rather belligerent ruler could rely on Philip the Good's assistance, if not as a participant in his wars, at least as a mediator to help end them in a manner favourable to Cleves. His son Duke John I of Cleves (1448–81) was on terms of intimate friendship with Philip the Good: he and his brother Adolf, lord of Ravenstein, had been more or less brought up at the Burgundian court. Both were honoured with membership of the Golden Fleece; both received handsome annual grants from Philip; both were provided with Burgundian wives, Adolf being accorded the perhaps dubious distinction of marrying a bastard daughter of Philip the Good, Anne de Bourgogne. In return for these and other favours John I of Cleves campaigned in 1452 against Ghent with Philip the Good

Adolf I, duke of Cleves = Mary of Burgundy, sister of Philip the Good

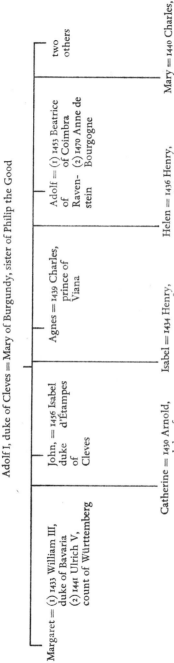

Margaret = (1) 1433 William III, duke of Bavaria (2) 1441 Ulrich V, count of Württemberg

John, = 1456 Isabel d'Etampes, duke of Cleves

Agnes = 1439 Charles, prince of Viana

Adolf = (1) 1453 Beatrice of Coimbra (2) 1470 Anne de Bourgogne of Ravenstein

two others

Mary = 1440 Charles, duke of Orleans

Catherine = 1430 Arnold, duke of Guelders

Isabel = 1434 Henry, count of Schwarzburg-Blankenburg

Helen = 1436 Henry, duke of Brunswick

Mary = 1449 James II, king of Scotland

Catherine

Margaret = Frederick I, count palatine of Simmern

Adolf of Egmont, = 1463 Catherine de Bourbon, duke of Guelders

5. BURGUNDY, CLEVES and GUELDERS

and in 1473 against Guelders with Charles the Bold, and John I and his father allowed Philip the Good to marry off John's nine or more brothers and sisters in the Burgundian interest. One married into the house of Württemberg; Catherine was married to the duke of Guelders; other sisters married into Brunswick and Schwarzburg-Blankenburg; Mary of Cleves was married to Duke Charles of Orleans.

All this and more was in the interests of Burgundy; but at least Cleves survived. It was otherwise with her neighbour Guelders which, offering effective resistance to the subtler type of Burgundian encroachment under Philip the Good, fell victim to conquest by Charles the Bold in 1473. The situation in Guelders was dominated by the constant disputes between Duke Arnold, who married Catherine of Cleves in 1430 but was firmly anti-Burgundian, and his son Adolf. Their quarrels were a standing pretext for Burgundian intervention. Adolf became a Burgundian protégé towards the end of Philip the Good's reign, accepting the Golden Fleece in 1461 and Catherine of Bourbon, sister of Charles the Bold's second wife Isabel of Bourbon, in marriage in 1463. Through him the Burgundian connection with Guelders was maintained until Charles the Bold arrested him and grabbed his duchy in 1473.

The other Burgundian ally in north-west Germany was the duke of Jülich, whose duchy was on the left bank of the Rhine. He also ruled the county of Berg on the right bank behind Cologne. Duke Adolf signed a treaty with Philip the Good in 1431. His successor Gerhard VII (1437–75) did nothing to oppose Charles the Bold when he laid siege to Neuss in 1474 and moved the Burgundian army and supplies for it through his territories.

All along the western border of the Empire minor princes were bribed or persuaded to enter the Burgundian orbit. Conspicuous among them in Philip the Good's reign were successive counts of Nassau; Ruprecht, count of Virneburg; counts Friedrich and Vincenz of Moers; and Wilhelm and Rudolf, margraves of Hochberg. Count Englebert II of Nassau, Ruprecht count of Virneburg and Count Friedrich of Moers were rewarded with the Golden Fleece. Under Charles the Bold Rudolf of Hochberg became governor of Luxembourg and counts John and Engelbert of Nassau were ducal lieutenants in Brabant.

Alliances were also maintained in the Empire at large. There was a special link in Philip the Good's reign with the counts of

Württemberg, two of whom visited Brussels in 1446. It was severed in 1474 when Charles the Bold arrested Count Henry, gaoled him at Luxembourg and then Boulogne, and tried to annexe his fief of Montbéliard. There was a special link, too, with the Habsburgs, which Philip the Bold had forged when he arranged for his daughter Catherine to marry Leopold of Austria in 1392 after fifteen years of intermittent negotiation. This brought the county of Ferrette or Pfirt, in Alsace, temporarily under Burgundian control, especially when Catherine of Burgundy was holding court at Ensisheim in 1406–11 during the last few years of her husband's life. Subsequent difficulties, chiefly over Ferrette, which had been restored to the Habsburgs, led to a brief and nearly bloodless Austro-Burgundian war in 1431, but good relations were maintained consistently after it. In 1469 Duke Sigmund of Austria-Tirol and Charles the Bold became close allies at St Omer, and Ferrette, along with much of Upper Alsace, was mortgaged by Sigmund to Charles the Bold, who thereupon took over its administration. The subsequent history of the Habsburg attachment is part of the story of the collapse of Burgundy – which it survived in the form of the marriage of Mary of Burgundy and Maximilian of Austria. The Burgundian dukes also maintained treaty connections at different times with the dukes of Bavaria, with the elector-palatine of the Rhine, with the archbishop of Cologne, and with other imperial princes.

We have examined the complex web of relationships which the Valois Burgundian dukes maintained with their more powerful neighbours, the rulers of France, England and Germany; the way in which they used the papal connection to extend their sphere of influence both in France and in the Empire; and the links they established with the minor princes on either side of the border. But what of the towns?

By and large it has to be admitted that the dukes of Burgundy failed to win the confidence, still less secure the co-operation, of those proud, exclusive, quasi-independent and wealthy urban oligarchies which had made their own way into history in the Europe of the middle ages. These towns had proliferated in the Low Countries, Italy and south Germany, but also in those very Franco-German borderlands which were straddled and more or less mastered and controlled by the Valois dukes of Burgundy. Admittedly some of them had been completely incorporated into the Burgundian state and do not concern us in the context of this chapter: Ghent, Bruges and Ypres; Malines and Antwerp; Amsterdam and Dijon – nearly all of which incidentally rebelled against the dukes at least once – were in this class. Then there were towns that were virtual enclaves in Burgundian territory so that they could scarcely avoid Burgundian pressures: Tournai, Liège, Besançon. Still others were aloof and powerful and relatively distant from Burgundian territory: Cologne, Frankfurt, Strasbourg, Basel and Bern were the most important. All were German-speaking and imperial. Mulhouse, Colmar, Metz, Trier and Aachen were in second line. It was these towns which remained sullen, distrustful onlookers of the growth of Burgundian power; it was they who conspired together in the end to engineer the destruction of Charles the Bold.

Tournai was a French city which was utterly dependent, economically, on good relations with the dukes of Burgundy, who controlled most of the country around it. On 1 July 1417 the town council expressed its dilemma in a delicate decision: 'Agreed that it was desirable for the town to hold out firmly for the king, provided that it could also remain in the good grace of my lord of Burgundy.' During much of the fifteenth century Tournai paid protection money to the dukes of Burgundy. For example under Charles the Bold the civic authorities paid the duke 10,000 francs per annum to be left in peace and quiet.

Besançon was an imperial city, but otherwise its situation was not dissimilar to that of Tournai. After 1386 the Valois dukes were its official guardians, receiving 500 francs per annum from the city for this service. Twice in John the Fearless's reign a scheme was seriously put forward for the transference of the lordship over Besançon to the duke of Burgundy. In return, the duke would make Besançon the administrative capital of Franche-Comté, giving it a chancery, an accounting office or *chambres des comptes*, a council, and transferring to it the Parlement or law court at Beaune. But nothing came of these projects, and it was not until after 1451, when a revolt in the city was success-fully put down by Philip the Good, that ducal power over Besançon was extended further.

Liège of course was very different from Tournai and Besançon. It was larger, more turbulent politically, more industrialized. It could only be mastered by military power and this was not readily available to its bishops, whose authority in their own capital city was repeatedly jeopardized or overthrown by the rebellious townspeople. When, in 1406, the rebels went so far as to elect an anti-bishop and set up a rival government to the bishop's, that prelate, John of Bavaria, turned for help to his ally and brother-in-law John the Fearless. A Burgundian army invaded the principality of Liège and the insurgents were decisively defeated on 23 September 1408 at Othée. Liège, however, was an episcopal city; it could by no means be annexed by the duke of Burgundy. It remained a thorn in his flesh, declaring war against Burgundy in 1430 and rebelling in 1465 against its bishop Louis de Bourbon and against his uncle Duke Philip the Good. Charles the Bold campaigned against the rebels of Liège in 1467 and forced them to accept a savagely repressive settlement; in 1468 he sacked and partly destroyed their city. These campaigns against Liège will be considered in more detail when Burgundian military power is discussed.

Although Burgundian relations with the larger and more distant German-speaking cities already mentioned form part of the history of the collapse of Burgundian power under Charles the Bold, contacts existed long before then. Cologne and Strasbourg were already greatly exaggerating the size of Burgundian armies in 1408 when John the Fearless attacked Liège. In 1434-5, when Philip the Good was threatened with a declaration of war by the emperor Sigmund, the duke wrote to Frankfurt, Cologne, Strasbourg, Nürnberg and Bern, all of which seem to have approved his pacific attitude. Furthermore, Philip the Good, who owned property in Cologne as duke of Brabant, was at Cologne in 1441 and at Bern in 1454. The climax of his more or less friendly relations with these towns was his treaty with Bern and some of her allies of 1467. At first this tradition was kept up by Charles the Bold. It was probably his harsh treatment of Liège which first really stirred urban animosity and suspicion against him.

The spider's web of Burgundian connections, though it was naturally most closely woven around the Burgundian territories themselves in the general area so far under discussion, extended far and wide to the very borders of Christendom. Many of the more distant threads were already fixed in Philip the Bold's time. He had an alliance or confraternity with King Martin I of Aragon and had hoped to marry one of his granddaughters to Martin's son Peter. In 1399 he sent an ambassador to King Henry III of Castile. He exchanged gifts with Giangaleazzo Visconti, duke of Milan, and visited him in person at Milan in

1391. He sent ambassadors to Florence and Sardinia. In connection with the crusade of Nicopolis he entered into close contact with King Sigmund of Hungary, the later emperor, and with Venice. He even intervened in the affairs of Poland and sent troops in support of Prince Ladislas, who had sought refuge in Dijon.

Contacts of this kind proliferated in the fifteenth century. John the Fearless exchanged embassies with King John I of Portugal and even sent him a portrait of himself painted by Jehan Malouel. Philip the Good sent Jan van Eyck to Portugal in 1428 to paint the portrait of Isabel, daughter of John I and sister of Prince Henry the Navigator, before marrying her in 1430. She lived at the Burgundian court, or in the Low Countries, until her death in 1471. Friendly relations with Aragon and Castile continued. John the Fearless used Scottish mercenaries in his armies and Philip the Good entertained some Scottish knights and squires, travelling with William, earl of Douglas, to dinner at Lille on 12 October 1450. They and their Burgundian hosts ate two hares, ten pheasants, a heron, four bitterns, 156 rabbits, seventy-two partridges, ten geese, twelve water-birds, thirty-four dozen larks, 231 chickens and fifty-six brace of pigeons. Of course all the Burgundian dukes had frequent contacts with the Hanseatic League, both economic and political; John the Fearless also negotiated with the Grand Master of the Teutonic Knights of Prussia.

In Italian affairs the Burgundian dukes were always quite closely involved. Contacts with Venice continued after Nicopolis, some of them commercial. In 1406 the Burgundian flag was briefly unfurled on the walls of Pisa; in 1413 John the Fearless had himself appointed the king of France's lieutenant in Genoa; in 1445 Philip the Good showed signs of interest in annexing that republic. Embassies went to and fro between Brussels and Naples; in the 1440s Burgundian ships appeared in the Mediterranean and the Black Sea. The Order of the Golden Fleece was again pressed into service to maintain these connections: John II, king of Aragon; Alfonso V, king of Naples and his successor Ferrante; Prince John of Portugal, duke of Coimbra, all accepted membership.

The ever-widening circle of Burgundian allies reached its climax, like almost everything else Burgundian, in Charles the Bold's time. He was proud of them; he paraded ambassadors at court almost like soldiers. On 15 January 1469, at Brussels, ambassadors from France, England, Hungary, Bohemia, Naples, Aragon, Sicily, Cyprus, Norway, Poland, Denmark, Russia, Livonia, Prussia, Austria, Milan, Lombardy *and others* were said to have been present at the ceremonial pardon of the Ghent rebels of 1467. In 1471 one of Charles the Bold's leading officials listed the duke's allies as follows: 'the pope, the emperor, the king of England, the king of Aragon, the king of Scotland, the king of Denmark, the king of Portugal, the dukes of Brittany and Austria, the house of Savoy, the doge and signory of Venice, the elector-palatine of the Rhine, the dukes of Bavaria, Cleves and Guelders, and my lords the archbishop-electors of Mainz, Trier and Cologne'. His camp outside beleaguered Neuss in 1474–5 became the diplomatic centre of Europe. But this delicately balanced and carefully maintained system of connections, part commercial, part political, part dynastic, which had helped for a hundred years to conserve and extend Burgundian influence through Europe, was brought down in ruins shortly thereafter.

CHAPTER FIVE

Rulers and Administrators

In this chapter and the next an attempt will be made to elucidate the mechanism of government of the Valois Burgundian state. How were the individual territories administered? How were decisions made and implemented? First, in this chapter, these problems will be examined in terms of the personnel of government: the dukes themselves, their wives, their lieutenants, governors and officials. Then, in the following chapter, the government will be investigated in terms of the regional and central institutions of the Burgundian state: the councils, the *chambres des comptes* or accounting offices, the Parlements or law courts, and the like.

By the fifteenth century the government of every European power was more or less bureaucratized. Central accounting offices and institutionalized royal councils had become established in the twelfth and thirteenth centuries. A class of expert financiers and legists with university degrees – professional civil servants – was rapidly extending its influence in ruling circles. But government at the topmost level was still almost exclusively personal. In Valois Burgundy, as elsewhere, the ruler himself took all decisions of importance, and this applies whether the particular decision was made inside or outside the council chamber. Of Charles the Bold, for example, we are told by a chronicler that he 'willingly listened to [his councillors'] deliberations but, after hearing everything, he followed his own opinion, which was usually contrary to what had been advised'.

To anyone with even the most superficial knowledge of Burgundian governmental records the impression that Charles the Bold intervened personally in almost all the details of government is overwhelming. The attentive Italian ambassador at his court noticed that he sometimes spent hours signing letters. He wrote out with his own hand the famous safe-conduct for King Louis XI to visit him at Péronne. Early in 1470 another observant Italian noticed that 'scarcely a day passes during which he does not spend an hour or two alone writing and drawing up his [military] ordinances'. The same personal touch, though not so pronounced, is found with John the Fearless. 'Bailiff,' he added in autograph at the foot of a letter, 'accomplish what I have written to you about or, if not, I shall show you how displeased I am.' Even the pleasure-loving easy-going Philip the Good kept complete control of everything that went on, so that when he was otherwise occupied, as for example with the festivities of the Burgundian patron saint on St Andrew's Day 1431, routine administrative matters had to be deferred. In 1450 the town clerk of Malines was kept waiting at The Hague for several days to have some letters sealed because Philip the Good was entertaining every evening. The duke's personal role in drawing up instructions for ambassadors is revealed in a remark by one of them, Hue de Lannoy, in a letter to Philip the Good: 'As for me, I have kept as nearly as I can to the terms you outlined to me in the garden of your house at Arras.'

The personal nature of government in the Valois Burgundian state by no means precluded the delegation of authority by the dukes. Regional councils tended to enjoy a certain autonomy conferred on them by mere geography. Provincial governors took office in different territories from time to time. Wide-ranging powers were given by Charles the Bold to lieutenants appointed to individual, or sometimes groups of, territories. This duke's lieutenant or *stadholder* in Guelders was empowered 'to do and cause to be done each and every thing for the good, honour, profit and utility of us and of our said land and of our subjects there which a good and loyal lieutenant can and ought to do and which we personally would do if we were present there'. Such appointments were manifestations, rather than diminutions, of the dukes' personal authority.

How far can one identify a family system of government in the Burgundian territories? Certainly the dukes' wives were energetic and capable and they were involved in public affairs of all kinds. They conducted negotiations, patronized artists, appointed their own people to ecclesiastical and other offices, amassed estates and requested taxes from the dukes' recalcitrant subjects. But no permanent family system developed. Philip the Bold's wife Margaret of Flanders, for example, lived in the duchy of Burgundy in the 1370s and acted as her husband's lieutenant there, but she ceased to play this role ten years before his death. The nearest thing to a real family system of government was that set up by John the Fearless, but it was short-lived. From 1411 onwards, while he was busy with French affairs, his son Philip, count of Charolais, later Philip the Good, ruled Flanders and Artois as his personal representative with the title 'lieutenant and governor-general'. And from 1409, John the Fearless's wife Margaret of Bavaria ruled the two Burgundies for him. She thought of herself as having wider powers than merely in these southern territories, for in official documents she styled herself 'Margaret, duchess of Burgundy, countess of Flanders, of Artois, of Burgundy palatine, lady of Salins and of Malines, having the government of the above-mentioned countries and places in the absence of my lord [the duke]'. No family government was indulged in by Philip the Good. Neither his wife Isabel of Portugal nor his son Charles the Bold were entrusted with genuine territorial lieutenancies, though Duchess Isabel undertook numerous governmental duties with considerable skill, and Charles became lieutenant-general in the Low Countries for his father briefly in 1454; his father's representative in Holland in 1462; and lieutenant-general in all the Burgundian lands in 1465-7 under his father's supervision. Nor did Charles the Bold set up any sort of family system of government, though his wife Margaret of York helped in the government of the Low Countries, notably in 1476.

Before the personalities and attitudes of the four Valois dukes of Burgundy are examined and compared it is as well to take note of their respective places of residence and their itineraries, for they were rather different in this important respect. Philip the Bold divided his time, in the 1360s, between Burgundy and France, and in the 1370s between France, Burgundy and the Low Countries including Artois. But increasingly, towards the end of his reign, France claimed his attention, and in the 1380s he was more often than not in Paris. Indeed, he spent more of his life in Paris than in any other town. John the Fearless was brought up in Burgundy and, apart from an occasional visit to the Low Countries, was there or in France most of the time until he succeeded his father as duke in 1404 at the age of thirty-three. Thereafter, he spent rather more than half his time in France, about one third of it in Flanders or Artois, and less than one tenth in Burgundy. Thus the first two Valois dukes demonstrated their French involvement by frequent and often prolonged stays in France. The second two dukes reversed this tendency. Philip the Good travelled about a great deal in the early part of his reign and even later; Dijon, Lille, Hesdin and even The Hague being favoured by long spells of residence. But in the 1440s and 1450s Bruges and Brussels emerged as rivals for the ducal capital. Brussels carried the day, becoming the duke's normal place of residence from 1459 until his death in 1467. Charles the Bold was much less sedentary but showed a marked preference for the Low Countries. Early in 1474 he paid the first visit of a Burgundian duke to their original capital of Dijon since Philip the Good's last visit there in the winter of 1454–5; but he never went there again. He resided for months at a time in the early years of his ducal reign at Hesdin, Bruges, Lille, Middelburg, The Hague and elsewhere. His last two years were spent almost continuously in the saddle, on campaign.

No really life-like portrait of Philip the Bold emerges from contemporary chronicles and records. The chronicles tell us of 'this valiant prince who undertook so many fine enterprises' without describing his person in detail. The records tell us that he wore scarlet leather slippers, slept in a woollen nightcap and had a portable clock which he hung on the wall of his room. But they do not reveal his personality. The writer Christine de Pisan, daughter of an Italian astrologer settled in France, who knew Duke Philip personally, says that he had all the princely virtues. He ruled wisely and well, worked hard and was well-informed. He was so 'devoted to the wellbeing and strength of the French crown that even in his old age he scarcely took any time for rest'. He was 'good-natured, amiable, as magnanimous as Alexander, noble and stately at court' and 'his people loved him dearly'. All this however is in an encomium of Philip's older brother the king of France Charles V – who is described as 'as liberal as Alexander' – written by Christine expressly for Duke Philip!

The famous Versailles Museum portrait of Philip the Bold and the likeness carved in stone on the portal of the church at the Charterhouse of Champmol outside Dijon by Claus Sluter both show Philip in the last decade of his life, that is in his late fifties. We see thin arched eyebrows, twinkling eyes, a long somewhat bulbous nose, rather heavy rounded cheeks and jaw and an expressive mouth with a slightly enigmatic smile. He looks a jovial, indulgent, sociable man, but with a certain firmness in the mouth indicative of determination. Such is the face of perhaps the most far-sighted, the most statesmanlike and the most successful of the four Valois dukes of Burgundy. For Philip the Bold laid foundations for Burgundian power on which his successors down to and including Charles the Bold could build. He put down the revolt in Flanders but then conciliated the Flemings and ruled them wisely. He maintained his position in France against growing opposition. He conducted foreign policy with skill and even vision. As for the extent of his power, it is notable that, at the turn of the century, in 1401–2, he controlled more territory than any of his three successors. After all, at that time he was undisputed master of France, he was ruler of the two Burgundies, Artois, Flanders, Limbourg, Rethel and Nevers – the last two were to be separated after his death from the main Burgundian dominions under a junior branch of his house – and he was regent of Brittany, Savoy and Luxembourg. Although he may not have been an administrative genius he took care to provide his lands with an effective, more or less unified, administrative structure. Militarily, on the other hand, he cuts a poor figure beside his successors. He did campaign in France as a young man in the 1370s, but ingloriously. He did launch the crusade of Nicopolis in 1396, but it was a failure. In 1386 he became the first of a long line of continental rulers who planned and prepared a grand attack on England but never crossed the Channel.

Although Philip the Bold's son and successor John the Fearless (1404–19) pursued his father's French connections and in general shared his political interests and outlook, he was a very different person. Gone is the prudent, open-handed, far-sighted, chivalrous prince; instead we have a cunning, unscrupulous, even violent, opportunist; a stealthy, suspicious, rather sinister, character who numbered assassination among his methods of dealing with political rivals and who was as devious and hypocritical as any of his fellow rulers, even including Henry V of England and Sigmund of Hungary. Admittedly he maintained the life of the court more or less as his father had left it, patronizing music, painting and sculpture. But he lived in fear of his life, locked himself up in a fortified tower – still standing in the rue Étienne Marcel – when in Paris, and employed a bodyguard. Unlike his father, he was a skilful and successful military commander with an interest in military matters which extended to the issue of detailed battle-orders before an encounter and to the reorganization of the artillery. Like his father, John the Fearless was concerned for the good government of his lands and interested himself in administrative reforms: he reorganized the system of taxation in Flanders, issued detailed instructions for his councillors, and even consulted his officials about proposed reforms. In a curious way one feels that this man, in spite of his involvement in bloodshed and violence, and the intermittent warfare he waged in France, was a sensitive and flexible ruler. He was on better terms with the Flemings than any of the other Valois dukes and managed to extract twice as much from them in taxation as his father had done. Though hopelessly entangled in French affairs he by no means neglected his own lands. He has been treated as a French prince by many historians and dubbed a traitor to the French crown, but he can only be fully understood as a Valois Burgundian.

Philip the Good has been better served by contemporary writers than any other Valois duke of Burgundy. His own court chronicler, George Chastellain, has left a convincing description of his person. He was tall, lean and bony, upright and well-proportioned, with a rather long weather-tanned face, long nose, high forehead, brown hair, expressive bushy eyebrows and large well-coloured lips. He dressed well, was good at riding, hunting and tennis, and indeed 'deserved a crown on the strength of his physical appearance alone'. Chastellain knew Philip towards the end of his life; so did the Flemish lawyer Philippe Wielant who observes that Duke Philip spoke little but to the point and was courteous to women, whom he respected. In his younger days he enjoyed dancing, feasting, jousting, falconry, tennis and archery. He certainly burnt midnight oil on many a court occasion, often only turning in at two in the morning or even later, but he was complimented by several contemporaries on his moderation at table. Bishop Guillaume Fillastre apparently admired his simple tastes in this respect: 'frequently he left partidges on one side for a Mainz ham or a piece of salt beef'.

Bishop Guillaume Fillastre, himself a bastard, son of an abbot and a nun, also commented on what he called Duke Philip's 'weakness of the flesh' and even tried to excuse the duke on the dubious grounds that none of us can be perfect, and to exculpate him by insisting that he never actually raped any of his sexual victims. Another courtier, Olivier de la Marche, mentions the duke's 'very fine troop of bastards of both sexes'. Philip the Good's illegitimate offspring has also engaged the attention of historians, most of whom have exaggerated their number; not to mention genealogists who have searched for and probably invented ducal bastards in order to confer a distinguished if illegitimate ancestry on certain people alive today who are proud to bear the surname de Bourgogne. For reasons of economy and convenience rather than merely for variety's sake, the duke's mistresses did not follow one another in succession, but a number were maintained at one and the same time in different places: at Lille, Bruges, Brussels and Arras for example. The progeny took their names from their mother's place of abode: Baudouin of Lille, Jehan of Bruges, etc.

Duke Philip provided husbands from among the higher nobility of his lands for his female bastards, and careers, usually in the church, for the males; but one of the former became a nun and an abbess, and two at least of the latter served the duke as lieutenant, governor, captain and councillor. The bastards were all referred to as 'bastards of Burgundy', and they must not be confused, for example, with the five 'bastards of Brabant', illegitimate children of Philip's predecessors as dukes of Brabant. In their enthusiasm to magnify or distort Duke Philip's sexual prowess historians have inadvertently attributed to him bastards of John the Fearless and other relatives of his. They have even invented a title 'Grand Bastard of Burgundy' and conferred it on Anthony of Burgundy as if it were some court office. But de Commynes calls him *le grand bastard* once only to distinguish him from his younger, likewise illegitimate, half-brother, Baudouin.

Although affairs of state were often deferred by Philip the Good until after his pleasure was gratified, documentary evidence shows that he by no means lacked a continuing personal commitment in the government of his lands. Even so, there is a striking contrast between his easy-going approach and the disciplined rigour of his energetic, hard-working son Charles the Bold, whose pastimes, according to Wielant, were 'to go in the morning from room to room to organize justice, war, finance and other affairs'. 'All this week,' wrote the Milanese ambassador on 31 December 1475, Duke Charles 'has been preoccupied with reorganizing the men-at-arms according to his new ordinances and making dispositions for, and drawing up the balance of, his receipts and expenses, so that he has scarcely eaten once a day.' Of course Charles differed from his father in many other ways. He had little or no interest in women. 'He turned the women's lodgings at court into a council chamber and an accounting office, saying that he would rather have the council and finances around him than women.' He left virtually no trace of illegitimate offspring and indeed may well have been a homosexual. Two courtiers who deserted him for Louis XI in 1470 justified their flight on the grounds of the 'most vile, detestable and dishonest things he indulges in against God our creator, against our law, and against all rules of nature'. Charles had a passion for things military which was quite foreign to his father, even though his father conquered more territory at the head of an army than he did. Charles fancied himself as a new Julius Caesar or Alexander. He liked nothing better than camp life. On the way back from the siege of Neuss he rode with his men all the way to Maastricht, showing the Italian ambassador

squadron after squadron and man after man. The trouble he takes is incredible. He always rides in his cuirass. All his pleasure, his every thought, is in men-at-arms: to make them look good and move in good order. He never dismounts until the whole camp is lodged and he has inspected all round the site . . .

There is a world of difference between Duke Charles's stern military dedication and the flamboyant way his father Philip the Good challenged enemies or rivals like Duke Humphrey of Gloucester and Duke William of Saxony to single combat.

Charles the Bold was violent, moody and cruel but scarcely deserving of the epithet Téméraire (Rash) given him by nineteenth-century French historians. As a matter of fact he invariably advanced into enemy territory with extreme caution. He was extraordinarily vain, and ostentatious in his behaviour and public appearances. He even outclassed his predecessors in sartorial extravagance. His gorgeous jewelled hats aroused curiosity and admiration; were they ducal, archducal or even regal? He loaded his gowns and robes with rubies and sapphires; pearls glittered all over his elaborate costumes and even on his armour. In contrast to his taciturn father, Charles loved making speeches and haranguing people, and specimens of his oratory have survived. He ruled with an element of authoritarian absolutism, disregarding the rights and privileges of others. At court he caused a stir when he took over the dispensation of justice in person, holding compulsory audiences for this purpose three afternoons a week which were none too popular with his courtiers. Contemporary stories make him a would-be world conqueror. A German parson reported 'that the duke of Burgundy claimed there were only three lords in the world, one in Heaven, that is God; one in Hell, the devil Lucifer; and one on earth, who will be he himself'. Both this cleric, Conrad

Stolle, and Johann Knebel at Basel believed that Charles's immodest ambitions would tempt him to undertake the conquest of the entire River Rhine. Their fears were perhaps not entirely unfounded.

In a world where the plight of most women was more or less servile, the authority and activity of the wives of the Valois dukes of Burgundy is striking. The names of Margaret of Flanders, Margaret of Bavaria, Isabel of Portugal and Margaret of York have already been mentioned in this connection. All of them were closely involved, at times, with the government of Valois Burgundy. Margaret of Flanders was the daughter of one of the most remarkable fourteenth-century rulers, the count of Flanders Louis of Male (1346–84). Margaret of Bavaria was the daughter of Albert of Bavaria, regent of Hainault, Holland and Zeeland. Isabel's father was King John I of Portugal, and Margaret of York's brother was King Edward IV of England. Every one of these four distinguished women would have been quite capable of ruling in her own right; indeed they often did take initiatives of their own. Isabel was mistakenly credited by ill-informed contemporaries with more influence than she actually possessed. She was certainly not so powerful 'that the duke had to give free rein to all her wishes', as one writer claimed. Nor was Pope Pius II altogether avoiding exaggeration when he wrote that 'this woman soon applied herself to increasing her power and, exploiting her husband's indulgence, she began to take everything in hand, ruling the towns, organizing armies, levying taxes on provinces and ruling everything in an arbitrary fashion'. However, documents show that she did help her husband in these and other matters.

More important for a duchess than governmental responsibility was procreation, for it was a vital concern of every ruler in those days to ensure the succession with a male heir and provide children of both sexes for marriage alliances. In this respect the first two Valois dukes' wives performed generously enough. Margaret of Flanders bore Philip the Bold three boys and three girls who survived the perils of childhood; Margaret of Bavaria was almost as prolific. But Isabel of Portugal, after bearing Duke Philip the Good three boys in the first four years of their marriage, only one of whom, Charles, survived, had no more children by him. His first two, short-lived, marriages had been childless. Least successful of all was Margaret of York, who bore her husband Charles the Bold no children at all in nearly ten years of marriage. His one and only legitimate child, Mary of Burgundy, was the daughter of his second wife Isabel of Bourbon.

Something has now been said about the rulers of Valois Burgundy and their wives; but what of the officials and others who administered it on their behalf? In the spring of 1385 Philip the Bold created a new central post of supreme importance in the Burgundian state. A Frenchman, Jehan Canard, who had risen to fame as a lawyer practising in the Paris Parlement, was appointed the duke's first personal chancellor. As 'chancellor of my lord the duke of Burgundy' he replaced the chancellors already existing in the individual territories of Burgundy and Flanders and became the effective head of the duke's civil service, indeed a sort of ducal prime minister. Jehan Canard, who was rewarded in 1392 with the bishopric of Arras, was the first of a line of distinguished Burgundian chancellors, though his successors were noblemen or burgesses rather than ecclesiastics. Just as Jehan Canard served throughout Philip the Bold's reign, so a Burgundian nobleman, Jehan de Saulx, lord of Courtivron, served as ducal chancellor throughout John the Fearless's reign and another Burgundian, the Autun burgess Nicolas Rolin, was Duke Philip the Good's chancellor from soon after Philip's accession as duke until the end of the 1450s. He died in 1461 aged eighty-two, having amassed a fortune in the duke's service, part of which he used to found and endow the famous hospital at Beaune, the Hôtel Dieu. Though documentary evidence shows time and again that he only carried out the duke's orders, Nicolas Rolin was believed by some contemporaries to be all-powerful at court. Chastellain quite erroneously claims that 'all the most important affairs of state were in his hands' and that 'this chancellor . . . had been ruling everything single-handed, making all important decisions of war and peace, and those concerning finance'. Nonetheless, the chancellor was quite certainly the most important and influential Burgundian official. Rolin was succeeded by another Burgundian, Pierre de Goux, who kept office under Charles the Bold until he died in 1471. The last chancellor of the Valois dukes was another Burgundian burgess, this time from Mâcon, Guillaume Hugonet. Four out of these five chancellors were Burgundian; the fifth was French; not one was from the Low Countries.

The chancellor was by far and away the best-paid of the duke's civil servants. Jehan de Saulx received an annual salary of

£2,000 of Tours – four times as much as the next-best-paid official, the treasurer and governor of finances. In addition, he was paid a daily wage of eight francs a day when away from one of his houses – at Couchey, Courtivron or Beaune – on ducal business. The accounts show that he scarcely took more than ten days' holiday each year; the rest of the time he was away from home and receiving his supplementary eight francs per day. So his total annual remuneration approached £5,000 of Tours. His predecessor Jehan Canard had been paid much the same amount by Philip the Bold.

Next in seniority to the chancellor were the governors or lieutenants appointed irregularly in various individual territories or, occasionally, groups of territories. These men were invariably chosen from the higher nobility or from neighbouring princely houses. Thus in the time of the first two Valois dukes Jehan VI, lord of Ghistelles, and William II, count of Namur, both served for a spell as governor or governor and captain-general of Flanders, and, in the county of Burgundy or Franche-Comté a local nobleman Jehan III de Vergy, lord of Fouvent, was governor. Under Philip the Good governors and lieutenants, with the exception of the *stadholder* of Holland, the governor of Luxembourg, and some others, were rather few and far between, but Charles the Bold made considerable use of these officers. They came for the most part from minor principalities inside the Burgundian sphere of influence, many of which we have already met with in a previous chapter as allies or client-states of Burgundy. Such were Adolf of Cleves, lord of Ravenstein, who served as the duke's 'lieutenant-general in all his lands and lordships' in the Low Countries in 1475–6, and Jaques de Savoie, count of Romont, who preceded Adolf in that office. Rudolf, margrave of Hochberg, count of Neuchâtel, was governor of Luxembourg for Charles the Bold; his uncle Jehan, count of Fribourg and of Neuchâtel, had been Philip the Good's governor of Burgundy. Count John IV of Nassau-Dillenberg and his son Engelbert alternated as seneschals or *stadholders* of Brabant in Charles the Bold's reign. These men were amply rewarded: Adolf of Cleves received an annual pension of 6,000 francs. Prominent among them at the end of Duke Charles's reign was a Picard nobleman Guy de Brimeu, lord of Humbercourt, who built up what amounted to a minor empire for himself along the River Meuse, based on his lieutenancy of Liège and his governorship of Namur and various other territories. He set up a council at Maastricht which became the administrative capital of this new territorial entity, and he ruled it like a king until the Ghenters cut off his head on 3 April 1477.

The men employed in the administration of the Burgundian state, numbering several hundred salaried persons in all, cannot be very accurately or meaningfully described with such modern names as 'civil service' or 'secretariat'. They were professional in the sense of being employed whole time, but they were for the most part unspecialized in that many of them performed both judicial and administrative duties. Nor had any specialized groups as yet emerged to deal expertly with such specific tasks as diplomacy and military affairs. Broadly speaking, each territory provided its own officials, Flemings serving the duke in Flanders, Dutchmen in Holland, and so on; while those employed in the central institutions of the Burgundian state were recruited almost without exception from the French-speaking territories or, in the early years, from France itself.

The most important categories of official were the councillors, the so-called *gens de finance* or financial officials, the secretaries and the bailiffs. Many of the councillors were legal experts with university degrees in civil and canon law. The secretaries and *gens de finance* were often from urban merchant families; the bailiffs were drawn from the nobility. There was considerable competition for the more lucrative posts in the ducal service: at Dijon there was a queue for vacancies among the *maîtres des comptes* or senior accounting officials. Thus in 1459 Philip the Good promised the next vacancy in the *chambre des comptes* there to a certain Mongin Contault, but in 1466 Charles, then count of Charolais, persuaded the duke to revoke this and promise the next vacancy to Jehan le Gros and the one after that to Jehan de Molesmes. So Mongin Contault was relegated, by ducal letters of 29 May 1467, to the third vacancy.

Naturally, the ducal civil service was riddled with nepotism and the families of civil servants frequently intermarried. Many examples could be cited of father succeeding son in a ducal office or of two brothers serving together. Thus Jehan and Pierre Blanchet, father and son, were ducal secretaries between 1363 and 1400; and, while Pieter van der Tanerijen was a *maître des comptes* in the Lille accounting office between 1394 and 1400, his brother Jacob was *procureur-général* of Flanders – a sort of public prosecutor – and a third brother Geraard was bailiff of the *salle* or feudal court at Ypres. On the staff of the Malines Parlement, the supreme Burgundian law court, when it was set up in 1473, which numbered forty-five persons, were three de Clugnys, two brothers and a nephew, and four other relatives of theirs. Some of the Flemish bailiwicks were almost becoming family possessions. In 1452 Diederik Mont followed his father-in-law as bailiff of the *salle* of Ypres but he resigned in 1462 in favour of his uncle. Other families spread their net over several such offices. The nobleman Frans van Haveskerke served between 1409 and 1419 as bailiff of Biervliet, Bruges, Alost and Ghent. His father Hustin was bailiff of Cassel and Sint-Winoksbergen; his brother Filips was bailiff of Sint-Winoksbergen between 1426 and 1428; his son Lodewijk was bailiff of Courtrai, Bruges and, again, Sint-Winoksbergen.

Important material and social benefits resulted from taking service as a ducal councillor or official. Perhaps the most immediate social advantage was ennoblement, which could be effected by ducal letters patent or by the king at the duke's request. At least four of Philip the Bold's *gens de finance* were rewarded in this way: Jehan d'Auxonne and Joceran Frepier, receivers-general of Burgundy; Amiot Arnaut, receiver-general of all finances; and the *maître de la chambre aux deniers* Hervé de Neauville. Ducal civil servants also enjoyed minor perquisites of robes, wine and the like as well as exemption from taxation. Many were provided with lucrative ecclesiastical offices. Four presidents of the great council succeeded one another during three quarters of a century (1410–83) as bishops of Tournai: Jehan de Thoisy, Jehan Chevrot, Guillaume Fillastre and Ferry de Clugny. Quentin Menart, ducal councillor, became archbishop of Besançon in 1439; Nicolas de Tholon and Robert Danguel, secretaries of Philip the Bold, both obtained bishoprics, of Autun and Nevers respectively. Philip the Good's councillor Anthoine Haneron was provost of St Donatian's at Bruges, according to Chastellain 'the finest and must lucrative non-episcopal benefice in all France', worth 2,000 Rhine florins per annum.

Quite apart from such very substantial recompenses for their services, many of the duke's officials were paid regular annual salaries and also, very often, supplementary daily wages. Under John the Fearless, for example, the two most important central officials after the chancellor, the treasurer and the receiver-general of all finances, were paid respectively annual salaries of £500 and £400 of Tours; ordinary councillors received £300;

maîtres des comptes £250 or £300; bailiffs £120–200. When away from home on ducal business daily wages were payable in addition, at a rate for councillors, of two francs per day. The leading financial official at this time was Jehan Chousat, native of Poligny in Franche-Comté, who was or became well enough off to found a collegiate church at Poligny and possess a town house in Paris where he once entertained the duke to supper. His annual salary was 500 francs, and his wages were 2½ francs per day. Between 1 December 1410 and 31 December 1411 he contrived to receive wages while absent from home for exactly 396 days! Thus in a good year he received well over 1,000 francs from the duke.

Some ducal employees, for example secretaries, received no annual salary or *pension* as it was called, being remunerated instead by a combination of daily wages and occasional monetary gifts. Most officials received such gifts from time to time and in many cases these gifts equalled the amount of the *pension*. Thus in 1396 two of the *maîtres des comptes* at Lille, with salaries of 250 francs, received gifts totalling 150 and 200 francs respectively. In the same year the councillor–*maître d'hôtel* Jehan de Poucques, with a salary of 300 francs, received a further 900 francs in gifts.

It is not easy to ascertain, on the basis of these figures, how well paid the Burgundian civil servants really were. It has been shown that, though marginally less well-off than their colleagues in the royal service, they were better-paid than the officials of other French princes like, for instance, the duke of Bourbon. It has also been shown that a fifteenth-century mason working in Dijon might hope to earn about fifty francs per annum – the same as, or even a little more than, many of the lowest-paid ducal officials, who however usually enjoyed other sources of income.

Fortunes could be and were made in the ducal service. Men like the chancellors Nicolas Rolin, Pierre de Goux and Guillaume Hugonet came from families of relatively modest means, but they acquired extensive estates, richly appointed houses and jewels, plate and illuminated manuscripts, as a result of their careers in the Burgundian civil service. Nicolas Rolin was perhaps outstanding in this respect, and he managed to provide supremely well for his three sons. Jehan Rolin became bishop of Autun and a cardinal; Anthoine, lord of Aymeries, Autun and Lens, served throughout Charles the Bold's reign as grand bailiff and captain-general of Hainault; Guillaume, lord of

Beauchamp, was captain of Dijon in 1475. One of Philip the Good's councillors and financial officials, Pieter Bladelin of Bruges, the founder and lord of Middelburg, was said by Chastellain to have been enjoying an income of 6,000 gold crowns per annum in rents alone. His fortune had been put together at the Burgundian court under Chastellain's very eyes.

The Burgundian civil service offered more than mere employment; it offered a career, for its different sections provided quite well-defined ladders of promotion. Take the case of the Flemish nobleman Robrecht van Capple, who served the first two Valois dukes in their capacity as counts of Flanders. Appearing first in 1387 as bailiff of Termonde, he moved to Veurne in 1390, remaining there till 1395 before being appointed water-bailiff of Sluis. But promotion came quickly. In 1396 he became bailiff of Ypres; in 1397 he was bailiff of Alost. Finally, after holding two other posts in succession, he crowned his twenty-four-year career in the ducal service by being bailiff of Bruges between 1407 and 1411. A bailiff might hope to better himself by transferring to the central administration of his particular territory or even to the central administration of Valois Burgundy as a whole. Thus in the duchy of Burgundy under Philip the Bold Guillaume de Clugny became a councillor at Dijon after serving as a bailiff, and in Flanders under John the Fearless Jan van den Berghe, who had begun his career modestly enough as bailiff of the lordship of Wijnendale, held in succession the bailiwicks of the Vier Ambachten, Courtrai, Veurne and other posts before becoming a councillor in the council of Flanders. He was still a councillor there when he died in 1439. Jan de Baenst did even better: after more than forty years in the duke's service he was appointed in 1460 a councillor in Duke Philip the Good's great council, though this may have been an honorary post only. Beginning his career in 1420 as receiver of Sluis, he became bailiff, then water-bailiff of Sluis; then bailiff of Veurne, *schout* or *écoutète* of Malines and finally bailiff of Bruges. A Flemish bailiff might also hope to take office as sovereign bailiff or receiver-general of Flanders.

As for the *gens de finances*, they could hope for promotion from a minor post of local receiver to the receiver-generalship of an entire territory or from a clerkship in one of the *chambres des comptes* or accounting offices to be a *maître* there. They might go further and crown their career by becoming one of the central financial officials, the treasurer–governor-general of finances or the receiver-general of all finances. Dreue Suquet began his career in 1395 as a clerk in the *chambre des comptes* in his home town of Lille. Soon he was a *maître des comptes* there, a post he held for some sixteen years before his promotion to be treasurer and governor-general in 1413. It was normal for the staff in each of the *chambres des comptes* – there were four under Philip the Good, at Dijon, Lille, Brussels and The Hague – to be quite separate, to be recruited locally, and to achieve promotion within their own organization. The *cursus honorum* here was from clerk to *auditeur* or auditor; from *auditeur* to *maître,* and from *maître* to *premier maître.* But among the personnel of the *chambres des comptes,* and among the receivers and receivers-general, there were numerous cases of the omission of at least one step in the ladder of promotion, as well as of exceptionally rapid promotion. Jehan Fraignot, in charge of the Chalon fairs in 1410, was receiver of the ʾailiwick of Chalon and receiver-general of the two Burgundies n 1415. Pierre Adorne was appointed receiver-general of Flanders in 1394 though he had not served in any subordinate post: he had, however, been treasurer of the town of Bruges since 1390.

The different categories of Burgundian civil servant were by no means homogeneous or even completely separate one from another. The most heterogeneous group were the councillors, for they included members of the great council, or central council, which perambulated with the court, and members of the regional councils at Dijon, Ghent, Mons, Brussels, The Hague and Luxembourg. The former were often famous and respected members of the higher nobility, close associates of the duke himself; the latter were obscure legal experts, or local magistrates. The former were recruited mainly from the duke's retinue, for example from among the court chamberlains, and were not in any sense professional civil servants; the latter were local people drawn from the lesser nobility and bourgeoisie. And there were full-time and part-time councillors at both the regional and the central level. In John the Fearless's reign two of the Ghent councillors, that is the permanent members of the council of Flanders, were Ghenters and one of these was dean of Liège as well as councillor. Another councillor, Daniel Alarts, had been a *maître des comptes* at Lille, and another had served as *procureur-général* of Flanders and as *maître* of the *chambre aux deniers,* the accounting office of the court. A fifth had been bailiff of Ghent. At Dijon in the same period Richard de Chancey, the *chef du conseil,* was also bailiff of Dijon and a *maître des requêtes* of the

duke, and other Dijon councillors were likewise part-time:
Jehan Couillier, who died in 1408, was dean of the ducal chapel
and *garde des chartes* or keeper of the muniments.

Like councillors, secretaries were recruited and employed in
all the Valois Burgundian territories. A number worked at court:
there were supposed to be seven there at the beginning of Philip
the Good's reign and fourteen in 1469 at the start of Charles the
Bold's reign. It was their task to draw up and sign the duke's
correspondence and they were often sent on confidential missions by the duke, usually, but not always, within his own
territories. Their remuneration equalled that of the less senior
councillors, so that they were on a par, roughly, with the *maîtres
des comptes*. At court, where the secretaries staffed the ducal
chancery, they were usually recruited directly from outside the
Burgundian civil service and they enjoyed few prospects of
promotion within it. Unlike the other officials employed in the
central government they were not mostly Burgundians, for a
high proportion of them came from the Low Countries or
elsewhere. Many were clerks in minor orders and some of them
were very successful in obtaining ecclesiastical benefices through
the good offices of the dukes. Martin Steenberch, for instance,
acquired fifteen livings. Although the backgrounds of many of
these secretaries remains obscure, it is clear that they were
predominantly of urban, bourgeois extraction. Only a few had
university degrees.

The bailiffs, in most respects except geographically, were a
reasonably homogeneous group of functionaries. Especially in
the two Burgundies, Flanders and Hainault, they were professional men who made their career in the bailiwicks, where
their duties were legal, financial, administrative and military.
In Flanders two important conditions were attached to their
employment: they had to be of legitimate birth, and they must
have no connection at all with the place where they were to
exercise their office. A less important condition was that they
were not allowed to own taverns.

Much has already been said about another large and amorphous group of Burgundian civil servants loosely referred to as
gens de finances, but something needs to be added about the
Italian bankers who operated alongside, if not actually inside,
the ducal civil service. For these Italians were used as financial
experts and advisers as well as suppliers of goods and of loans.
Two of them have achieved a certain renown: Dino Rapondi of

Lucca under Philip the Bold and Tommaso Portinari of Florence under Charles the Bold.

The Rapondi were a family of merchants and bankers of Lucca who had settled at Paris and Bruges in the second half of the fourteenth century. Dino Rapondi became in the 1370s one of the leading suppliers of luxury goods of all kinds to the royal and Burgundian courts. He advanced his first loans to Philip the Bold at this time; later he was rewarded or encouraged with the titles of ducal councillor and *maître d'hôtel*. Because he had business interests and offices in both Paris and Bruges he was admirably placed to help finance Philip the Bold's acquisition of Flanders and that duke's other enterprises. He was able to advance large sums to Philip in Paris and recoup himself in Flanders from taxes or other moneys owed to the duke. In 1383 he lent Philip money in return for the proceeds of a tax on Antwerp and of a fine which had been imposed on Ypres and other Flemish towns after their defeat at Roosebeke the year before. In 1391-4 he was responsible for the financing and construction of Sluis castle, one of Philip the Bold's most elaborate and costly building projects.

In these and other ways Dino Rapondi's wealth and skill contributed importantly to the formation of the Valois Burgundian state. He was much more to the duke than a mere banker or money-lender. In 1386 he went to Pavia to arrange a loan for Philip the Bold from Giangaleazzo Visconti. In 1392 he was away from his Paris house on ducal business, mostly in Flanders, for a total of over five months. He was still journeying on the duke's behalf in 1402, when he was too old to ride a horse, but had to travel in a carriage. Other members of his family assisted Philip the Bold: a brother Guillelmo lent money in 1369 for the duke's wedding to Margaret of Flanders; another brother Giacomo supplied Philip with books; a nephew Giovanni also lent money to Philip the Bold.

Tommaso Portinari, or Sire Thomas de Portunary as he is described in the Burgundian accounts, was Charles the Bold's Dino Rapondi. This Italian settled in Bruges was a descendant of Folco Portinari, father of Dante's Beatrice, and thus a respected citizen of Florence. He arrived in Bruges in 1439 as office boy in the Medici bank there and stayed half a century, becoming manager of the Bruges branch of the Medici bank when Agnolo Tani retired in 1464. He too became a ducal councillor and was frequently away on ducal business. It was he who had the new

Duke Charles the Bold's seal made at Bruges in 1467. He arranged the payment of ducal messengers to England and Rome in that year. He supplied the bulk of the de luxe materials and other things required for Charles the Bold's wedding to Margaret of York in 1468. At Trier in 1473, when Charles the Bold and the Emperor Frederick met in great state, Tommaso had an honoured place in the duke's retinue, being one of the nine courtiers issued for the occasion with robes of 'crimson-violet figured satin and pourpoints of crimson satin'. At the end of Duke Charles's reign Tommaso was playing an important role in the duke's military enterprises by transferring funds raised in taxes in the Low Countries thence via Geneva, Dijon and Besançon to pay the Burgundian army in the field. Historical research by no means confirms the story that Tommaso Portinari broke the Medici bank at Bruges by the irresponsible lending of enormous sums to Duke Charles, though he probably did exceed the limit of £6,000 credit he was authorized to allow Charles under his 1471 contract with Lorenzo il Magnifico.

What material bonds and what kind of loyalty held together this numerous but geographically scattered body of councillors, *gens de finances*, bailiffs, secretaries, legists and other officials and servants of the Valois Burgundian state? The remuneration of these people, in terms of annual salaries, daily wages, gifts, conferment of ecclesiastical benefices and so on was satisfactory if not lavish. It emanated from the duke himself and bound them to him personally even if they were paid out of regional or local funds. But many recipients of these ducal favours were indebted also to others for their livelihood, and the loyalties of many, especially in the higher ranks of the Burgundian civil service among the councillor-chamberlains of the court, were divided between the dukes and other lords, patrons, or benefactors. In Philip the Bold's reign Guy de la Trémoille, ducal councillor and chamberlain, in receipt of the very generous pension of 5,000 francs per annum from the duke, accepted other pensions at different times from the king of France, the duchess of Brabant, the count of Savoy, the ruler of Milan and even the pope. The income from these sources far exceeded that from his own estates.

Some noble families suffered a chronic dichotomy of allegiance between France and Burgundy. In John the Fearless's reign one member of the house of Chalon, Louis, brother of the prince of Orange, Jehan de Chalon, joined the Armagnacs and made war on the duke of Burgundy after Duke John had seized and annexed his county of Tonnerre. After the death of Louis III de Chalon, prince of Orange, in 1463, his succession was disputed between his three sons. The eldest, Guillaume, went to King Louis XI of France for 'advice, comfort and help'. The two younger, Hugues and Louis, took service with Charles the Bold. The classic example of this division of loyalty was furnished by the branch of the house of Luxembourg settled in Picardy and Artois. It came to a climax in the remarkable career of Louis de Luxembourg, count of St Pol, who tried to serve the interests of France and Burgundy at one and the same time, while also feathering his own nest. He ended his life on 19 December 1475 on the scaffold in the Place de Grève, Paris. His son, Jehan count of Marle, was a loyal Burgundian; another son, Anthoine, was Charles the Bold's councillor-chamberlain and lieutenant-general in the two Burgundies; a brother of his, Jaques, lord of Richebourg, also councillor-chamberlain of Charles the Bold, passed into French service after being taken prisoner by the French in 1475. Many other examples could be given: one brother of Savoy, Jacques, count of Romont, served Charles the Bold while another, Philip, count of Bagé and lord of Bresse, went over to Louis XI.

The problem of disloyalty to the dukes of Burgundy, or even open treachery, was aired from time to time at chapter meetings of the Order of the Golden Fleece. At the 1433 chapter Jehan de la Trémoille was accused of spying and even conspiring for the French. Charles the Bold had a complex about traitors. At the 1468 chapter when the three leading members of the Picard family of Croy were accused of all sorts of misdemeanours against the duke, one of the charges was that of disloyal relations with Louis XI. At the same chapter Henrik van Borselen, lord of Veere, Burgundian admiral of the fleet, was criticized for accepting office and pension from the king of France. At the 1473 chapter he was suspected of French sympathies, and Charles also complained that his own stepbrother, the bastard of Burgundy Anthony, had accepted monetary gifts from Louis XI.

As a matter of fact, though Charles the Bold kept imagining himself to be surrounded by traitors, the great majority of his officials and servants remained entirely loyal to him. A few minor figures, such as the writer of memoirs Philippe de Commynes, went over to Louis XI, but the rest remained firm in their allegiance – as their forbears had done under John the

Fearless. Only after the death of Duke Charles in 1477 and the annexation of the duchy to the French crown did many of the leading Burgundian civil servants and courtiers go over to France, among them Guillaume de Rochefort, who became chancellor of France, and at least three Knights of the Golden Fleece. But in those circumstances they had no option; service with Louis XI was their only chance of survival.

CHAPTER SIX

The Structure of Government

It has already been pointed out that the government of the Burgundian state was essentially personal. Everything was in the hands of the duke. Naturally therefore the organs of central government, forming the instruments he needed to implement his wishes and policies, were concentrated around his person. By far the most important of these was the court, for its main governmental function was to support, nourish and provide for the material needs of the duke himself, his chancery and secretaries, his councillors and ambassadors. Here the court will be considered in this light, as a governmental institution; later its contribution to literature and the arts will be examined.

Of course, like every other fifteenth-century court, the Burgundian court was always on the move. Yet an increasingly sedentary tendency was evident here, as elsewhere, especially in Philip the Good's reign. He maintained and enlarged the five principal ducal residences or palaces, at Brussels, Bruges, Lille, Dijon and Hesdin in Artois, which the Valois dukes had taken over from their predecessors, but allowed the magnificent Hôtel d'Artois in Paris, where the Burgundian court had been based during a large part of the reigns of the first two Valois dukes, to fall into disuse. At Lille, Philip the Good built an entirely new palace in 1452–63, and in these years too he extensively renovated the ducal palace at Dijon, adding the Tour de la Terrasse and the Salle des Gardes. At Bruges, money was spent on the Prinsenhof and on a smaller palace which Duke Philip bought and then restored for his more private use. At Brussels, where Philip the Good is said to have stayed for a total of 3,819 days, the Coudenberg palace was considerably improved during his reign, in part at the expense of the townspeople.

The castle at Hesdin in Artois, which was razed to the ground in the sixteenth century, had been fitted out at the end of the thirteenth century by Count Robert of Artois with a fine menagerie and aviary and a spacious park, as well as with a variety of curious mechanical contrivances or practical jokes.

Under the dukes of Burgundy the castle and its devices were carefully maintained and refurbished by a series of artists beginning with the renowned Melchior Broederlam of Ypres. There was a gallery containing three statues that could be made to squirt water, a distorting mirror, and a device which buffeted people about their heads and shoulders as they walked past. Its doorway was defended by a mechanism which squirted water up from below and another which could shower soot or flour from above. In one room rain, and even snow, thunder and lightning could be simulated. In another a wooden hermit could be made to speak. Elsewhere there was a box, and 'above the box a figure which makes faces at people and replies to their questions'. These and other mechanisms were in the care of a special official. Duke and court however were only occasionally at Hesdin. Philip the Good was there for a few weeks in 1435 and 1448 and a few days only in 1451-2 and 1461. Charles the Bold spent five months there in 1470.

Two documentary sources of evidence contain information about the material organization and size of the Burgundian court. First the *escroes* or daily accounts, entered on long strips of parchment, have survived in considerable number, 3,857 at least from Philip the Good's reign. From them we can learn the exact size of the Burgundian court on a particular day and the quantities of food it consumed. Already under Philip the Bold it often comprised some 250 or 300 persons and the same number at least of horses; later it could number anything up to a thousand or even more persons. As to the consumption of provisions, on 11 November 1460 when Philip the Good gave a dinner for the ladies of Brussels, this was recorded as follows: seventy-four dozen rolls, cress and lettuce, six joints of beef, forty-three pounds of lard, twenty-one shoulders of mutton, six-and-a-half dozen sausages, three pigs, tripe and calves' feet for making jellies, a bittern, three geese, twelve water-birds, four rabbits, twenty-two partridges, 159 chickens, sixteen pairs of pigeons, eighteen cheeses, 350 eggs, pastries, flour, cabbages, peas, parsley, onions, 100 quinces and 150 pears, cream, six pounds of butter, vinegar and oranges and lemons.

A second source of information about the court is the series of court or household ordinances. A comparison between the three issued by Philip the Good, in 1426, 1433 and 1438, and Charles the Bold's ordinance of 1469, shows how the permanent establishment of the court was steadily growing in size, from a total, excluding the chapel, of 234 persons in 1426 to 351 in 1438 and 440 in 1469. Not that all the courtiers and other persons mentioned in these ordinances served simultaneously; they did spells of duty in turn, for three or six months at a time. For example there were two barbers, each serving at court for half the year, and four of the *maîtres d'hôtel* or stewards were supposed to succeed one another, one in each quarter of the year. In 1469 there were 101 chamberlain-councillors, but only twenty-four were supposed to serve at court at any one time.

We are fortunate indeed in possessing a very full description of Charles the Bold's court in 1474 by the courtier-chronicler Olivier de la Marche, which shows that it had developed considerably since the 1469 ordinance. He describes first the chapel with its staff of forty; then the council, presided over by the chancellor; the dispensation of justice by the duke in his audience; the separate councils or departments for war and finance; and only then follows an account of the chamberlains and of the four main departments, offices or 'estates' as de la Marche calls them. These were the *paneterie* or bread pantry, the *échansonnerie* or wine-pantry, the *cuisine* or kitchen and the *écurie* or stable. Each was staffed by fifty squires and supervised by a *premier écuyer*. De la Marche also describes the duke's twelve war trumpets, the College of Heralds, complete with six kings-of-arms, eight heralds and four pursuivants, the sixty-two archers and 126 men-at-arms of the duke's bodyguard, besides the two minor court offices, the *fruiterie*, which was responsible for spices and candles as well as fruit, and the *fourrière,* which looked after lodgings and furnishings. This was the duke's court; one must not forget that the duchess often maintained a separate court of her own, similar to the duke's but smaller.

The leading courtier was the first chamberlain. Anthoine, lord of Croy, who held this office under Philip the Good, was succeeded in it under Charles the Bold by Anthony, bastard of Burgundy. The first chamberlain had to sleep near the duke, carry his banner into battle, and supervise the entire court. According to the ordinance of 1438 he was to be served twice a day with a plate of meat, two quarts of wine, and four small white and six small brown loaves or rolls. After 1437 he was the only courtier permitted to take meals in private.

Under Charles the Bold court discipline was tightened and indeed the entire court suffered a certain militarization. Later, in 1474-6, it was more or less converted into a branch of the army.

In the 1469 ordinance the chaplains and clerks were prohibited from 'all immoderate talking, chatting, conversation, mockeries, signs, derisions, games, laughing and other vain and frivolous things' during services. Every week at a special assembly the first chaplain had to see 'if there is anything to reform and correct in anyone's behaviour'. A chamberlain who misbehaved could be struck off the day's roll or *escroe*, thus losing his wages, and every day before supper a written return was made stating whether or not the chamberlains had 'served the duke at all times according to his ordinances'. Every Saturday evening the duke was furnished with a list of chamberlains who had been struck off the roll that week. Everyone was certainly kept on their toes.

The central officials and institutions of the Valois Burgundian state were comprised within the court. The ducal chancery, usually headed by the chancellor, and staffed by the secretaries, was essential for the drawing up of the duke's letters and ordinances. A body of *chevaucheurs* or mounted messengers had constantly to be on hand at court and, equally important, the court personnel, especially the councillor-chamberlains, had to be available to be drawn on for foreign embassies. As to the Knights of the Golden Fleece, twenty-four in number, they scarcely formed a separate governmental institution though, especially under Duke Charles, they enjoyed precedence and were sometimes seated separately at court occasions. Although only a few of them were normally at court at any one time, their importance is shown by the fact that, of the twenty-nine members of the great council listed in the 1438 ordinance, ten were Knights of the Golden Fleece. The Order was founded by Duke Philip the Good in 1430 and, though its seat was officially fixed at Dijon, its chapters were held in different towns, usually in the Low Countries. It had its own statutes, chancellor, treasurer, registrar or historiographer, and herald. The chief business at the chapters was the members' criticism of each other and of their sovereign the duke, and the election of new members, normally on the nomination, or rather instructions, of the duke. Charles the Bold held only two chapters, at Bruges in 1468 and at Valenciennes in 1473. At both he was criticized for working himself too hard, for speaking too sharply to his servants, for fighting too many wars and for not keeping his word.

In terms of the government of the Burgundian state the

grand conseil or great council was by far the most important part of the court after the duke himself. In spite of the existence of a ducal ordinance of 1446 purporting to set up a great council, one had in fact been in existence ever since Philip the Bold's time. Then, it was usually called merely the duke's council, though the phrase *grand conseil* does occur. Unlike the institutionalized councils at Dijon and Lille, it was at first amorphous in its membership, met irregularly, had no fixed meeting-place and had no clerk or registrar. The chancellor, when present at court, and a handful of nobles of the duke's retinue sat regularly in it; others attended from time to time. Gradually this informal group was institutionalized. In 1426 ten chamberlain-councillors were named as belonging to the great council. In the 1433 ordinance twelve such councillors were named, under a *chef du conseil*, Jehan Chevrot, later bishop of Tournai. They were noblemen drawn from both northern and southern French-speaking ducal territories, and they were now given regular hours: they had to meet twice daily before and after dinner. Evidence that a proportion of these councillors was often absent comes in 1446, when a ducal ordinance fixed the quorum at four or five. In the same document the councillors were instructed 'to take advice among themselves on the conduct of affairs' and the duke promised, not without hypocrisy, 'that from now on in these matters we shall neither do nor order anything which has not first been discussed and debated by our council and on which we have not had their advice'.

Charles the Bold's ordinance of 1469 ordered the great council to meet twice a day except on Sundays and feast days, on summer mornings from 7 to 10 o'clock and in winter from 8 to 11; and in the afternoons from 3 to 5 o'clock. Before meeting, the councillors were to attend mass, and immediately after the morning session the chancellor or president, with certain councillors previously named by the duke, was to visit Charles the Bold in his oratory and report to him on that morning's proceedings and those of the evening before. Membership of the great council was carefully defined and limited in this ordinance. Eight named chamberlain-councillors were to be regular members, also 'Monsieur the bastard' Anthony of Burgundy the first chamberlain, the five *maîtres d'hôtel*, the *maîtres des requêtes*, the marshal of Burgundy and one or two others. Prelates who were titular ducal councillors and a group of named ducal officers including the *stadholder* of Holland, the governor of

Luxembourg and the sovereign-bailiff of Flanders were allowed to attend on occasion. And naturally the duke permitted himself to 'bring or cause to be brought any other persons with him when it is his pleasure to attend in person'.

Presumably one can attach more credence to the 1469 ordinance than to Olivier de la Marche's evidently rather idealized picture of the *grand conseil* of Charles the Bold – unless its composition had been changed by 1474, when he wrote. According to de la Marche, the council comprised the chancellor, a bishop to be head or *chef* of the council in the chancellor's absence, four notable knights, eight *maîtres des requêtes* and fifteen secretaries and other officers and servants. Apart from the duke, no one else was allowed to sit in the council except those specially ordered there, the Knights of the Golden Fleece, and the *maîtres d'hôtel*.

The great council was a law court as well as an advisory and indeed also an administrative body. It heard cases on appeal from most of the duke's lands, though it never became the exclusive appeal or supreme court simply because cases in the duchy of Burgundy and the county of Flanders could be and frequently were taken on appeal to the Paris Parlement, and some territories possessed sovereign courts of their own, such as that at Mons in Hainault. Moreover, appeals lay from the great council to the Paris Parlement. The judicial business of the great council grew rapidly from the mid-fifteenth century, and under Charles the Bold much of it was diverted to a separate judicial section or committee of the council which was fixed at Malines in June 1473 and converted into the Malines Parlement at the end of that year. Some, too, of the council's judicial business was taken over by Charles the Bold in person in the audiences he held twice or thrice weekly 'to hear and deal with all the petitions sent to him especially by poor and humble people'. Criminal justice was reinforced in Duke Charles's reign by a central official based at court called the provost of the marshals. He was supported by a contingent of troops and was empowered to seek out and arrest criminals. His jurisdiction extended throughout all the duke's territories and in all his towns; indeed everywhere except at court where the *maîtres d'hôtel* held sway. Since the law courts of one territory had no jurisdiction in the next, the provost of the marshals fulfilled an important role by virtue of his ability to pursue a Flemish criminal into Brabant or a Hainaulter into Namur.

Is there any truth in Olivier de la Marche's description of Charles the Bold's war council in 1474? If this really was a more or less permanent institution in his reign it could only have been so in the last two or three years. It certainly did not exist under earlier dukes. According to de la Marche the duke had appointed four knights as war councillors or military advisers. They held council with the first chamberlain, the chancellor, the marshals, the master of the artillery and some others, and two secretaries made a written record of their proceedings. What a pity it has not come down to us!

Although the financial administration of Valois Burgundy was by no means fully centralized, central financial officials existed from the start and a central financial council evolved under the last two dukes. The official responsible for court expenses, the *maître de la chambre aux deniers,* first appears in 1377, and from 1381 there was an unbroken succession of these officials except between 1426 and 1431. The *chambre aux deniers* was staffed by the *maître* himself, a *contrôleur de la dépense de l'hôtel,* and two or more *clercs des offices de l'hôtel,* and it met daily to record the court's expenses. A *maître d'hôtel* normally had to be present to verify them. The *clercs des offices* wrote up the daily accounts, called *escroes;* the *contrôleur* was responsible for the monthly accounts called *contrerolles;* and the *maître* made up an annual account and submitted it for audit to the Dijon *chambre des comptes.*

The *maître de la chambre aux deniers* was responsible only for court expenses. The other central financial officials had wider-ranging responsibilities. The receiver-general of all finances was at the apex of a hierarchy of regional receivers-general and local receivers but, as we saw in an earlier chapter, he by no means centralized all the receipts and expenditure in his accounts. Still, he was an authentic central official, the senior receiver, more concerned with the financing of the central administration than any other receiver. Alongside him was the treasurer or treasurer and governor of finances, who did not keep an account but acted as a sort of auditor, verifier and authorizer of payments of all kinds. He was the supreme head of the ducal financial system and his duties included the supervision of the receiver-general of all finances and the other receivers.

The central financial administration so far described, put together by Philip the Bold, survived more or less intact until the end of the history of Valois Burgundy. Admittedly there were breaks, when some other organization was tried and found wanting. For instance between 1426 and 1429 the offices of receiver-general of all finances and treasurer were abolished, apparently in an effort to save money on salaries. The council was to have done their work, but it did not, so they reappeared. However, during Philip the Good's reign a sort of financial section or committee of the great council made its appearance at court: from the late 1440s on a group of three to six special financial councillors – *commis sur le fait des finances* – supervised the finances and their administration. When Charles the Bold's large-scale military activities necessitated the appointment of a new central financial official keeping separate accounts of his own – the war treasurer or *trésorier des guerres* – he joined this central financial council or *chambre des finances*, which Olivier de la Marche describes as forming part of Charles the Bold's court in 1474. According to de la Marche the four chief members of this office or department of finance were the *maître de la chambre aux deniers*, the *trésorier des guerres*, the *argentier* or treasurer, and the receiver-general of all finances. Some of what he tells us about the finances themselves is certainly erroneous, but it is easy to believe the substantial accuracy of his statement about this financial council that 'the duke came there often. He knew perfectly well what he received and what he spent. He himself sat at the end of the table and reckoned along with the others.'

An entirely new central financial institution was created by Philip the Good in about 1430 called the *épargne*. It was a sort of private ducal savings bank with a central and a regional organization into which funds were diverted for the duke's personal use and for hoarding in his castle at Lille. At the head of this curious organization, which was swept away by Charles the Bold in 1468, was a receiver-general and keeper of the *épargne*.

In spite of their allegedly lavish expenditure, in spite of the debts some of them have been accused of incurring, and in spite of their repeated and often somewhat radical measures to obtain ready cash by slashing the councillors' salaries and raising forced loans from their officials, the Valois dukes of Burgundy were among the wealthiest rulers of their day. Their financial organization had evolved piecemeal, over the years, in a way that made it very like that of France. Even though it was clumsy and inefficient, it provided the dukes with revenues which were adequate for most of their purposes. They were of two main types, ordinary and extraordinary. Ordinary revenues were made up of the rents and dues levied in the duke's domain or according to his traditional rights: rents, sale of produce, judicial fines, fees for the use of the duke's seal, and the like. Extra-ordinary revenues comprised taxes or *aides* specially voted in the form of lump sums by the Estates of a single province or territory, and then divided up among the households or hearths of the area. Certain other sources of revenue would likewise have been defined as extraordinary, especially loans and, of great importance for the first two Valois dukes, annual grants and cash gifts from the French crown.

The mammoth task of analysing the duke's total revenues to ascertain what proportion of them was ordinary and what extraordinary, and what proportion came from each territory, has not yet been undertaken. It has been shown that, taking the history of Valois Burgundy as a whole, rather more than half (actually 57½ per cent) the receipts recorded in the accounts of the receiver-general of all finances were ordinary revenues; but the actual proportion of ordinary revenues in the duke's income as a whole was at first very much higher than this. Later it dropped. Thus in Philip the Bold's reign about one eighth of the ducal revenues came from *aides* or specially voted taxes, and in John the Fearless's time the figure was one seventh or one sixth. Under Philip the Good and Charles the Bold extraordinary revenues increased in relative importance but probably never made up as much as a half of the total. As to the proportion of receipts from each territory, this has not been established with any certainty. However, it seems likely that the two largest single contributions to the revenues of the Valois dukes were made by the counties of Flanders and Holland; next came Brabant, then Artois and Hainault, and lastly the duchy of Burgundy. Revenues from other territories were quite in-significant.

The history of *aides* in Valois Burgundy emphasizes the imbalance between the two groups of territories in the relative size of their contributions to the ducal treasury. Philip the Bold persuaded the tight-fisted Flemings to vote him additional sums of money or *aides* on six different occasions. Together they totalled over half a million francs, which amounted to some £30,000 of Tours annually during his twenty years as count of Flanders. The Estates of the duchy of Burgundy voted him *aides* on eleven occasions, but their approximate annual yield, spread over the same years 1384–1403, amounted only to some £18,000 of Tours. In the second half of Philip the Good's reign the Flemish *aides* were bringing in as much as, if not more than, they had under Philip the Bold, but the Estates of the duchy of Burgundy were contributing only some £6,000 of Tours per annum. Artois on the other hand, which had voted less than £14,000 of Tours under Philip the Bold, was voting some £23,000 of Tours annually between 1442 and 1462. And of course by then the situation had been transformed by the Burgundian annexation of Holland, which paid more in *aides* than Flanders and indeed than any other single territory, as well as of Hainault and Brabant. Charles the Bold managed to extract a great deal more money in *aides* each year from his subjects than his father had done, but the imbalance between the northern and southern territories was still very evident. Thus while the northern territories were producing 500,000 crowns per annum at the end of the reign, the southern lands could manage only £100,000 *estevenants*, which were of approximately equal value to the crowns.

The increasing share of ducal revenues provided by *aides* was partly a function of the evolution, especially in the northern territories, of a regular system of *aides* which soon began to make nonsense of the idea inherent in their original definition of 'extraordinary'. In other words, these specially voted taxes soon became regular and ordinary annual payments. At first, in most cases, the entire sum of money voted as an *aide* was levied at once and in the course of a single year. Then, it became the practice for the Estates to vote a much larger sum and agree to it being levied in instalments, usually annual, over a period of years. This had happened in Brabant in the late fourteenth century, before the Burgundian dukes took over; it became normal in Hainault about the middle of the fifteenth century. In Artois the traditional 'ordinary' *aide* of £14,000 of Tours was supplemented from time to time by an 'extraordinary' *aide* of the same amount. In 1451 for the first time these Artois *aides* were voted for a term of years: three *aides* of £14,000 of Tours each annually for a period of three years. By the time of Charles the Bold all the northern territories were voting *aides* in this way, for a period of years, and in 1473 the States General accorded him a simultaneous and concurrent *aide* from them all together of 500,000 crowns annually for six years. In the same year the Estates of the duchy of Burgundy, for the first time in their history, voted an *aide* to run for a period of years, in this case six.

The *aides* formed an important part of the income of the Valois dukes of Burgundy. How did they spend their money?

As with receipts, so with revenues, it is difficult to extract the sort of quantitative data from the ducal accounts that we should most like to have. At the end of his reign, out of an approximate total annual revenue of about 400,000–450,000 francs or pounds of Tours, Duke Philip the Bold seems to have been spending rather more than half on the court. Of these court expenses, which included payments for robes, for the duchess's court, for gifts, for tapestries, jewels and so on, about 100,000 francs was needed annually for the day-to-day running costs of the court, mainly in food, wages and transport. Since the court was in large measure, as we have seen, an administrative institution, a proportion of expenditure on it should certainly be classified as administrative. The next largest single item of expenditure after the court was made up by the wages and other remuneration of councillors and officials. This probably totalled some 100,000 francs per annum under Philip the Bold. His other recurring expenses were relatively insignificant: warfare probably cost him less than 5,000 francs per annum. This pattern of expenditure, set by the first Valois duke, was followed by the others, except that John the Fearless and Charles the Bold spent a great deal more on their armies. It takes no account of those costly special projects which all the Valois dukes indulged in at irregular intervals. Philip the Bold spent some half million francs ransoming John the Fearless and his companions after they fell into Turkish hands in 1396 at the battle of Nicopolis, and bringing them home. How much he spent on the crusade itself is not known with any certainty. The rebuilding of Sluis castle and the building of the Tower of Burgundy at Sluis cost him at least 160,000 francs, and a similar sum was disbursed on his other great building project, the Charterhouse of Champmol. Philip the Good also spent lavishly on particular undertakings: his illuminated manuscripts, for example, and court festivities like the Feast of the Pheasant in 1454. At the end of his reign, though, he had managed to save, leaving his son a very substantial treasure stored away in the castle at Lille.

A great deal of work remains to be done on the finances of the Valois dukes of Burgundy, but enough is now known for us to be sure that their financial administration, for all its shortcomings, was reasonably effective and that their finances were in good shape. Indeed, the dukes seem to have been able to find means to pay for almost any enterprise they chose to undertake, however costly it might be. Often short of ready cash, they raised forced loans from their own officials or borrowed from their towns, or found some other means of providing it. Their credit stood high. Even Charles the Bold could still obtain goods on account right at the end of his reign. This financial strength, which enabled them to hold court, to patronize the arts, and to make wars in the way they did, derived in the main from the wealthy urban communities in their territories, above all from the great towns of the Burgundian Low Countries, Ghent, Bruges, Antwerp, Malines, Brussels, Amsterdam and a host of others.

So far in this chapter the topics discussed have all of them been closely connected with the court. That, and the other institutions so far described were more or less authentically central. Furthermore, most of them were in existence throughout the entire time-span of Valois Burgundy. Three other institutions which ought to be mentioned before we pass to an examination of the regional or provincial administrations of the Burgundian state are the States General of the Burgundian Netherlands, the Parlement of Malines, and the *chambre des comptes* of Malines. They were in a sense central, because they centralized and tended to unify and integrate the northern group of territories; but they were by no means central in the same sense as the court, the great council and the finances, because the southern territories were altogether outside their sphere of influence. Moreover, these quasi-central institutions were of limited importance because they evolved or were set up late in Burgundian history and two of them survived only for a very short time.

Nearly every single one of the territories which together made up the Burgundian state had possessed its own Estates. These representative institutions, whose chief function was to vote taxes or *aides*, naturally continued in existence under the Burgundian dukes. We shall be examining them in their regional contexts in the second half of this chapter. As to the States General, an assembly which intermittently brought together at Lille, Ghent, Bruges, Brussels or elsewhere representatives from the individual Estates of the different northern territories, although its Acts have been printed from 1427 onwards, its origins can be traced earlier. Thus in 1425 a joint assembly of the Estates of Brabant, Holland and Zeeland was held. On the other hand, most recent historians will concede the title 'States General' only to the assembly held at Bruges in January 1464 and those subsequent to it. In reality there was no such thing as a first meeting of the States General; it evolved.

The States General was called into being by the duke as a matter of administrative convenience. The unification of the coinage of the Burgundian Low Countries in the years after 1433 and other monetary problems were of prime importance in its emergence. In 1463–4 it discussed the arrangements which might be needed if the duke went off on crusade. In 1465 the individual delegations were each asked to vote a special *aide* to finance the war of the League of the Public Weal in France. A further development took place in Charles the Bold's reign. The States General was summoned in 1471 to apportion between the different territories the *aide* of 120,000 crowns per annum for three years voted the previous year by the separate provincial Estates. But in 1473 the duke approached the States General directly for a global *aide* of 500,000 crowns per annum for six years. In 1476 the States General opposed the duke's demands; after his death it came into its own.

At the end of 1473 Duke Charles the Bold issued a group of ordinances at Thionville in Luxembourg. One was military and will concern us in a subsequent chapter; another set up the Parlement of Malines; others established new quasi-central financial institutions. It may be that these new judicial and financial organs were not so much intended as central institutions for the existing Burgundian state, but rather to provide a centralized administration for the new kingdom, apparently the kingdom of Frisia, of which Charles the Bold had hoped to be crowned king at Trier in November 1473. The new financial institutions were all established at Malines in Brabant. A *chambre des comptes* staffed by a president, nine *maîtres*, six *auditeurs* and four clerks was to replace the existing *chambres des comptes* at Lille and Brussels – that at The Hague had been abolished or transferred to Brussels in 1462. A *chambre du trésor* was to look after the revenues of the domains and a *chambre des généraux* was to administer the *aides*; each to be run by two officials, one speaking French and the other Netherlandish, called *trésoriers* or treasurers and *généraux* respectively. These two offices were to be subordinate to the *chambres des comptes*, which, besides the routine duties laid down for it, was also made responsible for the coinage; indeed it was expressly instructed to summon a meeting of financial and monetary experts to try to reduce the chaotic state of Netherlandish monetary affairs into some kind of order.

The Parlement of Malines was perhaps Duke Charles the Bold's most radical and most characteristic creation. Although it was only a step in the natural process of unification in the Low Countries and only a logical extension of the development of a separate judical section of the ducal great council, nonetheless it was much too farfetched, too logical, too revolutionary indeed, to be acceptable, still less really workable. No wonder it disappeared with its creator three years only after its inception. Organized on the lines of the Paris Parlement, its personnel included two presidents, four knights who were members of the great council, six *maîtres des requêtes* and twenty councillors. Charles the Bold set it up as the 'sovereign court and Parlement for all our duchies, counties, lands and lordships' in the Low Countries. As such it was scarcely legitimate: it infringed imperial rights, it usurped or threatened to usurp some of the jurisdiction of the Paris Parlement, and it constituted a blatant attack on the Hainault law court at Mons which had always been considered as a sovereign court. Charles the Bold's motives in establishing this new court were explained in the preamble of the ordinance: 'princes have been instituted by divine providence to rule principalities and lordships so that the regions, provinces and peoples are joined together and organized in union, concord and loyal discipline by them, on behalf of God our creator'. Since this 'union and public order can only be maintained by justice', the duke is setting up a new law court to expedite the administration of justice hitherto undertaken in his great council.

So much, then, for the quasi-central institutions set up by Charles the Bold in the very last years of the history of Valois Burgundy. They and the authentically central institutions of court, chancery, great council and the central financial administration formed part of the framework of Burgundian administration. The provinces had their own institutions with wide powers which enabled them to administer the different Burgundian territories without continuous prompting from the central government. This decentralized, almost federal, governmental structure was partly a mere historical accident: Burgundy had been put together through a process of aggregation and each territorial unit had maintained its own organs of government. But in part this devolution of powers was a matter of administrative convenience in an age of limited transport facilities. We see the same process at work in Burgundy's neighbours: in

France, separate Parlements at Grenoble, Bordeaux and Toulouse; in England, separate Councils of the Marches and of the North.

The duchy of Burgundy was the dynastic and historical nucleus of the Valois Burgundian state; the administrative centre of the duchy of Burgundy was the ducal council at Dijon. It existed before the Valois dukes took over in 1350, and in the 1360s we find it writing to the duke with news about what was happening in the duchy, levying taxes, and taking measures to preserve law and order. The membership, duties and indeed everything about this council were ill-defined and flexible. It was not even, like the ducal councils elsewhere, an exclusively administrative and judicial body, for it was never properly differentiated from the *chambre des comptes* at Dijon. Right through the period of the Valois dukes the two acted as a single body and indeed for a long time there was no separate council chamber at Dijon, the council's meetings being held in the room where the accounts were kept, that is the *chambre des comptes*, in a building next door to the ducal palace. Thus at Dijon decisions were recorded as made 'by messieurs of the council and the accounts' and even the judicial sessions of the council, when it sat on Sundays after mass as a law court, were held in the *chambre des comptes*. Its members, up to six councillors and three to five *maîtres des comptes*, were invariably local people, and from 1400 its meetings were presided over by a president.

Within a year or two of his acquisition in 1384 of the counties of Burgundy and Nevers, bordering on the duchy of Burgundy, Philip the Bold had extended the competence of his Dijon council over them. Thenceforth it acted as a unifying force and a central institution for the entire southern group of territories. Ducal ordinances, too, were issued which applied in both the duchy and county of Burgundy and a single financial official, the receiver-general of the duchy and county of Burgundy, was responsible for the ducal revenues in both territories. Thus, although Nevers, with its associated barony of Donzy, passed in 1404 to a junior branch of the Valois Burgundian house, a very real measure of centralization was achieved in the remaining southern territories long before Charles the Bold's ill-starred attempts to integrate the northern territories.

The judicial system in the two Burgundies was well developed by the mid-fourteenth century and was scarcely altered by the Valois dukes. A hierarchy of courts was based on the petty tribunals of provosts and castellans. From these courts appeals lay to the bailiffs' assizes, held monthly in different places in each bailiwick; and from them in their turn appeals in the duchy went to a special court of appeal which sat at Beaune about six times a year. The Parlement of Beaune, meeting more or less annually, was the supreme court of the duchy; a similar Parlement or law court at Dole acted as supreme court for Franche-Comté. There was an important difference between them: appeals lay from Beaune to the Paris Parlement, whereas the Dole Parlement was sovereign.

For administrative and judicial purposes the duchy of Burgundy was divided into six bailiwicks: Dijon, Autun, Auxois, La Montagne or Châtillon, Chalon and Charolais. Franche-Comté was divided after 1422 into three: Amont, Aval or Poligny, and Dole. In each bailiwick a receiver – instituted by Philip the Bold in 1366 – was responsible for the collection of ducal revenues. The bailiff was thereafter chiefly a judicial and police officer, but he acted in all sorts of ways as the local representative of ducal authority. He assembled the men-at-arms of his bailiwick in time of war; he published and implemented the duke's ordinances; often he had to attend the council in Dijon. Assisting him in his duties were up to fifty subordinate officials – lieutenants, councillors and sergeants.

In both the duchy and the county of Burgundy the Estates had evolved by the mid-fourteenth century into well-established institutions whose chief function was to vote taxes or *aides* at their ruler's request. The county of Charolais too had its own quite distinct Estates. Only the duke could convene these Estates. In the duchy they comprised some twenty clerics, two from each of the ten principal religious houses; about the same number of nobles, summoned individually; and about sixteen or twenty urban delegates, two from each of the main towns, forming the Third Estate. In Franche-Comté there were normally only two Estates, clergy and commons, and these met separately in each bailiwick up to 1420. Really, we know very little about them, but the history of the Estates of the duchy is much better documented. After 1386 they normally met in Dijon. They fulfilled their function of voting taxes at regular intervals throughout the fifteenth century and they even had some influence over the officials appointed to levy them. Sometimes they raised objections; sometimes they even dared make stipulations. On occasion they arrogated a political role to themselves. In 1428 they talked about sending a deputation to Philip the Good 'to beg and request him to be pleased to consider getting married, so that he could have an heir'. In 1431 they petitioned him to abolish the council at Dijon. He actually agreed to this request in return for an *aide*, but the councillors refused to disband and were later officially reinstated by the duke. In 1460 the Estates of the duchy presented a whole list of grievances to the duke, who conceded their points here and there. However, effective political power escaped them altogether.

In spite of opposition from Franche-Comté Charles the Bold succeeded in creating a sort of States General of the two Burgundies by summoning all the Estates to a single assembly. At Salins on 8–10 July 1476 the combined Estates of the two Burgundies, after listening to a lengthy harangue by the great duke himself, voted him funds for the defence of his lands – and theirs – against the Swiss and their allies who had just decisively defeated him in two pitched battles.

In the Low Countries the adjoining counties of Flanders and Artois formed the original nucleus of Burgundian expansion. Here, administrative institutions had evolved during the half century prior to Philip the Bold's accession as count in 1384 on lines parallel to those described at Dijon. These institutions were similar simply because, in Flanders as in Burgundy, they were based on French models. After all, both territories formed part of the kingdom of France. During the reign of Philip the Bold's father-in-law Louis of Male (1346–84) a sort of standing committee of the Flemish comital council had begun to function at Ghent and, after 1379 when the count was driven out of Ghent by the revolutionaries there, at Lille. Thus a sedentary, institutionalized *chambre du conseil*, staffed by full-time salaried professionals, similar to the one Philip the Bold had found at Dijon when he took over the duchy of Burgundy in 1363, was already functioning at Lille when he became count of Flanders. Furthermore, a *chambre des comptes* or accounting office for Flanders had emerged at just the same time and was established at Lille in 1382 in permanent quarters in the Palais de la Salle, with facilities for the conservation of its muniments, which were mainly accounts.

Just as Philip the Bold's ordinance of 11 July 1386 reorganizing the *chambre des comptes* at Dijon was the result of an investigation by and advice from two officials of the French royal accounting office at Paris, so on 6 July 1385, the same duke appointed one of

the same two French officials, Jehan Creté, along with a group
of experts of his own, one of them from the Dijon *chambre des
comptes*, to advise on the administration of Flanders and the other
northern territories. They recommended a permanent council
and a *chambre des comptes* at Lille 'for the government of the lands
of Flanders, Malines, Antwerp and Blaton and the counties of
Artois and Rethel'. These two institutions, though they had
already existed, were established anew by a ducal ordinance
of 15 February 1386. Two councillors were given special responsibility for justice and for the administrative personnel of
Flanders and the other lands; one of them was to act as president.
Three financial councillors or *maîtres des comptes* were appointed.
Later, numbers were substantially increased: by the end of
Philip the Bold's reign, in 1404, there were five judicial councillors,
two of them presidents, and four *maîtres des comptes*.

Apart from the greater degree of separation at Lille, especially
after 1389, between council and *comptes*, these administrative
institutions at Lille were almost identical to those at Dijon, at
least during Philip the Bold's reign. Important changes occurred
thereafter. The council was moved into Flanders proper, or
'Flemish Flanders', by John the Fearless, who established it
first at Oudenaarde, then at Ghent, Thereafter it was mainly at
Ghent, though with spells at Courtrai, Ypres and elsewhere. The
accounting office remained at Lille and its authority was enhanced when, from 1419, the auditing of the central accounts of
the Burgundian state, those of the *maître de la chambre aux deniers*
and the receiver-general of all finances, was transferred to it
from Dijon. A further change occurred in 1409 when the law
court called the *audientie* or audience, which had been held under
Philip the Bold some six times a year in different Flemish towns,
was allowed by John the Fearless to cease to exist. The *chambre du
conseil* or council of Flanders took over its attributions and
functions and became the supreme Flemish court, judging
crimes against the count and his officers at first instance and
developing an important appellate jurisdiction.

Although behind closed doors French continued to be the
language of the council of Flanders, John the Fearless had to a
large extent met the aspirations of the Flemings by transferring the council to Flemish-speaking Flanders and by making
provision, in an ordinance of 1409, for the use of Flemish in its
public or judicial sessions. The councillors were an independent-
minded self-important group of men. In 1419 they threatened

three absentee councillors that they would report them to the duke if they did not attend within eight days. In 1420 they informed Simon de Fourmelles that he must make up his mind whether or no he wished to continue as their president and let the duke know. In 1433 they complained to the receiver-general of Flanders that their wages had not been properly paid. If this was not done at once they had resolved to 'adjourn all the cases in progress before the council and cease to attend it'. The ordinance of 1409 had instructed them to meet 'every working day in the morning and sit till dinner', hearing cases on Monday, Tuesday and Thursday and holding council on other days. Among other things they were instructed to 'inform the duke and his chancellor of all important events happening in Flanders'. A strike would have jeopardized the entire administration of the county.

The financial administration of Flanders and Artois was similar to that of the two Burgundies. During most of the period a single receiver-general of Flanders and Artois, answerable to the Lille *chambre des comptes*, was responsible for the comital revenues. Local receivers, one in each bailiwick, existed in Artois but not in Flanders, where the bailiffs were responsible for rendering accounts annually to the Lille accounting office. The accounts themselves were modernized by Philip the Bold: from 1385 they were written in French instead of Flemish and entered in registers instead of on unwieldy rolls.

In Flanders especially, older, in some cases ancient, institutions survived side-by-side with more up-to-date developments. Some of them, like the *audientie* and the chancellorship of Flanders, died natural deaths; others, like the regional feudal courts at Lille, Ypres, Douai and elsewhere, and the central feudal court at Lille called the *chambre légale*, persisted. Side-by-side with the modernized financial organization of bailiffs and receiver-general dependent on the relatively new-fangled *chambre des comptes* at Lille was an older financial administration responsible for a substantial part of the domanial produce and revenues. The officials who levied these receipts were responsible to a separate financial or accounting office, fixed at Lille by Philip the Bold, called the *chambre des rennenghes*.

In both Flanders and Artois the backbone of the administration was formed by the bailiffs – some sixteen in Flanders and twelve in Artois. As in Burgundy, the bailiffs were responsible for justice and held courts. They had to carry out the count's commands, assemble troops, and keep the council informed of everything that happened in their own areas, which in Flanders were known as castellanies. There was a senior or sovereign bailiff in Flanders who had been instituted first by Louis of Male in 1372. Under the Valois dukes of Burgundy he became the chief executive and judicial officer of the county, acting along-side the *procureur-général*, who was a sort of attorney-general or public prosecutor. A number of local officials in Flanders were virtually bailiffs but went under other names – the *écoutète* or *schout* of Antwerp for example. Unusual was the water or mari-time bailiff of Sluis. His jurisdiction extended over the estuary leading up to Bruges called the Zwin as well as the harbour of Sluis. He had six sergeants to help him patrol these waters, enforce port regulations and see that goods were unloaded where they should be. Despite his name, his headquarters were at Mude, opposite Sluis on the other bank of the Zwin.

A régime of Estates had emerged in fourteenth-century Artois which closely resembled that of the duchy of Burgundy. From 1361 the three Estates assembled almost annually in Arras to vote an *aide*, which had become fixed at 14,000 francs. They continued thus through the fifteenth century, meeting more frequently however, and voting more money. There were actually some 150 meetings in Philip the Good's forty-eight-year reign. Political power these Estates lacked, though they were sometimes courageous enough to reduce their vote or send a deputation to the duke to insist on their penury.

Of all the constituent territories of the Valois Burgundian state, Flanders possessed the most active, the most powerful and indeed the most interesting representative institutions. Its Estates were assembled for the first time at Lille in September 1384 by Philip the Bold: prelates, nobles and deputies of the towns, in the presence of the duke himself. They were convened again by him on some half-dozen occasions to discuss religious affairs, domanial rents, the quarrel between him and Ghent. They never voted taxes. Their situation and role remained unchanged through the fifteenth century. Called into being in the first place by the duke, they continued to meet in-frequently and to lack any real purpose or power. The real representative institution of medieval Flanders was not the Estates but the meetings or *parlementen* of the so-called Four Members or *vier leden* of Flanders. They had evolved spontane-ously in the fourteenth century and remained extremely active throughout the history of Valois Burgundy. In Philip the Bold's reign *parlementen* were held, on average, thirty times a year; in Charles the Bold's nine-year reign some 200 meetings took place, not all of them of the Four Members on their own, but virtually all including deputies from the Four Members.

Who and what were the Four Members of Flanders? Three of them were urban – the three largest towns in Flanders, Ghent, Bruges and Ypres. The fourth was the Franc of Bruges or *het Brugse Vrije*; it comprised the castellany of Bruges, effectively the countryside around Bruges. These four had become the voice of Flanders; the accepted representative institution in a county which had for years been so dominated by its great cities as to become virtually a federation of city-states. They sent deputations to the count – or duke in the Burgundian period – with complaints of all kinds on behalf of themselves and their fellow Flemings; they helped their ruler to negotiate commercial treaties with England and the Hanseatic League; above all they had successfully arrogated to themselves alone the right to vote *aides* on behalf of the entire county of Flanders.

John the Fearless was confronted at the beginning of his reign with a petition from the Four Members asking him to reside 'in some Flemish town of his choice', to respect the 'privileges, rights, laws and customs of the Flemings', to transfer his council of Flanders from Lille to Flemish Flanders, and to reply to the Four Members' requests in Flemish. In Philip the Good's reign the prestige and influence of the Four Members was somewhat eroded. This was due to the addition of Brabant, Hainault and Holland to the Burgundian state as well as to serious internal divisions in Flanders. The Four Members, indeed, were divided among themselves by commercial rivalry and civic particularism. In 1436 Bruges was even at war for a time with the Franc of Bruges. Social disturbances, especially at Ghent in the 1440s and 1450s, likewise undermined the power of the *parlementen*. This decline was accentuated by Charles the Bold: in Philip the Bold's reign only 10 per cent of the *parlementen* were convoked by the duke; in 1467–77 a good half of them were summoned by Charles the Bold. Nonetheless, they continued active to the end, still retaining more power than any other representative institution on Burgundian territory.

The administrative institutions of the duchy of Brabant, which lay between Flanders and Holland and included within its borders the towns of Nivelles in the south and s'Hertogenbosch

in the north, had been adapted to the Burgundian pattern long
before Philip the Good became duke of Brabant in 1430. Indeed
Anthony of Burgundy, John the Fearless's younger brother,
had made progress along these lines even before he was proclaimed duke at the end of 1406. He borrowed Burgundian and
Flemish officials like Pierre de le Zippe, Jehan Chousat, Simon de
Fourmelles and Jaques de Lichtervelde. He employed one of the
maîtres des comptes at Lille, David Bousse, to establish a *chambre des
comptes* or *rekenkamer* at Brussels in 1404. Later, Burgundian financial
officials like the ex-receiver-general of all finances, Jehan
Despoullettes, held similar posts in Brabant, and John the
Fearless encouraged Anthony to set up a Burgundian-type
council at Vilvorde and to appoint a Burgundian-type chancellor, Pierre de Camdonck, in 1408. Thus, though John the
Fearless failed to get hold of Brabant in 1416 after Duke Anthony's
death at Agincourt, he had helped to lay down administrative
foundations for the subsequent integration of Brabant into the
Valois Burgundian state.

The Burgundian administration of Brabant differed in one
important respect from those of Burgundy and Flanders: it
retained under Philip the Good its own chancellor and chancery
with its own seal and its own staff of secretaries. This was a result
of the insistence of the Estates of Brabant, which did their
utmost in 1430 to preserve their duchy's autonomy in the face
of Burgundian annexation. The chancellor, keeper of the great
seal of Brabant and president of the council of Brabant, was
head of the administration of the duchy. The Estates had laid
it down in 1430 and Philip the Good had accepted, that he should
be a native of Brabant and that he should be proficient in Latin,
French and Netherlandish. However, his office was swept away
in 1467 by Charles the Bold.

The *chambre du conseil* or council of Brabant, over which the
chancellor of Brabant presided, was very similar to the council
of Flanders. Like it a court of law as well as an advisory and
administrative body, it had become well established in the years
before Philip the Good became duke of Brabant. He put the
finishing touches to it in an ordinance of 29 December 1430.
Naturally, Philip the Good kept in being the Brussels *chambre des
comptes*. He issued ordinances fixing the wages of its staff, regula-
ting its auditing procedures, and even exempting from tolls
provisions on their way to it. Its connections with its parent
institution, the *chambre des comptes* at Lille, were closely maintained,

ensuring administrative uniformity if not unity between the territories of Brabant and Flanders. Thus Barthelemi a la Truye, who began his career in 1411 as an *auditeur* in the Lille *chambre*, became a *maître* there in 1413 but was transferred to the Brussels *chambre* as *maître* in 1430. From 1436 he was *premier maître* or *eerste meester* of both *chambres des comptes*. In 1463 the competence of the *chambre des comptes* of Brabant at Brussels was extended over the counties of Holland and Zeeland and the duchy of Luxembourg. Ten years later it was abolished by Charles the Bold.

In other respects too the administration of Brabant was in line with that of other Burgundian lands. Public order was maintained and justice administered by the seneschal and *drossart* at the centre and by the bailiffs locally, and, until Charles the Bold abolished his office in 1469, a receiver- or rentmaster-general of Brabant supervised and to some extent centralized the collection of revenues by the local receivers, one in each of the four 'quarters' of the duchy: Antwerp, Brussels, Louvain and s'Hertogenbosch.

The Estates of the duchy of Brabant, nobles, clergy and deputies of the towns, meeting usually in Brussels, had been in a position to exercise real political power during the succession crises of the late fourteenth and early fifteenth centuries. In the 1390s they had successfully opposed Philip the Bold's attempts to take over their duchy himself; only in 1401 did they at last agree to his younger son Anthony inheriting it after Duchess Joan's death. In 1416 they resolutely opposed John the Fearless's demand that they should appoint him regent of Brabant for Anthony's children John and Philip, and in 1430 Philip the Good was compelled to make important concessions to the Estates before they accepted him as duke. But, like the other Burgundian Estates, the Estates of Brabant could not avoid becoming a mechanism for voting taxes, though they did their best to lay down conditions. In 1451, for example, an *aide* for six years was only granted in return for a written promise on the part of the duke to limit the number of ducal officers in Brabant and not to seek any additional *aides* while the current one was being levied. But bargains of this sort implied little political power in the Estates, and Charles the Bold's promises to them, enshrined in a formal document at his accession to the duchy, just as his father's had been, were disregarded with impunity.

We need to bear in mind, when examining the governmental structures of the different Burgundian territories, that, while

Flanders and Burgundy formed part of Valois Burgundy throughout the whole of its approximately one-hundred-year history, from 1384 to 1477, Brabant and Holland-Hainault only became Burgundian half-way through this period, in about 1430. Holland had been for many years closely integrated administratively with the geographically contiguous county of Zeeland; it had been united with Hainault under a single ruler ever since 1299. But under the Burgundian dukes, while Holland and Zeeland were treated for the most part as a single unit, Hainault was different. It was indeed, from its annexation in 1427, regarded and treated as a quite separate territory. Nor were any important changes made to its existing institutions.

The supreme – and theoretically sovereign – law court of Hainault continued to sit in the administrative capital of the county, Mons. Revenues from its fines, for rape, theft, kidnapping, abduction of women, insulting ducal officers, etc., continued to contribute towards meeting Hainault's administrative expenses. At Mons, too, the council of Hainault controlled the administration and acted as a law court, exactly like the councils of Flanders and Burgundy. The head of the administration of Hainault, who was also president of the council of Mons, was the bailiff of Hainault. His status improved steadily under the Valois dukes. Soon known as the grand bailiff, he acted also as captain-general and, in 1467, Charles the Bold gave him the title of 'grand bailiff and captain-general of Hainault'. After 1473 he was ducal lieutenant there as well. This office was filled by a line of distinguished noblemen: in Philip the Good's reign, Jehan de Croy, lord of Chimay, was succeeded by his son Philippe de Croy, lord of Sempy; under Charles the Bold the Burgundian Anthoine Rolin, son of Philip the Good's chancellor Nicolas Rolin, was grand bailiff of Hainault. He was responsible, in particular, for the publication and implementation of the duke's instructions, for convoking the Estates of Hainault, for the recruitment and equipping of troops, and for acting as the link between the local administration in Hainault and the central administration of the Burgundian state. In this last capacity he had to undertake frequent journeys to the duke or to the chancellor or other leading representatives of the duke in the Low Countries. In October 1453 he had to arrange for the transport to Duke Philip the Good at Lille 'on a pack horse, of the third section of the chronicles of the Belgians and the fourth part of the chronicles of Froissart, which the duke had had made at Mons by the late Master Jehan Wauquelin and which he had ordered to be brought to him; there were ninety-one quires which weighed a great deal'. The bailiff of Hainault's activities are all recorded in the detailed accounts which he kept and submitted for audit, from about 1435 onwards, to the *chambre des comptes* at Lille.

Likewise audited at Lille, after 1438, were the accounts of the receiver-general of Hainault, who had been appointed by Philip the Good in 1427 as head of the county's financial administration on the lines of the financial organization in the other Burgundian territories. However, his office was abolished in 1463. The accounts of the half-dozen administrative districts or castellanies into which Hainault was divided – Blaton and Feignies, Bouchain, Le Quesnoy, Maubeuge and Bavai, Mons, and Valenciennes – were aslo submitted to Lille. After 1463 the officials who kept them became receivers in their own right instead of mere 'lieutenants of the receiver of Hainault' as they had been before then. The county of Hainault, like other Burgundian territories, continued to keep its own archives except for the accounts, which are still at Lille; and there was a 'keeper of the charters' at Mons, just as there was at Dijon, Poligny, Lille, Brussels and elsewhere.

The Estates of Hainault were rather similar to those of Artois in many respects, but they had given way more readily to the ruler's pressure for an *aide* voted occasionally and levied over a period of years rather than voted and levied annually. For this reason they met less frequently, especially after 1450. On the other hand, they did secure control of the levying of their own *aides*. Their protests to the duke, however, were mostly disregarded, even in 1450 when they reinforced them by refusing to send deputies to the States General.

Perhaps the most immediately prominent feature of the Burgundian administration of Holland-Zeeland was the office of *stadholder*. Admittedly, *stadholders* had been appointed on a temporary basis before, by Count William VI, but Philip the Good made this office permanent. The *stadholder* was in effect a governor and president of the council of Holland rather than a lieutenant or personal representative of the duke, and his office differed very little from that of grand bailiff of Hainault. It was held, between 1433 and 1440, by Hue de Lannoy, lord of Santes, a nobleman from the castellany of Lille; and between 1448 and 1462 by his cousin Jehan de Lannoy. He was followed by

Louis de Bruges, lord of Gruuthuse, who was *stadholder* of Holland throughout the reign of Charles the Bold. None of these was Dutch, though the last spoke Netherlandish and married a Dutch wife; but governors in Valois Burgundy were seldom natives of the territories they governed.

The council or *raad* of Holland at The Hague, which only later acquired the rather grandiose name of *het Hof* – the court – of Holland, had appeared in the years before Philip the Good became count. During his reign it developed a strongly collegiate nature, acting as a law court and as an administrative body, and it was provided by him with a registrar and, in 1434, a *procureur-général*. The central administration of the county was completed by the rentmaster- or receiver-general, who was at the same time a member of the council. His office survived until its abolition by Charles the Bold in 1469.

At first, from 1432, the financial administration of Holland was under the control of the *chambres des comptes* of Lille and Brussels, and the rentmaster-general, Godscalc Oom, and the other Dutch accounting officers presented their accounts and were responsible to Barthelemi a la Truye, *maître des comptes* at Brussels, and his colleagues. But when he died, in 1446, a separate accounting office, the *rekenkamer*, was established for Holland-Zeeland at The Hague. Thereafter, between 1447 and 1463, the twin institutions of *raadkamer* and *rekenkamer* functioned side-by-side at The Hague, just as the *chambres du conseil* and *des comptes* did at Brussels and at Dijon. The reasons for the abolition of the Dutch *rekenkamer* in 1463 remain obscure; thereafter the Dutch accounts were audited in the Brussels *chambres des comptes* until, ten years later, it in its turn was abolished, or transferred to Malines.

In one respect the county of Zeeland remained distinct from Holland throughout the Burgundian period. It had its own Estates, though these met together with those of Holland on important occasions when matters of general interest were discussed. In each county there were two Estates only, nobles and representatives of the towns. In political influence the Estates of Holland and Zeeland fell between the more active and powerful Four Members of Flanders and the less powerful Estates of Brabant, Hainault, Artois and the other French-speaking territories. Their *aides* were voted for periods of up to ten years at a time, but they seem to have made up for the absence of an annual wrangle over taxation to discuss other matters, of political rather than fiscal significance. And sometimes they successfully resisted their ruler's demands. In 1437 they stoutly refused the *stadholder's* request to help their duke in his war against the English. They signed treaties with foreign powers; they participated in commercial and monetary legislation. In 1462 they persuaded the duke to promulgate a whole series of judicial and administrative reforms, mainly affecting the council of Holland. The Estates of Holland and Zeeland were, then, a force to be reckoned with, though a direct hostile confrontation between them and their French-speaking Burgundian rulers never occurred.

The duchy of Luxembourg only became Burgundian in 1443 but its administrative institutions needed little or no modification to bring them into line with those of the other Burgundian territories. The senior ducal officer was the governor and captain-general, who was given extensive powers and the handsome annual salary of 1,000 Rhenish florins. After 1452 this office was held by Anthoine, lord of Renty and of Croy, the brother of the grand bailiff of Hainault. During most of Charles the Bold's reign the governor of Luxembourg was Rudolf, margrave of Hochberg or Hachberg near Freiburg im Breisgau, count of Neuchâtel in Switzerland and lord of Rötteln in the Breisgau. From 1474–7 there was a ducal lieutenant in Luxembourg too: Claude de Neuchâtel, lord du Fay, a nobleman from Franche-Comté. As elsewhere so in Luxembourg, the principal administrative institution was the council with its registrar and, after 1461, *procureur-général*. The president of the council of Luxembourg first appears in 1452. Inevitably, there was a receiver-general of Luxembourg whose accounts were audited, before 1462, by a *maître* of the Lille *comptes* and thereafter at Brussels.

Unlike the Estates of most of the other Burgundian lands, those of the duchy of Luxembourg were dominated by the nobles. In 1451, for example, the sixty nobles must have enjoyed a very preponderant voice against the five abbots – all that there was of the Estate of the clergy – and the thirteen town deputies. The Estates of Luxembourg, like those of Brabant and Hainault, had played an important part in the succession crises of their territory in the first half of the fifteenth century but, once it was under firm Burgundian rule, their power declined. Indeed, they were convened only occasionally, seldom voted *aides*, and in general willingly accepted and deferred to the Valois Burgundian dukes.

Such then was the administrative structure of the Valois

Burgundian state. Below the level, as it were, of the central institutions based on the court, were the institutions belonging to the different territories and groups of territories. Of these territories, only Hainault and Luxembourg were administered more or less on their own as separate units. Brabant was in many respects combined with Limbourg. Flanders and Artois (with Boulogne and the Somme towns), Holland and Zeeland, and the duchy of Burgundy (with Charolais) and Franche-Comté, were in each case more or less integrated into a single whole. Though each of these units tended to keep its own administrative traditions, recruit its own personnel, and enjoy a wide measure of local autonomy, all were bound together by a common subordination to the duke and the central government, as well as by the remarkable degree of uniformity which had developed in their institutions and procedures. By and large, the governmental machinery described here was assembled into a working whole by Philip the Bold in 1384-7, comprising at that time the two Burgundies and the counties of Artois and Flanders. Then, about half a century later, Philip the Good added further units which had the effect of enlarging the whole structure but by no means altered its essential character. Charles the Bold tried to enlarge it still further and to alter its nature by centralizing policies, but he failed.

CHAPTER SEVEN

Military Power

Fifteenth-century political structures were such that success depended on a line of able rulers, an effective bureaucracy, sound finances and military power. Valois Burgundy was fortunate in the first of these for, unlike France and England, it had no minors or mental deficients among its hereditary rulers and it experienced no succession crises. It was also fortunate in its bureaucracy and in its finances. But what of its military power? At the end of 1407 a merchant made this statement in a letter to the authorities of Lucca: 'you may be quite sure that the duke of Burgundy will remain the most influential and powerful prince in the kingdom [of France]. His power is based on the troops he can raise in his lands. He can muster so many that he fears no one.' What follows may be regarded as a commentary on this assertion.

Not until right at the end of their history did the Valois dukes of Burgundy try to maintain a standing army permanently in being. Instead, like every other ruler, they raised individual armies for individual campaigns. In order to understand how these armies fulfilled their purpose we need to consider their size and composition, the procedure and tactics of their troops in battle, and the generalship of their leaders the dukes.

How big were the armies of the Valois dukes of Burgundy? Excluding non-combatants, John the Fearless's largest army was probably the one he assembled at the end of the summer of 1417 for an attack on Paris, which numbered some 10,500 men. No information is so far available on the size of the army Philip the Good mustered for the Ghent campaign of 1453, but it must have been comparable to the 1417 army. His projected crusading army, of 1455–6, was put at 6,300 combatants. Under the first three dukes, the Burgundian armies were probably seldom larger than this and often smaller. The situation changed under Charles the Bold. He may have had 15,000 combatants with him when he attacked Liège in 1467; but at Neuss, in spite of reports of 30,000 or more men in the Burgundian camp, the documents only allow us to credit him with 12,000 combatants or so. At Murten in 1476, too, Duke Charles's army was probably only some 12,000 strong. The Valois dukes, then, normally fielded some 5,000 men; 10,000 could be assembled if need be; more than that only with difficulty. The Burgundians could always be outnumbered by the French; Charles the Bold was out-numbered by the Swiss and their allies. The dukes suffered this serious military disadvantage: their armies were on the small side.

What was the composition of the Burgundian armies? Their nucleus invariably comprised the nobles or mounted men-at-arms with their men, who were legally obliged to turn out because they were ducal or comital vassals, though they were paid for their services. These heavily armed knights brought with them mounted archers and crossbowmen and mounted swordsmen. Infantry, in the shape of contingents of pikemen from the towns, especially of Flanders, sometimes formed an important, if unreliable, section of the ducal army. Its numbers nearly always had to be increased by the hiring of mercenaries, often English archers, as well as by persuading an ally or two to bring troops. An analysis of four of John the Fearless's armies shows that 38 per cent of his men came from Flanders and Artois, 33 per cent were provided by allies or were hired as mercenaries, and 29 per cent came from the two Burgundies. That is, one third of his troops had to be found from outside his own lands. This proportion probably held under his successors, even under Charles the Bold, who used large numbers of Italian mercenaries after 1472. For example at the siege of Neuss there were probably about 2,000 Englishmen and about 2,000 Italians, out of some 12,000 in all. The Burgundian armies were thus essentially heterogeneous in composition, but the heavily armed and armoured knight, usually but not always mounted, was normally their most effective and numerous fighting element. These men came from Artois and, even more, from the two Burgundies; and right to the end the two Burgundies were still providing the armies of Charles the Bold with an élite corps of heavy cavalry.

Though little evidence of it has survived, care was usually taken before a battle to arrange the troops and, sometimes at least, to give them detailed instructions on battle procedure. Charles the Bold drew up orders for the battle of Brustem on the evening before the engagement and rode round his men the next day just before the battle, giving them their instructions. The same duke described in a letter to Claude de Neuchâtel, his lieutenant in Luxembourg, written on 27 May 1475, exactly how he had posted his army before advancing towards the enemy on 23 May. It was divided into two battles, one behind the other, each arranged with infantry in the centre and mounted men-at-arms on the wings. The centre of the first battle comprised pikemen and archers in two contingents; 'the pikemen were intermingled with the archers, who were in groups of four, so that there was a pikeman between each group of archers'. The contingents of men-at-arms on either side of them were each supported by a separate reserve contingent of men-at-arms. The second battle was drawn up similarly, except that the household troops with their own reserve contingent behind them occupied the centre, with archers on either side of them. Here again, there were men-at-arms on the flanks. The arrangement of the much larger army Charles led against the Swiss a year later, in May 1476, was not very different. There were now no fewer than eight battles, in six of which an infantry corps, usually 500 strong, was to advance between cavalry corps on either wing.

John the Fearless, expecting an encounter with his French enemies in September 1417 near Paris, issued an exceptionally interesting plan of action which has fortunately survived. It seems to be unique. The marshal and his men in the van are to keep reconnoitring ahead and reporting back to the duke. If the enemy takes up position near Paris, whence they can easily receive supplies, they are on no account to be attacked. A body of 1,000 picked cavalry is to be ready to withdraw to one side of the van on the enemy's approach. If they see any disorder in the enemy's ranks, such as mix-up between their cavalry and infantry, these men are to attack at once. If the enemy advances in good order they are to withdraw further to one side, ready to attack when called on, possibly on the enemy's rear. In the event of an enemy attack, the entire van will take up defensive positions on foot with the archers and crossbowmen in front of them. The marshal commands the van; the duke the main army. Other instructions covered the dispositions of the main army, the rearguard and the baggage train.

These battle orders undoubtedly reflect John the Fearless's considerable military ability; he may have drawn some useful conclusions from his defeat at Nicopolis. He was probably the best general of the four Valois dukes of Burgundy. Note how, in his only important pitched battle as duke, he routed the Liègeois at Othée by means of a brilliantly organized flanking movement. Note how, throughout the same campaign, he kept a substantial strategic reserve in being behind him on the borders of Brabant. By contrast, his father Philip the Bold seems to have had no military talents, nor is there any reason to suppose that his son Philip the Good possessed qualities of generalship. At the battle of Gavere, fought against Ghent on 23 July 1453, Philip the Good managed to endanger his own life by his foolhardy enthusiasm to do battle in person, though he was fifty-seven at the time. Incredibly, after the battle he was gullible enough to allow a patriotic local guide, who was asked to lead him and his men onwards to Ghent, to take him back to his own camp by a roundabout route!

How far does Charles the Bold deserve his nearly undisputed reputation for military talent? He certainly liked nothing better than camp life, and Italian observers noted his profound interest in the art of war. The Milanese ambassador Panigarola reported on 12 May 1476 that 'all day yesterday the duke stayed locked in his room drafting certain [military] ordinances'. And the same ambassador says, writing of the skirmish on 23 May 1475: 'I was in the field during this engagement and I saw the duke applying himself in person here and there admirably in organizing and commanding. He has a mind like Caesar's.' Charles the Bold, then, was indubitably a military enthusiast. But, since he lost his most important battles, his reputation as a military genius must depend on the way he transformed the clumsy, antiquated, ill-organized Burgundian army into a much more effective fighting force and established it for the first time on a permanent footing.

The idea of creating a standing army of companies of ordinance, that is, of permanent cavalry squadrons set up and regulated in every detail by ordinance, was borrowed from elsewhere, for the Burgundian companies were said by a contemporary to be modelled partly on those of France and partly on those of Venice. Charles the Bold's ordinance of 31 July 1471, issued at Abbeville, established this new force in the first place, though it had been planned since 1469. It was first used in battle against the French in the summer of 1472. At this time the companies of ordinance were twelve in number. Each was supposed to comprise 100 men-at-arms and 300 archers, mounted; and 100 pikemen, 100 culverineers, and 100 archers, on foot – a total of 700 combatants per company, or 8,400 fighting men in all. But in fact, in the spring of 1472, most of the companies were short of at least 100 men, many of them culverineers and archers. Later the number of companies was increased to twenty. By the time Charles the Bold used his army against the Swiss and their allies in 1476 it was mainly composed of troops of the ordinance. Those employed on the 1476 campaign were arranged in twelve heavy cavalry corps of 100 men-at-arms each, twenty-four or more light cavalry corps of 100 mounted archers each, and at least three infantry corps, each 1,000 strong.

In the remarkable military ordinances of Abbeville (13 July 1471), Bohain-en-Vermandois (13 November 1472) and Thionville (autumn 1473), Charles the Bold became the first military commander to introduce systematic rules of discipline, compulsory drill and effective training and manoeuvres. The chain of command was laid down in detail; the men's armour, arms and uniforms were carefully prescribed; a roll call was instituted so that the captain or *conducteur* (compare Italian *condottiere*) 'can check, whenever he takes the field with his ensign, that all the men-at-arms and other troops of his company are present'. Regulations were issued governing the use of ensigns, one for each *conducteur* of a company, cornets for the captains of squadrons, bannerols, and other emblems to ensure ready identification of officers in the field by their men. The duke's men were forbidden to swear, blaspheme and play dice. Nor were they allowed to appropriate individual women camp-followers to themselves. Instead, each company was allowed a maximum of thirty women – in common. Discipline was further tightened in May 1476: disobedience on the march or in battle was to be punished with death; there was to be no violation of churches or women even in enemy territory; and the officers were 'to see that all prostitutes and ribalds are expelled from their companies for this campaign, and to make their people drink more water to keep them cool'.

These last measures were clearly wartime ones. In peacetime 'in order that the troops may be better trained and exercised in the use of arms and better practised and instructed when something happens' the captains were to take their men-at-arms into the fields from time to time and make them practise charging with the lance in close formation and withdrawing and rallying on the word of command. The archers were to practise dismounting and drawing their bows, and attaching their horses together by the bridles and leading them behind them. They were 'also to march briskly forwards and to fire without breaking rank. The pikemen must be made to advance in close formation in front of the archers and kneel at a sign from them, holding their pikes lowered to the level of a horse's back so that the archers can fire over them as if over a wall.'

Charles the Bold made other notable changes in the Burgundian army. He employed English troops, mainly archers, in larger numbers than ever before. At the siege of Neuss and apparently throughout the last two years of his reign, Sir John Middleton served as *conducteur* of one of the ordinance companies, which was almost certainly entirely composed of Englishmen. Right to the bitter end, on the frozen battlefield of Nancy, at least ten companies of mounted English archers, each of 100 men when at full strength, fought in the Burgundian army. Even more important was the introduction in 1473 of Italian captains and mercenaries in large numbers, who made up the strength of the ordinance companies and provided them with expert *conducteurs*. In spite of determined efforts, Charles failed to obtain the services of the most famous of all the quattrocento Italian *condottieri*, Bartolomeo Colleoni, the superb equestrian statue of whom by Verrocchio still stands in Venice. This seventy-year-old veteran, though he lived in semi-retirement in his castle of Malpaga, was still captain-general of the Venetian army, and the Venetians would not let him go off north of the Alps in case, in his absence, they were attacked by their old enemy the duke of Milan. But the duke of Burgundy did manage to hire a host of other Italian *condottieri* with their contingents, mostly from Naples and Lombardy. Often they were family concerns: Troylo da Rossano and his two sons; Jacobo de' Vischi and his two sons; and, most important of all, Cola de Monforte, count of Campobasso, also with two sons. The contract between Cola and Duke Charles, signed on 10 November 1472, was for 400 four-horse lances, 400 mounted crossbowmen, and 300 infantry, to serve for three years at 82,800 crowns per annum; a small army in fact.

Charles the Bold transformed the court or household (*hôtel*) forces into a corps of élite troops who were given pride of place in the Burgundian order of battle. The nucleus of these household forces consisted of forty or so mounted chamberlains and gentlemen of the duke's chamber with the ducal standard and the duke himself. Its main military force was the guard. The chronicler Olivier de la Marche, Charles's captain of the guard, talks about a bodyguard of sixty-two archers and a guard of 126 men-at-arms and 126 archers in November 1474, and a recently unearthed roll dating from 1474–5 gives the names of these 252 men, and some others. Later the guard and the household force as a whole were augmented. In May 1476 there were four 100-strong companies of 'ordinary household infantry' while the guard now included four 100-strong companies of mounted English archers, and another four companies of mounted English archers were attached to it. In all, the household troops numbered over 2,000 combatants at that time, which was the eve of the battle of Murten.

A word ought to be said about the Burgundian artillery, which was carefully reorganized by John the Fearless. It was he who first appointed a single artillery master for all the Burgundian lands and obliged the officials at Dijon to keep a special artillery book containing copies of documents concerning artillery and inventories of the duke's cannons. The rate of fire of fifteenth-century cannons was too slow for them to be of much effect in a pitched battle. In some sieges they may have been of decisive importance, but even this is doubtful. Charles the Bold was supposed to have had the finest artillery in Europe, but Liège and Nijmegen were certainly not reduced by Burgundian artillery bombardment, and Beauvais and Neuss held firm in spite of it. Charles took well over 100 cannons with him on each of his Swiss campaigns. Most of them fell into Swiss hands and some are preserved to this day in six Swiss museums. They were certainly up-to-date, but little can be deduced from these surviving pieces because most of them were kept in use for years after 1476 and modernized either then or later in the process of restoration.

To what purposes were the Burgundian armies put? They were used to conquer and annexe territories, to put down rebellions or support Burgundian allies against rebellions, to defend Burgundy against her attackers, to make war in or against France, to fight England, and for crusades. A Burgundian fleet, too, could be brought into being and was used at different times against England and France, and Burgundian naval vessels even penetrated as far as the eastern Mediterranean and the Black Sea. It goes without saying that, of the four Valois dukes of Burgundy, Charles the Bold was by far and away the most active exponent of military power. However, each of his three predecessors, but especially John the Fearless, repeatedly found it necessary or desirable to make use of military power as an instrument of policy. Let us examine, first, the dukes' use of their army for the conquest of new territories.

Military conquest was a traditional means of acquiring new territory, although it was seldom used entirely on its own. Some other means was brought into play as well; or at least some additional pretext was found for the proposed annexation. Indeed Philip the Bold, who put together the territorial nucleus of the Burgundian state by the pacific means of his own marriage to Margaret of Flanders, never used an army to acquire new territory. His methods were purchase, diplomatic or economic pressure, deceit, or whatever; not force. But John the Fearless made effective use of the Burgundian army in the annexation of the royal town and dependent lands of Mâcon in September 1417, and in the annexation of the county of Tonnerre, which however was later returned to its owner Louis de Chalon. Furthermore in 1416 he seized the county of Boulogne by force from George de la Trémoille. But Mâcon and Boulogne were relatively minor gains.

Under Philip the Good the Burgundian Low Countries were more than doubled in size, and Luxembourg represented a further significant territorial gain, for it was nearly as large as the duchy of Burgundy. This great extension of Burgundian power was brought about mainly by military action. Admittedly the exiguous county of Namur was purchased, and the extensive duchy of Brabant was acquired through diplomacy; but all the other territories added by Philip the Good to the Burgundian state were conquered, though in every case the conquest was reinforced or justified by dynastic or other pretexts or claims.

The hardest-fought, most notable and longest-lasting territorial conquest in the military annals of Burgundy was surely that of Holland by Philip the Good. It necessitated five separate campaigns between September 1425 and summer 1428. Not that the Dutch were united against him. On the contrary, the merchants and burgesses of Rotterdam, Leiden, Amsterdam and Haarlem and other mainly urban elements of the population supported Philip, while the rural aristocracy and a few of the towns – notably Gouda, Oudewater and Schoonhoven – supported Jacqueline of Bavaria, daughter of Count William VI of Holland. In part, therefore, the Burgundian conquest of Hol-

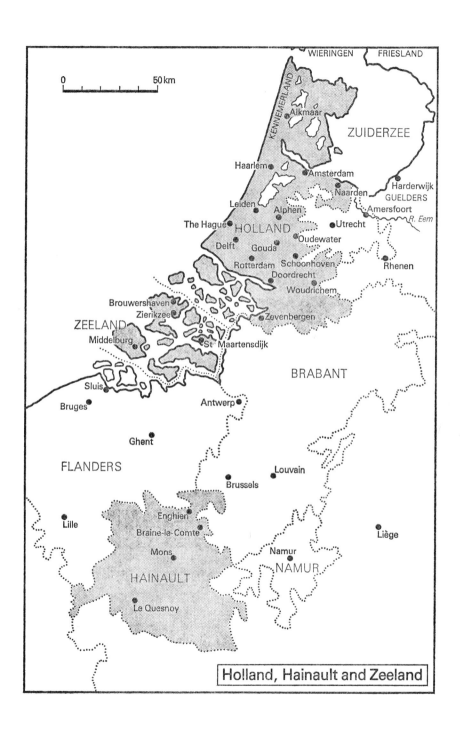

Holland, Hainault and Zeeland

land was a civil war. In the battle of Alphen, fought on 22 October 1425, Jacqueline's supporters attacked and defeated a Burgundian army consisting mainly of the citizen levies of Haarlem, Amsterdam and Leiden. During that winter English forces, sent by Duke Humphrey of Gloucester to assist Jacqueline, disembarked in Zeeland and a pitched battle was fought at Brouwershaven near Zierikzee on 13 January 1426 between Philip the Good in person with a number of Picard and Burgundian men-at-arms and contingents from Dordrecht, Delft, The Hague and other Dutch towns on the one side, and a mixed army of English and Zeelanders on the other. Duke Philip won, and soon afterwards Zierikzee recognized him. Still, much of Holland remained loyal to Jacqueline, and Alkmaar and the coastal strip of North Holland went over to her in 1426 and had to be reconquered by Philip at the end of the summer. The winter of 1426-7 was taken up with the epic siege of Zevenbergen, a stronghold of Jacqueline's in the extreme south of Holland. Both castle and town had been on an island since the floods of 1421, and the place was blockaded by a circle of Burgundian ships anchored offshore. Its surrender on 11 April 1427 was chiefly due to a quarrel between the defenders of the castle and the townspeople over the sharing of provisions between them.

Even after the fall of Zevenbergen, Jacqueline's fleet still cruised undefeated in the Zuiderzee, and she had enlisted a more effective ally than the English in the shape of Bishop Rudolf von Diepholz of Utrecht. Although her fleet was defeated off the then island of Wieringen, and Philip the Good established strongpoints at Naarden and Harderwijk on the southern shore of the Zuiderzee, the winter campaign of 1428-9 was by no means a Burgundian success, and Jacqueline was only forced to surrender much later, in the summer of 1428, after Duke Philip had laid siege to her headquarters of Gouda, and after other events had intervened to undermine her further resistance to the Burgundian conqueror.

Besides Holland, Luxembourg was added to the Valois Burgundian state through military action. It was at the end of August 1443 that Philip the Good marched out of Dijon in battle order to wrest the duchy from the hands of its Saxon claimants. No field army was mustered against him and most of the towns willingly surrendered to the invading Burgundians. At Thionville and Luxembourg, however, garrisons of Saxon soldiers prepared to resist. While tentative peace negotiations

were begun at Flörchingen, a Burgundian escalader was sent
to investigate the defences of Luxembourg. After several failures
because of the vigilance of the watch, he managed to fix a rope
ladder with iron hooks at one end to the battlements, using a
contraption of sticks which fitted into each other end to end.
He entered the town and made a thorough inspection of the
defences and the movements of the watch. The point chosen
for a night attack was a postern gate which was used by the
townswomen for going into the moat to spread their washing
out to dry. On what was supposed to be the darkest night of the
year, 21–2 November, a few hundred picked men assembled
shoeless in the moat. Breaking open the locks and bars of the
postern with an enormous pair of pincers twelve feet long, they
startled the inhabitants at two o'clock in the morning by running
through the streets yelling 'Long live Burgundy!' on their way
to seize the market place. The town was theirs, and the citadel
surrendered a few days later. Thus the duchy of Luxembourg
became a Burgundian province overnight.

The military might of Burgundy was likewise successfully
employed by Charles the Bold in the conquest of new territory.
It was by no means barefaced; as with Philip the Good so with his
son Charles, the naked aggression of invasion and occupation
was concealed or blurred behind a smokescreen of diplomacy,
or at least justified dynastically or financially. In the case of
Guelders, Duke Arnold had mortgaged the duchy to Charles
the Bold shortly before he died on 23 February 1473; his son Adolf
was in a Burgundian prison. The attack, which was made jointly
with Charles's ally of Cleves, was launched from Maastricht on
9 June 1473. It was similar to Philip the Good's conquest of
Luxembourg in that there was nobody to field an army against
the duke of Burgundy. All he had to do was to lay siege to the
few defended places. On 21 June Charles the Bold was in Venlo,
which had held out against his artillery for only a few days.
But Nijmegen offered a much more determined resistance to
Duke Charles than the town of Luxembourg had to his father
thirty years before. It only surrendered on 17 July after three
weeks of siege. By the first week of August Charles was in
Zutphen while his men went off to visit the ladies of Deventer
who, according to a Burgundian chronicler, were 'extremely
gracious, taking pleasure in entertaining strangers'. Guelders
was Burgundian.

Charles the Bold's conquest of Lorraine in 1475 followed a

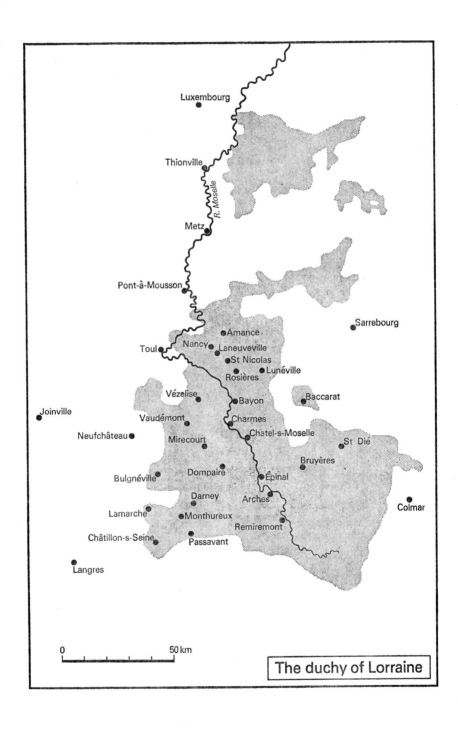

The duchy of Lorraine

Luxembourg

Thionville

R. Moselle

Metz

Pont-à-Mousson

Sarrebourg

Amance

Toul Nancy Laneuveville

St Nicolas

Rosières Lunéville

Vézelise Bayon Baccarat

Joinville

Vaudémont Charmes

Neufchâteau

Mirecourt Chatel-s-Moselle

St Dié

Bruyères

Dompaire Épinal

Bulgnéville

Darney Arches

Lamarche Colmar

Monthureux

Châtillon-s-Seine Remiremont

Passavant

Langres

0   50 km

similar pattern. Duke René II's allies were carefully neutralized by diplomacy. Again, no one was powerful enough to resist the Burgundians in the field. While Anthony, bastard of Burgundy, moved northwards from Burgundy in the first days of September 1473 into the south of Lorraine, Charles crossed the northern frontier of the duchy on 23 September and, marching past the capital, Nancy, was at Laneuveville south-east of it at the end of the month. A few places, like Charmes and Dompaire, offered resistance; their garrisons were brutally hanged after surrendering. Épinal fell on 24 October and Vaudémont soon after. With impeccable strategy Charles mopped up all the pockets of resistance before turning his attention to the well-fortified city of Nancy. It held against him for a month only. The duke entered the town on 30 November, the feast day of the Burgundian patron, St Andrew. He had reached the peak of his power, but his annexation of Lorraine is the last entry in the catalogue of Burgundian conquests. Nor did it prove of any duration, for the duchy slipped out of Charles's control in less than a year and he never really succeeded in reconquering it.

The Burgundian army, besides being employed in the conquest of new lands, was also used to put down rebellions, and these campaigns constituted the half-dozen most critical and decisive wars in the history of Valois Burgundy. Some of the revolts were against the duke himself, others were aimed at his neighbours or allies. All of them were urban in character; the towns concerned were Ghent in 1379–85 and 1449–53; Liège, in revolt against its bishop, in 1408, 1430 and 1465–8; and Andernach, Neuss and Cologne, in revolt against the archbishop of Cologne, in 1473–5. Other rebellions occurred but did not require military action on a large scale.

Ghent was one of the largest towns north of the Alps in fourteenth-century Europe. Its numerous cloth-workers had been in a state of intermittent turmoil since the late thirteenth century, and serious revolts had occurred, especially in 1359–60, before the Burgundian period. The same was true, on a smaller scale, of Ypres, where risings had occurred in 1359, 1367, 1370, 1371 and 1377, and of Bruges, which had experienced disturbances in 1351, 1367 and 1369. There was nothing very unusual or surprising, therefore, about the revolt at Ghent in 1379 which began in early September when the rioting weavers killed the bailiff and burnt down Louis of Male's castle at Wondelgem; especially as it nearly coincided with two other revolutions, the revolt of the Florentine cloth-workers in 1378 and the so-called Peasants' Revolt in England in 1381. Troops from the duchy of Burgundy, under the command of Guy de Pontailler, first appeared in the Low Countries in the autumn of 1379, but they only acted as an escort for Philip the Bold, numbering a mere 200 men-at-arms. The contingent sent in summer 1381, however, took part in Louis of Male's siege of Ghent. In May 1382 the rebels of Ghent seized Bruges, and Louis of Male's situation became critical in the extreme. A major campaign was mounted by Philip the Bold to restore his father-in-law's authority in the county of Flanders, making use of the French army and king, as well as all available forces from Burgundy, perhaps 1,500 men. At the battle of Roosebeke, fought on 27 November 1382, the Flemings were decisively defeated, and Ghent was forced thereafter to continue her rebellion alone. When in the following year her English allies laid siege to Ypres, Philip the Bold again came to the rescue with a combined Franco-Burgundian army; his own contingent probably numbering 6,000–7,000 men. Warfare in Flanders continued intermittently until the peace of Tournai was signed at the end of 1385.

It was well over half a century before the Burgundian army was called out again in force to quell a rebellion against the duke. Once more the offender was Ghent, which this time had been provoked into defiance of the duke by Philip the Good's demands for a salt tax, his attempts to intervene in the civic elections, and by other unwarranted interference. The situation deteriorated when, in the winter of 1451–2, the common people set up a revolutionary government in Ghent after seizing power, subverting the constitution, and murdering some supporters of the duke. That summer Philip the Good made a rather half-hearted attempt to invest Ghent, using troops from Picardy and Holland, while Ghent tried, but failed, to enlist the support of Bruges and the other Flemish towns. Eventually, on 18 June 1453, Duke Philip set out from Lille to attack Ghent with all his available forces. The plan was to batter the outlying fortified places into submission with artillery or seize them by assault; then to advance on Ghent itself. It went like clockwork. The castles of Schendelbeke, Poeke and Gavere surrendered after bombardment by the Burgundian artillery. In hanging or strangling their garrisons Philip the Good (in this way as in so many others) was setting an example which his son Charles was to follow in similar though better-known circumstances. It was in an attempt to raise the siege of Gavere that the Ghenters marched out in force on 23 July 1453. Too late to save their comrades in the castle, who had been murdered that very morning, they advanced against the ducal forces but were decisively defeated on the battlefield of Gavere. Rejecting advice to destroy the town of Ghent, Philip the Good contented himself with imposing terms which seriously reduced her independence and her authority over the surrounding countryside.

Ghent revolted again, in 1467, but military intervention was not required on that occasion to reduce her to submission. While she was an irritating urban thorn in the flesh of the dukes of Burgundy another town, almost equally large and powerful and even more politically turbulent, was intermittently in arms against another ruler. This was Liège, on the River Meuse between Namur and Maastricht, which in the fourteenth century experienced just the same internal upheavals as Ghent. Indeed in 1384, at the very time when the weavers of Ghent were in open revolt against their ruler, the craft guilds of Liège virtually seized control of their city in defiance of the authority of their ruler, who was also their bishop. For Liège was the capital and natural centre of one of those overgrown territorial bishoprics which were an important feature of the European political scene. The principality of Liège was comparable to the *Sticht* of Utrecht or the *Stift* of Cologne; the prelates of Basel and Geneva, Mainz and Strasbourg, enjoyed similar territorial powers. But the principality and city of Liège were of very special importance to the dukes of Burgundy.

The River Meuse, or Maas as its lower reaches were called, was one of the great arteries of Burgundian trade long before Charles the Bold made it a Burgundian river. The common people of Liège were the natural allies of the working classes of Ghent and other Netherlandish towns, and the city of Liège was a natural symbol and focal point of urban hostility to the dukes of Burgundy and other rulers. Furthermore the principality, which lay directly between Brabant and Limbourg, was, after 1430, an enclave in Burgundian territory. Right from the start, too, it was within the Burgundian sphere of influence and its successive bishops were either Burgundian allies or subject to Burgundian pressures. John of Bavaria (1390–1418), whose sister Margaret had married John the Fearless in 1385, appeared in the Burgundian army which Philip the Bold mustered in Paris in 1401 with a contingent of seven knights and forty-five squires 'more like Hector or Achilles than a prelate' as a chronicler put it. When his successor Johan von Heinsberg (1419–55) was persuaded into declaring war on Philip the Good in 1430, he did it in the politest possible manner. Referring to Burgundian hostilities against Liège, he explained that 'for this reason, most high, noble and puissant prince, after my humble salutations and excuses, I must again inform you of these things and, should they be continued, opposition will be made thereto so that my honour may be preserved'. Later Bishop Johan von Heinsberg had to sign a treaty with Duke Philip in which he promised to help the duke make war on his own city of Liège whenever the duke might find this necessary. But at least Johan von Heinsberg contrived to rule Liège without provoking it into revolt. Not so the relative of Philip the Good who succeeded him, Louis de Bourbon (1456–82), who was an unashamed Burgundian puppet.

The first occasion on which the military might of Burgundy was used to put down a revolt in Liège was in 1408. In September 1406 the people of Liège, increasingly restive at John of Bavaria's attempts to extend his episcopal authority, and indeed perhaps fearful that he might try to convert the principality into a hereditary state, had replaced him by a revolutionary government of their own. A *mambour* or regent in the shape of the local nobleman Henry, lord of Perwez, was chosen to administer the secular affairs of the principality and he promptly annexed or conquered most of it from John of Bavaria, while his son Thierry de Perwez became bishop, or rather anti-bishop. John of Bavaria at once enlisted the aid of his brother-in-law the duke of Burgundy, and John the Fearless sent him a contingent of troops from the duchy of Burgundy in January 1407; too late to prevent the castle of Bouillon, which was virtually the last toehold in the principality still held by the bishop, from falling into the hands of the rebels. Bouillon was actually the centre of an isolated territory to the south of the rest of the principality. Now, John of Bavaria was left with no more than Maastricht to defend, of which he was part-owner only. This place likewise was outside the principality, on its eastern border. He was besieged there in the winter of 1407–8. It was the hardest winter in living memory. The ink froze on the desk of the clerk of the court of the Paris Parlement and, when he placed his ink-well on the fire, it froze in his pen. The sea froze over between

Flanders and Zeeland. On 7 January 1408 the lord of Perwez was forced by this great frost to raise his siege of Maastricht.

John of Bavaria was again besieged in Maastricht in the summer of 1408. Militarily powerless, he had to rely on diplomatic pressure to persuade his brother-in-law John the Fearless and his brother William, ruler of Hainault and Holland, to bring an army to rescue him. During the siege both sides used unconventional weapons. Bishop John sent out letters inviting the moderate elements in the rebel army to overthrow their extremist leaders and return home. The only reply he received was a 'document' made from the bark of a tree and 'sealed' with a lump of cow dung. The rebel leaders did all they could to stop John of Bavaria's relatives from coming to his aid. They dispatched forged royal letters to John the Fearless ordering him not to intervene in the affairs of Liège, and they sent out bogus pilgrims to spread the false news of the surrender of Maastricht and the flight of John of Bavaria. Other sham pilgrims appeared inside Maastricht, reporting that they had travelled through France, Burgundy, Picardy and Flanders without seeing a trace of troops being mustered to help the citizens and their bishop, and strongly advising them to surrender.

A first attempt to raise the siege of Maastricht was made by John the Fearless in August 1408, but the 366 men-at-arms and 267 archers he sent then apparently did little more than devastate the country around Maastricht. He assembled his main army near Tournai and reviewed it at Nivelles in Brabant on 15 and 16 September. Here a French ambassador arrived with instructions to prohibit Duke John from advancing further. Although this time the royal initiative was genuine, John the Fearless refused to comply with it. Instead he persuaded the ambassador to join his army against Liège. The ambassador was only too glad to do this; he had secretly brought his armour with him, packed in baskets. John the Fearless provided some for his attendants. He crossed the frontier of the principality of Liège with his brother-in-law William of Bavaria and their combined forces on 20 September 1408, leaving his brother and other ally Duke Anthony of Brabant at Tirlemont, so that his Brabanters could act as a strategic reserve. In response to this invasion, the lord of Perwez raised the siege of Maastricht on 22 September, took his men back to Liège, then marched them out again on 23 September to oppose the invaders at Othée, between Liège

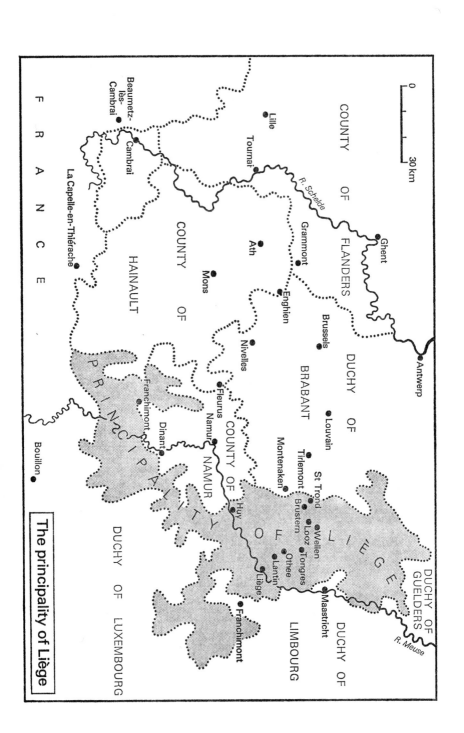

The principality of Liège

and Tongres. When the Liègeois failed to attack, John the Fearless took the initiative by sending a flanking force to attack the enemy's rear while he himself with the main army assaulted their front. In spite of a spirited resistance, the militia of Liège were forced to give ground. Eventually they dispersed and fled, suffering heavy losses. The battle of Othée was a resounding Burgundian victory, though William of Bavaria's forces and those of the count of Namur formed a large section of John the Fearless's army, perhaps 3,000 of a total of 8,000. The revolt of Liège collapsed; the great city surrendered and handed over 500 hostages to the victors. The terms they imposed were extraordinarily harsh. All guilds in the city of Liège were to be abolished; Duke John the Fearless and Count William of Holland-Hainault were to have rights of free passage through the principality and along the River Meuse with or without troops; their coins were to be legal currency in the principality; and so on. The treaty indeed was so severe that it was never properly implemented. John the Fearless had a special tapestry made illustrating his victory – the second great pitched battle in Burgundian military history, after Roosebeke.

In spite of the bishop of Liège's declaration of war on the duke of Burgundy in 1430 there was little fighting at that time; possibly it was an outbreak of plague which brought the brief hostilities to an end. Only after the accession as bishop in 1456 of Philip the Good's youthful and irresponsible nephew Louis de Bourbon, an eighteen-year-old undergraduate at Louvain University, did civil war and rebellion again threaten the principality. On 27 August 1457 a cleric at Cambrai recorded that the duke of Burgundy was about to set out on 'an expedition against the Liègeois who were in revolt'. Burgundian troops had actually been mobilized in Hainault, Flanders and elsewhere, and Philip the Good was on the brink of invading Liège on his nephew's behalf. Though the particular crisis blew over, the general situation deteriorated. The bishop was exiled to Maastricht, and the houses of his friends in Liège were looted and burned. He retaliated by excommunicating his own flock, which appealed for protection against him and his ally Philip the Good to the king of France. In 1461–3 both Philip the Good and Louis XI took their turn in trying to negotiate a settlement between the bishop and the city of Liège. In 1463 a papal legate tried his hand. All these efforts proved fruitless.

In 1465 the pattern of events of 1406 was in part repeated. A *mambour* or governor-regent was chosen by Liège in the person of Marc von Baden, brother of Karl, margrave of Baden. Marc probably hoped to supplant Louis de Bourbon as bishop of Liège. After all another brother of his, Georg, was bishop of Metz and a third, Jacob, was archbishop of Trier. He arrived at Liège on 1 August 1465 with three German counts, 400 knights in red uniforms, and an enormous bombard, in time to join the Liègeois in an invasion of the Burgundian duchy of Limbourg which King Louis XI had persuaded them to undertake. At this moment Philip the Good's son and heir Charles, then count of Charolais, was campaigning near Paris in alliance with other French princes against the king of France in the war of the League of the Public Weal. But Marc von Baden and his men soon went home, Louis XI made peace with Charles and his princely allies at Conflans early in October, and Liège was left to its fate.

The fate of Liège, against the background of the final months of Philip the Good's reign and the opening years of Charles the Bold's, was to be the target of four successive military campaigns conducted by Charles in person, in the first two as count of Charolais, in the second two as duke of Burgundy. Ostensibly undertaken to help Louis de Bourbon regain control of his principality, their real aim was to destroy the power of the rebellious populace of Liège which constituted a standing threat to the authority of princes, and to extend Burgundian influence over the principality. These campaigns were launched in November 1465, August 1466, October 1467 and October 1468. Each of the first three was followed by a peace settlement: the treaties of St Trond signed on 22 December 1465, of Oleye signed on 10 September 1466, and of Brustem signed on 28 November 1467. The fourth was followed by the systematic sacking and burning of the city of Liège.

These campaigns against Liège of 1465–8 constituted the nearest thing in Valois Burgundian history to a real war in anything approaching the modern sense of a series of hostilities over an extended period. After the failure of a surprise attack on Dinant at the end of November, the 1465 campaign was brought to a close without serious fighting by the peace of St Trond. But Dinant was excluded from this settlement. It was supposed to have incurred the special displeasure of Charles, count of Charolais, because some of its citizens had hanged him in effigy and alleged that he was not Philip the Good's son at all, but a bastard child of the previous bishop of Liège, Johan von Heinsberg, and Duchess Isabel of Burgundy. Charles probably resented this slur on the otherwise irreproachable reputation of his mother, though the Dinanters may be forgiven for their imputation against Bishop Johan: other sources credit him with up to sixty bastards. In spite of further negotiations in the first half of 1466, Philip the Good decided to besiege Dinant, and his son Charles entered it victoriously on 25 August 1466. His men sacked and burned it, and this act of violence was sufficient to persuade Liège to accept the terms of the peace of Oleye, which meant accepting the duke of Burgundy as hereditary protector-guardian of the city and principality of Liège and paying a heavy fine.

The succession of Charles the Bold as duke of Burgundy on 15 June 1467 only exacerbated the growing hostility between Burgundy and Liège. Bishop Louis de Bourbon and some of his clergy had withdrawn from Liège to Huy, while partisans of the revolutionary leader Raes de Lyntre paraded in the streets of Liège with the words 'Long live Liège!' embroidered on the sleeves of their red uniforms. In July and August a number of moderate leaders were executed at Liège by the extremists and a ducal secretary was arrested there. Soon, the Liègeois were raiding Burgundian territory in neighbouring Limbourg; on 16–17 September Raes de Lyntre and his men seized Huy, the bishop having escaped to Namur. War had begun.

Charles the Bold resolved on a mass attack on the rebellious city and he set out from Louvain to take the field on 19 October 1467 with a fanfare of trumpets. On 20 October a force of some 900 combatants was sent off in advance of the main army to try to recapture Huy, but failed. The reaction of the rebels to this and other Burgundian raids was to march out of Liège in battle array with the banner of their patron saint St Lambert and a statue of Our Lady. They took up defensive positions at Brustem on 28 October, causing Charles the Bold to abandon his preparations to besiege St Trond and turn to attack Brustem instead. This he did on the afternoon of 28 October. Battle was joined with an artillery bombardment, but the shots of each side went over the heads of the other. The Liègeois defenders were inconvenienced but not injured when the Burgundian cannon brought down branches of trees as thick as legs and arms onto their heads. Nor could the Burgundian cavalry make any impression on the heavily defended village. At this juncture,

Charles ordered his archers to dismount, and they fought their way into the enemy lines on foot so that the Liègeois were forced to flee, leaving most of their baggage and artillery in Burgundian hands. It was a decisive enough victory but, instead of following it up, Charles's troops dallied on the battlefield, robbing the corpses, amassing loot, and eating and drinking the wine, cheese, bread and salt meat left behind by the Liègeois. Only on 11–12 November did they begin to take up quarters on the outskirts of Liège, after Heers, Looz, St Trond, Wellen and Othée had fallen to them. By this time internal convulsions at Liège had resulted in the resumption of power by moderate elements, and the peace dictated by Charles the Bold on 28 November was reluctantly accepted by this new government. It repeated many of the terms of the treaty imposed after Othée in 1408, but went further. The existing law courts and judicial arrangements at Liège were all abolished, and cases in future were to be judged 'according to reason and written law, without regard to the bad styles, usages and customs' formerly in use; the bishop's court was removed elsewhere; a large fine had to be paid; and an attempt was made to completely demilitarize the city: no arms of any kind, no artillery, no defensive walls and gates, were to be allowed her. Naturally, the duke of Burgundy continued as hereditary *advocatus* or guardian of the city and principality.

Liège belonged to the church and could not be incorporated outright into the Burgundian state. Nevertheless, in the winter of 1467–8 Louis de Bourbon, who had in the past been forced to share power with the people, was forced to share power with the duke of Burgundy, in the person of his lieutenant-general in Liège, the Picard nobleman Guy de Brimeu, lord of Humbercourt. Then, in the spring of 1468, both Louis de Bourbon and Charles the Bold had to accept the intervention of a papal legate sent to arbitrate the disputes at Liège, Onofrio de Santa Croce, bishop of Tricarico. While these three were arguing at the end of the summer of 1468, the rebels of Liège, encouraged by their hope that Duke Charles would soon be at war with and would be defeated by King Louis XI of France, seized power again in Liège to shouts of 'Long live the king and a free Liège'.

This time the fate of Liège hardly hung in the balance. It was an open city, most of its fortifications having been demolished during the previous winter, and Charles was determined to destroy it in spite of Bishop Onofrio's well-meaning efforts to arrange a peace settlement. Nevertheless the first Burgundian attack was rebuffed at Tongres by a night attack on Charles's captain Guy de Brimeu. That very day, 9 October, King Louis went to see Duke Charles at Péronne and a Franco-Burgundian settlement followed. This left Charles free to divert the substantial army which had just arrived from his southern territories for the proposed war against France. Instead, he could now use these troops to help him punish Liège. The duke was even able to persuade the king to accompany him in person on the expedition against Liège; persuasion which was no doubt reinforced by Louis de Bourbon's relatives, for his sister Jeanne and three brothers, Charles, archbishop of Lyons, John duke of Bourbon, and Pierre lord of Beaujeu, all took the field with Louis XI and Charles the Bold. Indeed the expedition took on the appearance of a Boubon family rescue operation.

The campaign of 1468 was brief but hard fought. The rebels of Liège delivered a series of desperate but useless counterattacks on the advancing Burgundians. On 9 October, when they struck at Tongres, they took Guy de Brimeu prisoner for a time. On 22 October they struck again, this time at the village of Lantin. Late on 26 October they sallied out a third time and attacked the Burgundians while they were taking up quarters in the suburbs of Liège, and very early on 27 October they attacked again, wounding Guy de Brimeu among others. Finally, in another night attack, on 29–30 October, they penetrated the Burgundian lines and came near to killing or capturing the king and the duke of Burgundy in their lodgings. On Sunday 30 October, even before the great bombard was fired as the signal for the general assault, some of Charles's men had entered the city. There was little or no organized resistance; there were no defences to man. Looting continued all that day while the troops from the duchy of Burgundy, much to their annoyance, had to remain, on ducal orders, fully armed and drawn up in battle order in the market place. When the looting was over large sections of Liège were systematically demolished and burned. An arch of the only bridge over the Meuse at that time was broken down, and a ducal garrison was installed in a castle which Charles the Bold had built near the town centre. Liège was as near as possible Burgundian; no further revolts are on record during the remainder of Duke Charles's reign.

The last Burgundian war waged on rebels against a prince's authority was the siege of Neuss in 1474–5 – a military and political event of epic proportions which dazzled Europe at the time and has impressed posterity ever since. Though it ended in costly military failure, it was a brilliant display of Burgundian power which greatly enhanced Charles the Bold's prestige.

In many important respects the Neuss campaign was similar to those of Liège. The Burgundian dukes had had their eyes on the archbishopric of Cologne just as they had on the bishopric of Liège. When a vacancy occurred at Cologne in 1463 Burgundian ambassadors arrived to plead the cause of a Burgundian candidate for the archiepiscopal throne. They were snubbed, but the successful candidate, Ruprecht of Bavaria, was soon turned into a Burgundian ally and client. In the 1465 treaty between them Philip the Good swore to be Ruprecht's 'true, faithful and perfect friend'. Soon after this the archbishop sent the duke the somewhat unusual gift of a lion. Just as Louis de Bourbon's episcopal authority at Liège was threatened by rebellion, so before long at Cologne Ruprecht of Bavaria found himself opposed by his own cathedral chapter and, even more, by the chief towns of his archbishopric, Cologne and Neuss. Just as the rebels at Liège in 1406 and again in 1465 had appointed a local nobleman or neighbouring ruler as their guardian, so on 29 March 1473 the opposition to Ruprecht chose Hermann, landgrave of Hesse, 'captain and protector' of the *Stift* of Cologne. Naturally too, just as Louis de Bourbon at Liège had applied for support to the duke of Burgundy, so Ruprecht of Bavaria sought military aid from Charles the Bold, visiting him in person to this end at Zutphen in August 1473 and at Thionville in December. Even so, at Cologne as at Liège, practically everyone, including the duke of Burgundy tried to mediate, and it was only at the end of June 1474 that Charles the Bold finally decided on a military expedition 'to bring the rebellious subjects of the archbishop of Cologne back to his obedience'. Long before this he had had himself declared protector of the *Stift* of Cologne just as he and his father had been guardians of the principality of Liège.

Even though Charles the Bold liked to think of himself (and indeed was thought of by many contemporaries) as a new Alexander the Great, a universal conqueror who would bring the Germans to heel and subject the entire River Rhine to his rule in a single decisive campaign, he was realist enough to limit his immediate political aims to the maximum possible extension of Burgundian influence along the great river and to proceed with the utmost military caution. Before setting out on campaign he made sure of the neutrality of neighbouring powers and secured his lines of communication through friendly Cleves and more or less friendly Jülich-Berg. Instead of trying to attack or lay siege to Cologne itself, which was larger and defensively much stronger than Liège, he selected Neuss, which had been the most consistent and determined element in the revolt against archiepiscopal authority, as his prime target and first victim. Contemporary observers mostly thought that this relatively small place would soon fall to the Burgundian army and artillery. Nijmegen, similar in size and defensive possibilities, had fallen in three weeks even though its first fortifications had been constructed by Julius Caesar. Why should Neuss – apart from the fact that it had survived a boasted thirteen sieges – do better? But contemporaries were wrong. Neuss held out from 30 July 1474 until Charles eventually withdrew between 13 and 27 June 1475.

The secret of Neuss's achievement in successfully defying one of Europe's largest and best-organized armies, not to mention the Burgundian artillery, lay partly in her topographical situation, for she was protected by a branch of the River Rhine on one side and surrounded on the others by excellent moats. Moreover her walls and gates were strong and in good order and she had had time to prepare fully for a long siege: a numerous garrison of soldiers from Hesse manned her walls; enough cattle were taken into the town to provide fresh meat until Christmas; the tall trees surrounding the local monastery, the Oberkloster just outside the walls, had been felled and taken into the town; and the lead had been stripped off the abbey roof to make cannon-balls. Even so the defenders were credited with almost superhuman powers of organization. All their provisions were said to be kept in two houses under armed guard and a strict rationing system 'as with boys at school' was enforced. They had divided themselves into three groups. While one slept, another ate, and a third remained on guard. Supernatural aid was also provided or imagined for them, for their patron saint Quirinus appeared in person to help and encourage them. Nonetheless the valiant defenders of Neuss were in a bad way during the last months of the siege. Their gates had been rendered into mounds of rubble. Their only communication with the outside world was an occasional letter concealed in a cannon-ball with a long streamer or marker ribbon attached to it, which was fired out of, or into, the town with a cannon. Sometimes these messages splashed into the Rhine and were lost. Their

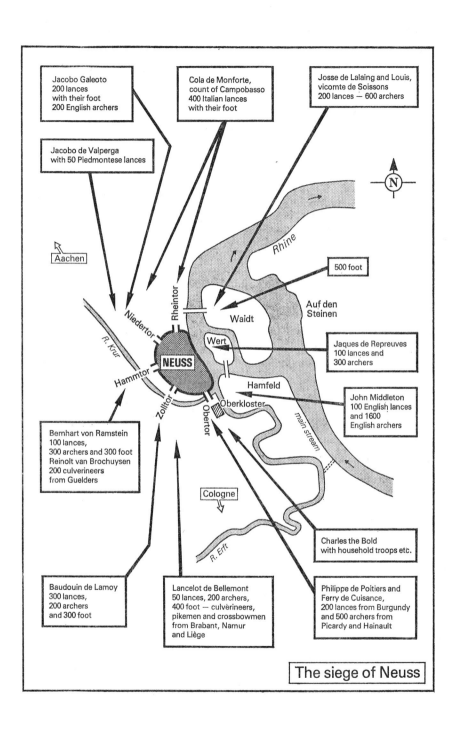

Jacobo Galeoto
200 lances
with their foot
200 English archers

Cola de Monforte,
count of Campobasso
400 Italian lances
with their foot

Josse de Lalaing and Louis,
vicomte de Soissons
200 lances — 600 archers

Jacobo de Valperga
with 50 Piedmontese lances

Aachen

Rhine

500 foot

Niedertor

Rheintor

Waidt

Auf den
Steinen

R. Krur

Wert

NEUSS

Hammtor

Hamfeld

Jaques de Repreuves
100 lances and
300 archers

Zolltor

Obertor

Oberkloster

main stream

John Middleton
100 English lances
and 1600
English archers

Bernhart von Ramstein
100 lances,
300 archers and 300 foot
Reinolt van Brochuysen
200 culverineers
from Guelders

Cologne

R. Erft

Charles the Bold
with household troops etc.

Baudouin de Lamoy
300 lances,
200 archers
and 300 foot

Lancelot de Bellemont
50 lances, 200 archers,
400 foot — culverineers,
pikemen and crossbowmen
from Brabant, Namur
and Liège

Philippe de Poitiers and
Ferry de Cuisance,
200 lances from Burgundy
and 500 archers from
Picardy and Hainault

The siege of Neuss

food supplies dwindled fast after the New Year in spite of some successful foraging raids on the Burgundian camp. They ate every single horse, rat and other animal they could lay their hands on.

The supernatural, or at least an element of incredulity, was likewise introduced by contemporaries on the Burgundian side. Duke Charles was described in his famous portable wooden pavilion not reposing on a bed, but reclining in a chair with his armour on and 'following the noble and exalted characteristics of the lion' sleeping with his eyes open. His forces completely encircled and effectively blockaded the town; some of his men were posted on islands in the Rhine, others were in boats brought from Holland. He and his courtiers lodged in the Oberkloster. He was supposed to have erected more temporary buildings outside the walls of Neuss than there were houses inside it. The Italian ambassador Johanne Petro Panigarola, who arrived at the siege in March 1475 when it was eight months old, claimed that Neuss had some 3,000 'stout defenders with good artillery' facing some 30,000 Burgundians. 'To tell the truth my lord,' he wrote to his employer the duke of Milan, 'this undertaking at Neuss is a difficult thing and, according to people expert in the art of war, it will take a long time to have it by force.'

In the same dispatch Panigarola reports that the duke 'could have the place on terms but he doesn't want this; he wants it at discretion. He is in close touch with the emperor and the German princes concerning a settlement.' As a matter of fact the Emperor Frederick III had, in his habitual dilatory fashion, been lethargically assembling the imperial army as if intending, at some indeterminate point in the distant future, to try to raise the siege. But, as Panigarola reported already in March, before this relieving expedition had got under way Charles was trying to extricate himself by means of a negotiated peace. He was by no means obstinately maintaining the siege of Neuss in a 'do or die' mood of desperation, as some people liked to think and as de Commynes asserted. But his offers of March, repeated in April, to withdraw peacefully provided Neuss was neutralized and a peace mediated between the archbishop and his rebellious subjects, were rejected. Thus the great siege continued into May while Frederick III contrived to advance as slowly as possible towards it. Leaving Cologne eventually on 6 May, he still managed to dawdle *en route* to Neuss, so that his army only made contact with the Burgundians, whose camp at Neuss was a mere twenty-four miles downstream from Cologne, on 23 May. Some skirmishing took place on that day, but thereafter the emperor and his men remained in a defensive encampment and, apart from a serious skirmish on 16 June, no further fighting interfered with the peace talks. These were protracted by procedural and other difficulties, but the air was cleared when a papal legate saved the honour of both sides by commanding both Frederick and Charles to lay down their arms on pain of excommunication. Even then an argument developed, for neither side wished to be the first to retreat. Charles pleaded for an exactly simultaneous withdrawal; Frederick insisted that Charles must first withdraw three miles towards his own lands. Then, after a pause of three days, he, Frederick, would withdraw. This, in the event, was more or less what happened on 27 June 1475. Having astonished Europe first by failing to take Neuss, and then by maintaining his siege for so long in the face of imperial opposition, Charles the Bold rode off informing Panigarola that he planned to spend the next six months on campaign, and he kept his word. In spite of his failure to take Neuss and the expenses and losses incurred by the siege, Burgundian military power and political standing were unimpaired.

So far we have discussed the use of Burgundian military power in conquering new lands and in suppressing rebellions. Holland, Luxembourg, Guelders, were annexed through military conquest; rebellions at Ghent, Liège and in the *Stift* of Cologne were suppressed or opposed by the Burgundian army. But it was also used, though for the most part to less good effect, in the wars which every power in those days fought from time to time with her neighbours. Burgundian wars against England were very few and far between. Indeed between 1387 and 1477, when the two powers were more or less permanent allies, there was only one short war, in 1436. Right at the start of Valois Burgundian history, however, Philip the Bold had married Margaret of Flanders in 1369 against English competition and from that year onwards he joined in his brother King Charles V's campaigns against the English, though without achieving any startling military successes. In 1369 he was appointed commander of a projected French invasion of England, but this was forestalled by an English counterattack from Calais which Philip failed to brush aside though he was bold or foolhardy enough to challenge the English captain John of Gaunt to a single combat. However, the parties failed to agree on procedure. Some years later, in September 1377, Philip the Bold made an attempt to conquer Calais on behalf of the crown of France, but he achieved nothing. Such was the rather slender Burgundian contribution to this part of the Hundred Years War.

In 1383 Philip the Bold became more directly involved in a confrontation with the English. An expeditionary force under Henry Despenser, bishop of Norwich, crossed to Flanders in support of the rebels of Ghent and laid siege to Ypres. Now it was the turn of the French to fight on Burgundy's behalf, but King Charles VI and his men, brought by Philip the Bold, who was the king's uncle, arrived in Flanders to find the English army already dispersing. They easily took the last few places still held by the enemy: Bergues, Bourbourg and Gravelines. Again in 1384–5 England intervened in Flanders in support of the Ghenters and even sent a *rewaert* or regent to Ghent with several hundred English troops. In these circumstances it is not surprising that Philip the Bold was behind a French plan to invade England in 1385, which was deferred until 1386. Elaborate preparations were then made at the embarkation port of Sluis in Philip the Bold's newly acquired county of Flanders for a massive onslaught on England. Provisions were assembled, including 500 barrels of wine; a collapsible wooden fort was constructed at Rouen, but much of it was captured at sea by the English while it was on its way to Sluis; and the renowned Flemish artist Melchior Broederlam painted the duke's motto in gold letters all over the mainsail of his ship. In September, over a thousand ships and a powerful Franco-Burgundian army were waiting at Sluis, but the expedition never set sail. Bad weather and contrary winds were the reasons, or excuses. According to a report submitted by the captains to the French royal council in mid-November, 'the sea is damnable, the nights are too long, too dark, too cold and too wet. We lack provisions. We need a full moon and a favourable wind.' They went on to explain that England's harbours and coasts were perilous and that the fleet had too many old ships and too many small ones.

After this farce, Philip the Bold took up the negotiations which he had been conducting intermittently with the English ever since 1375, and the Anglo-Burgundian alliance became an almost permanent feature of the political structure of fifteenth-century Europe. Only once, in 1436, soon after the Peace Congress of Arras, when Philip the Good made what may at first have

looked like an effective peace settlement with King Charles VII
of France, was this alliance (then strained by economic irritations
on either side) broken by warfare. On this occasion the English
authorities reacted to the duke of Burgundy's new-found
French connection by embarking on a diplomatic offensive
against Burgundy and by permitting acts of piracy against
Burgundian shipping. This English hostility coincided with the
emergence of an old enemy of Philip the Good, Duke Humphrey
of Gloucester, as the most powerful figure in the English
government. It was he who had married Jacqueline of Bavaria
and tried by force of arms to prevent Philip from annexing
Hainault and Holland at a time when Burgundy and England
were officially allies. Now he had himself appointed royal
lieutenant of the king of England in Calais, Picardy, Flanders
and Artois, and prepared to invade Flanders by sea. Philip the
Good, aware of this threat, decided to strike the first blow by
laying siege to Calais, and the civic militia of the Flemish towns
began taking up their positions round this important English
continental possession early in July. Soon they were conquering
the outlying strongpoints while the ducal heavy artillery was
brought from all parts; the bridge on the main road through
Châtillon in Burgundy was badly damaged by its passage.
Calais, however, was no ordinary town. It could only be
effectively blockaded by sea, and Philip the Good's fleet was
very late in arriving. When it did at last anchor off the harbour
on 25 July it maintained its blockading stations for only two
days, then set course for home. The Flemish militia were furious
and, when the reinforcements promised by the duke failed to
arrive and the English made some vigorous sorties against them,
they too decamped and made for home. Thus the Burgundian
siege of Calais melted away on 28 and 29 July 1436. The disappointed
duke partly excused this military failure on the grounds that
his dispositions were 'an encampment only, and not designed
for a siege . . . and we neither fired artillery against the town
nor did we make the customary preliminary summons to the
defenders'.

Duke Humphrey's invasion of Flanders followed in the first
half of August. By-passing defended places like Bourbourg
and Gravelines, he and his men spread fire and destruction
through rural West Flanders. At Poperinge, his point of furthest
penetration, he had himself proclaimed count of Flanders on
15 August, then set fire to the town. By the first week in

September he was in Calais again laden with plunder – in time to be taken off by his fleet, which had cruised along the Flemish coast and devastated parts of it as far as the island of Kadzand. No effective defence could be found against these depredations; the men of Ghent refused to turn out in force even when the duchess of Burgundy's special emissary implored them to 'defend the boundaries and frontiers of their own land, together with their own possessions and belongings, their privileges, rights and liberties, their lives and the lives of their women and children, as well as the honour and good renown of their posterity'. All they produced was a contingent of 100 archers. The Anglo-Burgundian peace was soon patched up, though not before Philip the Good had tried, and failed, in 1438, to drown the English out of Calais by breaching one of the sea dykes. There were no further significant hostilities between England and Burgundy apart from some desultory fighting at sea in 1470 between Charles the Bold's subjects and the earl of Warwick's fleet.

More frequently, though still rarely, the Burgundian army was used to fight the French. John the Fearless, the character of whose rule was at times as military as that of Charles the Bold, relied on his army to maintain his power in France against the allied French princes who became known as the Armagnacs after one of their number, Count Bernard VII of Armagnac. On one occasion only did he lead an army outside France, when he attacked the rebels of Liège in 1408. In the autumns of 1405, 1410 and 1411 his troops were assembled in Paris to defend it against Armagnac attacks, but there was little or no fighting. In 1412 John the Fearless attacked and laid siege to the Armagnac town of Bourges, but his own forces were outnumbered on this campaign by the royal troops with them, for both the king and the dauphin accompanied him. The siege of Bourges was cut short by a negotiated peace. Early in 1414, after he had had to flee from Paris in August 1413, the duke of Burgundy led his troops on a dashing but unsuccessful bid to recapture the capital, and in 1417 he organized and led another campaign in the Paris area which likewise failed in its main objective of taking Paris. Other campaigns fought in John the Fearless's reign were defensive. There was fighting in the duchy of Burgundy, but on the front-iers only. On two occasions, in 1411 and again in 1414, the Armagnacs assembled troops in Picardy with a view to invading the Burgundian lands in the Low Countries. In 1411 John the

Fearless assembled his men at Douai and then, reinforced by his brother Anthony's men from Brabant and the militia of the Flemish towns, he counterattacked with considerable success, forcing the Armagnacs to evacuate Ham on the Somme, which fell to him on 14 September. He decorated its walls and towers with 3,000 Burgundian banners and went on to take Péronne, Nesle and Roye. In 1414 the Armagnacs were rather more successful; they conquered Bapaume and laid siege to Arras, capital of the county of Artois. This time it was they who had possession of King Charles VI, but John the Fearless seems to have taken the precaution of garrisoning Arras with troops from Franche-Comté and from England who could fight against the king of France with a clear conscience; he was not their suzerain. The siege was abandoned early in September 1414 and the exhausted and bedraggled French troops made their way back to Paris looking 'as if they had been in gaol for six or eight months on bread and water', according to a chronicler there.

John the Fearless was the only one of the Valois Burgundian dukes who used his military power chiefly against the French. His son Philip the Good turned his back on French affairs, and serious Franco-Burgundian warfare only occurred early in his reign as a kind of aftermath of Duke John's campaigns. But, while John the Fearless fought no pitched battles with the French, Philip the Good was the personal victor of the battle of Mons-en-Vimeu fought on 31 August 1421, and troops from the duchy of Burgundy were victorious in the battle of Bulgnéville, in Lorraine, on 30 June 1431. Both these pitched battles represented serious French setbacks, but they were isolated and indecisive. Moreover, the Burgundians had been defeated by the French in the battle of Anthon in Dauphiny on 11 June 1430 and Philip the Good had had to abandon the siege of Compiègne that same summer. By this time there was no longer any serious military confrontation between France and Burgundy. Peace talks had been going on for some time, and continued. The rest of Philip the Good's reign, until 1465, was characterized by a kind of armed peace, a state of permanent mutual distrust and irritation, between France and Burgundy.

Thanks to the fabrications of contemporary chroniclers, in particular the coolly mendacious de Commynes and the romantically fanciful Chastellain, Charles the Bold has gone down in history as the mortal enemy of King Louis XI of France.

The two are thought of as locked in deadly and inevitable combat. But in actual fact both rulers had other irons in the fire and, though Charles the Bold loved to conjure up visions of the destruction of French royal power at the hands of himself and his allies, most of his military activities were directed elsewhere. His territorial conquests and the campaigns of Liège and Neuss have already been mentioned; his last three fateful campaigns against the Swiss and their allies will be described in the final chapter. Against France, he conducted only two wars of aggression, in 1465, before he became duke, and in 1472; and two defensive campaigns against French invasions, in 1471 and 1475. In these wars the same ground was fought over as was disputed in John the Fearless's time; Paris was surrounded by Charles and his allies in 1465 as it had been by John in 1417; the French attacked Arras again in 1475 as they had done in 1414; and Nesle and Roye were taken by Charles in 1472 as they had been by John in 1411.

The war of the League of the Public Weal in 1465 was the last and most serious of a series of revolts of the French princes against the growing power of the French crown. 'Seven dukes, twelve counts, two lords, one marshal, 51,000 men-at-arms – all against King Louis and the city of Paris,' was how a Parisian diarist recorded it at the time. Charles was merely one of the seven dukes. His main motive in participating in the war was the recovery of Péronne, Roye and Montdidier, which his father had ceded to Jehan, count of Étampes and Nevers, and the so-called Somme towns (Abbeville, Amiens and St Quentin were the most important), which his father had ceded to the French crown two years before. It is not surprising therefore that before marching towards Paris to join the other French princes, Charles seized and conquered as many of these places as he could. The only pitched battle of the war was fought on 16 July 1465 at Montlhéry not far south of Paris. Nobody has ever discovered who won, for part of each army was left apparently victorious on the field and part fled. The battle was fought between the royal and Burgundian forces, and Louis XI and Charles, then count of Charolais, were both present in person. It was a disorganized affair from the start and it is certain that neither Louis nor Charles knew exactly what happened. Charles claimed in a message to his mother the dowager duchess Isabel that his artillery had killed 1,200–1,400 of the advancing French troops, and he admitted losses of three or four hundred of his own men. He did not disclose to her that he had been wounded in the neck and very nearly taken prisoner. Nor evidently was he able to admit to himself that the whole affair had been bungled almost disastrously and that he was gravely at fault both strategically, in fighting the king without his allies and their troops, and tactically in personally pursuing a group of French fugitives for several miles off the battlefield because he thought the king was among them. Nevertheless the battle of Montlhéry surrounded the count of Charolais with an aura of invincible military might. His reputation was made.

In spite of belligerent pretences and preparations on either side at various times, it was not until early in 1471 that the Burgundian army was used again against France. In a surprise attack, Louis XI had recaptured Amiens, St Quentin, Roye and Montdidier. Charles counterattacked by seizing Picquigny, town, castle and bridge over the Somme, and he laid siege to Amiens in March. But then peace negotiations intervened. The French had invaded Hainault too, and raided Franche-Comté. As to the duchy of Burgundy, this was formally but only theoretically confiscated to the French crown on 24 February. Two days later, French troops invaded it from the south but were rebuffed.

The savage attack which Charles the Bold launched on France in June 1472 was partly a war of revenge and partly of reconquest. The duke opened hostilities by sacking Nesle and recapturing Montdidier and Roye on the frontier. Then he marched deep into French territory and laid siege on 27 June 1472 to the town of Beauvais. Why were the Burgundians forced to raise the siege of this place after twenty-five days? Probably not merely because of the heroism of her womenfolk, who were subsequently granted by the king permission to wear whatever clothes they liked and to precede the men in civic processions. The real reasons for the failure of the siege of Beauvais were that it was well garrisoned with 1,000 men-at-arms and 4,000 archers and that, before Charles had invested it completely, abundant provisions and other supplies were taken into it, including 100 barrels of the finest wine sent by the town of Orleans. Even though something like a quarter of the total length of wall surrounding Beauvais had been reduced to rubble by Charles's artillery, his assaults were of no avail. History was to repeat itself two years later at Neuss. The remainder of the 1472 campaign was equally indecisive, though it continued favourable to

Burgundy in the sense that most of it was fought on French soil. According to one of his captains, in 1472 Duke Charles had 'had the finest and largest army that ever entered France, though it is nothing to what he intends to have next season'. But, in the following year, Charles was busy conquering Guelders. The next and last Franco-Burgundian conflict was that of May 1475, when Louis XI delivered simultaneous attacks on Charles the Bold's northern and southern territories as well as a naval attack on Dutch ports and shipping. In the north the French recaptured some of the disputed Somme frontier places; in the south they won a pitched battle at Guipy near Château-Chinon on 20 June 1475. But these French invasions were by no means pressed home, and the truces which had expired on 1 May, when Louis had opened his attacks, were soon restored.

One further use of Burgundian military power remains to be considered: the crusade. It was strikingly different from the other uses we have been considering. In conquering territories, putting down rebellions and fighting neighbouring powers the Burgundian army was more or less successful: it held its own at least. But the one and only Burgundian crusade, the Nicopolis (modern Nikopol) expedition of 1396, was a disastrous failure.

During the course of the fourteenth century, while the Ottoman Turks were systematically swarming into the Balkans and threatening to overwhelm large parts of Christendom, the popes and the western powers contented themselves with a succession of crusades scarcely worth the name. Led by minor adventurers instead of Europe's leading monarchs, who were busy with their own affairs or preoccupied with fighting each other, most of these crusades were actually harmful to Christendom, and some were positively beneficial to the Turks. In 1306–8 the island of Rhodes was seized, not from the infidel, but from the Christian Greeks of the Byzantine Empire. In 1365 the sack of Alexandria considerably damaged western trade with the East and provoked counter-measures against Christians. In 1366 the count of Savoy, Amadeus VI, led an expedition which, usefully, took Gallipoli from the Turks, but was then diverted against the Christian kingdom of Bulgaria, accelerating its collapse and conquest by the Turks. Some Burgundian knights and squires accompanied the count of Savoy on this crusade. Duke Louis of Bourbon's expedition to Tunis in 1390 was utterly futile in almost every respect, though it, too, provided crusading experience for a handful of prominent Burgundian noblemen.

This was also available on the frontiers of Prussia and Lithuania, where an annual crusade, which had become a kind of tourist attraction for western noblemen, was still being organized by the Teutonic Knights against the unfortunate Lithuanians, even when they were converted to Christianity after 1386. In Prussia then, in Tunis, and in the Balkans, and in 1393 also in Hungary, Burgundian noblemen acquired crusading experience, often with the help of ducal subsidies.

The kingdom of Hungary was seriously threatened by the Ottoman advance into the Balkans. In 1395 King Sigmund sent an embassy to the West seeking military assistance in the form of a crusade. Philip the Bold was the only western ruler who responded not, as he had at first intended, by going in person, but by sending his twenty-four-year-old son John, then count of Nevers, with a body of picked Burgundian and Flemish men-at-arms accompanied by many French and some English contingents. Among the Flemings were five bastard uncles of John of Nevers, illegitimate sons of his grandfather Louis of Male. The general idea of the Nicopolis crusade, to protect the Christian kingdom of Hungary against the Ottomans by a major campaign along the Danube, was an excellent one. Though Sigmund advised playing a waiting game and permitting the sultan Bayazid to cross the Danube into Hungary before they attacked him, the Burgundian crusaders made up their minds to carry the war at once into enemy territory. They crossed the Danube by Orsova and laid siege to an important Ottoman stronghold south of the river, Nicopolis. Bayazid hurried to relieve the town, and contrived to arrive with a large army within some four miles of it without the crusaders becoming aware of his approach. This may have been because Jehan Boucicaut, marshal of France and one of the most famous soldiers of the age, had ordered that anyone found guilty of spreading alarm and despondency by announcing the approach of the enemy was to have his ears cut off!

The battle of Nicopolis was fought outside the town on 25 September 1396. The Burgundian crusaders, acting on the battle orders previously drawn up by Philip the Bold, insisted, against Sigmund's advice, on taking the van and insisted too on launching an all-out cavalry attack on the Turkish positions. They exhausted themselves cutting through rank after rank of Turkish foot and horse, without waiting for their Hungarian allies under Sigmund to come to their support, but were finally surrounded and overpowered when Bayazid sent all his un-committed reserves, which had been hidden by a hill, against them. Sigmund escaped down the Danube with a handful of his men; all the Burgundian and French leaders were killed or captured.

The great advantage of a crusade was that it brought its leader prestige and renown whether it succeeded or, as was the general rule with most of them, whether it ended in disaster. Thus John of Nevers, whose ransom cost Philip the Bold several hundred thousand ducats, was welcomed home early in 1398 with an extraordinary outburst of enthusiasm. He was acclaimed everywhere as a conquering hero with gifts, festivities, municipal deputations. He marched proudly into Lille on 19 March preceded by three minstrels and a trumpeter. He made a triumphal progress through the Flemish towns. So the Nicopolis disaster ended in a blaze of glory. Valois Burgundy had become a European power.

The fact that John the Fearless had actually taken part in a crusade must have meant a great deal to his son and grandson. Philip the Good teetered on the crusading brink on several occasions and even Charles the Bold fancied himself as a crusader. As a matter of fact Philip the Good was born in the very year of the Nicopolis crusade, which had, of course, been led by his father and organized by his grandfather. As a five-year-old he is said to have dressed up as a Turk in the park at Hesdin. In the early years of his ducal reign he subsidized several minor expeditions to the East, and when the Knights Hospitallers of Rhodes sought help against the Egyptians he sent a small Burgundian fleet into the Mediterranean which assisted with the defence of Rhodes in 1442. In 1444 and 1445 Burgundian galleys operated against the Turks in the Bosporus, on the Black Sea and on the Danube; they also committed acts of piracy against the Genoese and others. But the fitting-out of a few ships was not a crusade. Ten years later, at the Feast of the Pheasant in Lille in February 1454, Philip the Good made his famous vow to go on crusade in person. He went further and promised to take on the Grand Turk in single combat. No doubt he was flushed with wine on this occasion, but he had, after all, issued similar chal-lenges in the past to Duke Humphrey of Gloucester and the duke of Saxony.

The vow of the Pheasant was sworn in 1454, less than a year after the news of the fall of Constantinople to the Turks had

reached the West. Crusading talk, crusading plans, even preparations, continued thereafter at the Burgundian court for at
least a decade. A detailed report was drawn up, probably in
1455-6, on the possible routes the projected crusade might take;
what finance, equipment, troops would be needed; what
shipping required, and so on. According to this uniquely interesting document, 'everyone ought to be prepared from now on,
so as not to be taken unawares'. It claimed that 'four secretaries
will be needed, two knowing Latin and German and the others
Latin, French and Dutch'. If the route selected was via Italy
boats would have to be provided at Chalon

to take the infantry, both archers and others, with some of the Picard men-
at-arms to escort them and accompany the artillery and the rest of the
baggage as far as Aigues-Mortes. These boats will have to be bought, for they
cannot return against the Rhône [current], so they will be sold, if possible at
a profit, at Aigues-Mortes.

While that section of the army would continue from Provence
to Naples by sea, the duke and most of his cavalry would cross
the St Bernard and Mont Cenis Passes. If the chosen route was
via Germany, the troops would rendezvous at Ulm, those from
the southern lands crossing the Rhine bridges at Basel and
Breisach and most of those from the Low Countries passing
through Lorraine and over the bridge at Strasbourg. From
Regensburg passage would be down the Danube, in 300 boats,
taking a month at best to reach Belgrade. All this was meticu-
lously costed.

In the late 1450s and early 1460s there was a veritable craze for
crusading among European princes and popes. But, though
everyone took the cross, nobody actually went. Philip the Good
seemed on the verge of going, but Louis XI is supposed to have
dissuaded him. Instead, he decided to send, not his son Charles,
but his bastard son Anthony. On 20 April and 4 May 1464 eighty-
two volunteers marched out of Ghent in black uniforms with
crusaders' crosses on their chests and silver Gs for Ghent on
their backs. Their names were set down in full by a proud local
diarist, but they got no further than Marseilles. It was the
nearest Philip the Good came to launching a crusade.

Apart from the last campaigns of Charles the Bold, which will
find a place in the final chapter of this work, we have now
briefly reviewed the military history of Valois Burgundy in
terms of the uses to which the ducal armies were put. Used
carefully and when needed, Burgundian military power was

adequate under the first three dukes. It continued adequate in the early years of Charles the Bold's reign. He defeated Liège just as his father had defeated Ghent; he conquered Guelders just as his father had conquered Holland. His subsequent military downfall was brought about, not so much by inadequacies in the Burgundian military machine as through his own tragic blunders.

CHAPTER EIGHT

The Court and the Arts

In an earlier chapter the court was considered as an instrument of government, in so far as it supplied the venue, the personnel, the material needs, of the central administrative machinery of the Burgundian state. Here we have to examine the court as a centre of cultural activity; as a supplier of the duke's personal requirements; as a provider of entertainment; as a workshop of etiquette and ceremony; and as an organization for projecting far and wide a magnified and resplendent image of the duke of Burgundy.

Both the duke and his entourage of courtiers were wealthy connoisseurs and potential patrons of the arts. The duke commissioned tapestries and paintings, ordered fine books, paid for sculptures and founded religious houses; all on the grand scale. His courtiers did the same things in a more modest way. The dukes maintained around their persons a lavish display of material splendour, they lived in surroundings of extravagant luxury, because such was the fashion among rulers in those days. Thus, while the kings strove to outdo each other in this kind of magnificence, the dukes, and not least the dukes of Burgundy, did their best to emulate them, and the courtiers in their turn imitated the duke. Nor, among the courtiers, should the councillors and senior officials of the dukes be forgotten. Nicolas Rolin the chancellor, Jehan Chevrot and Ferry de Clugny councillors, and the *audiencer* Jehan le Gros the Younger, were all clients of Roger van der Weyden. The first three of these, as well as several others, possessed or commissioned de luxe illuminated manuscripts. Ducal councillors founded religious houses and colleges, had their tombs carved by the best sculptors available, and, towards the end, cultivated Italian connections, just as the dukes themselves did. However, in what follows attention will be focused on the activities of the dukes. Naturally, they emulated each other in cultural and artistic attitudes. There was only one spark of originality in this respect among them – Charles the Bold's passion for Italy.

The great Belgian scholar Georges Doutrepont remarked long ago on the popularity at the Burgundian court of prose versions of earlier medieval epic poems, especially in the time of Duke Philip the Good. These romances of chivalry, which celebrated the often bizarre adventures of legendary knights of long ago, were not only commissioned and read by Philip the Good and his courtiers; their contents inspired actual events at court. It was in works like the *Vows of the Heron* and the *Chronicle of Naples* that Philip the Good must have found the idea of a solemn vow pronounced on a pheasant at a ceremonial banquet. The duke's tapestries figured King Arthur, Doon de Mayence and Aimeri de Narbonne, all of them the renowned heroes of twelfth- or thirteenth-century *chansons de geste* or romances. The Lancelots, the perilous forests, and the miraculous or magical springs of the Arthurian and other romances were re-created at the Burgundian court at jousts or deeds of arms like the Deed of Arms of the Tree of Charlemagne held at Dijon in 1443. Heroes of the mythical past with a Burgundian connection were naturally most in demand at the Burgundian court. Girart de Roussillon, legendary first duke of Burgundy, became a hero of literature in the twelfth century. He had the merit, from the modern Burgundian point of view, of having quarrelled with the king of France. Philip the Good commissioned a prose version of his adventures which is now one of the most sumptuous illuminated manuscripts in the Austrian National Library at Vienna. Gilles de Chin was an old-time warrior of Hainault whose whimsical exploits were recounted in a thirteenth-century poem of which, too, Philip the Good possessed a prose version. This *Chronicle of the good knight Messire Gilles de Chin* was a romance, but it served as inspiration and model for the *Book of the deeds of the good knight Messire Jaques de Lalaing* which was a chronicle, or rather a biography, of a real-life fifteenth-century Burgundian courtier. Jaques de Lalaing really did live the life of one of the mythical knight-errants of romance. This hero of chivalry was almost a reincarnation of Gilles de Chin; his Arthur was Duke Philip the Good, who sent him to travel through Europe. He issued challenges and jousted wherever he went. In 1448 he was in Scotland, where at Stirling he measured his strength and skill against James earl of Douglas and was found somewhat wanting. He journeyed to Portugal. At Naples he was thwarted of combat by King Alfonso V, who prohibited his subjects from taking on the Burgundian knight because of his fraternal alliance with Duke Philip the Good. Messire Jaques's most famous exploit was a deed of arms called the *Fontaine aux pleurs*, the Fountain of Tears, which he staged at Chalon on the island in the Saône in 1449-50. Here for an entire year he stood by to fight all comers at the river crossing. At the fountain he placed his pavilion; the Lady of the Fountain with a unicorn; a herald; and three shields, white, violet and black, each sewn with white tears. The challenger touched the white shield for a duel with battle-axes, violet was for swords, and black for a mounted combat with lances. Elaborate regulations for the contests were drawn up and published but they only attracted a trickle of chivalrous adventurers, kindred spirits of Messire Jaques de Lalaing. Reality impinged dramatically on all this make-believe when Jaques was killed at the age of thirty-two by a rebel cannon-ball during the Ghent campaign of 1453.

If the romance of chivalry was a characteristic element in Burgundian court literature, so was the writing of history, though there was, of course, no firm contemporary distinction between the two genres. Many of the most informative and famous fifteenth-century chronicles were written by Burgundian courtiers or employees. The official chronicler George Chastellain and the courtier-captain of the guard Olivier de la Marche have already been mentioned among the sources of information of Burgundian history; so has the ducal secretary Edmond de Dynter. That notable observer of contemporary events at Arras, Jaques Duclerq, was a Burgundian official, and two other Burgundian courtiers, Jehan Lefèvre and Jehan de Wavrin, both of them councillor-chamberlains of the duke, wrote vivid personal accounts of the events in which they were involved. Nor should the *Geste des ducs de Bourgogne* be forgotten for, in spite of its poor verse, it is a historical source of the first importance for the reign of John the Fearless up to 1411.

Each of the four Valois dukes made a distinctive contribution to literature even though their cultural interests were almost slavishly imitative. Philip the Bold was partly responsible for two notable works on falconry and the chase. Gace de la Buigne started his verse *Delights of the Chase* for the duke's instruction as a young man and completed it later at the duke's request. Later on Gaston Phoebus, count of Foix, dedicated his *Book of the Chase* to Philip, whom he acknowledged to be 'the master of all of us who are interested in hunting'. Duke Philip also patronized poets like Christine de Pisan and Eustache Deschamps, and he

commissioned works from the well-known writer Honoré
Bonet, author of the treatise on the laws of warfare called *The
Tree of Battles*.

The literary history of John the Fearless is full of curiosities.
The best-known is *The Justification of the Duke of Burgundy*, which was
read aloud to the French court by a doctor of theology of the
University of Paris, Jehan Petit, on 8 March 1408. The performance
is said to have taken four hours. This extraordinary work was
also circulated around Europe in copies both illuminated and
plain. It is an elaborate and bombastic justification of tyrannicide
and, in particular, a defence of John the Fearless's assassination
of Duke Louis of Orleans in Paris on 23 November 1407. 'The deed
was perpetrated for the safety of the king's person and that of his
children and for the general good of the realm', argued Jehan
Petit. 'My thesis is the following syllogism. It is permissible and
meritorious to kill a tyrant. The duke of Orleans was a tyrant.
Therefore the duke of Burgundy did well to kill him.' Other
works connected with John the Fearless are a tract advising
princes not to dabble in fortune-telling, which was dedicated to
him in 1411; the memoirs of a Burgundian spy at the French court,
Pierre le Fruitier or Salmon; and that extraordinary pastoral
poem in which John the Fearless, Louis of Orleans and others
appear as quarrelling shepherds, divided into Burgundian lions
against Armagnac wolves, called the *Pastoralet*. It was written
'in honour and praise of the most noble and most excellent
prince John, duke of Burgundy, count of Flanders and of
Artois, who in his time was most valiant and intrepid'.

Duke Philip the Good's taste in literature was certainly not
limited to the romantic heroes of chivalry. He and his courtiers
virtually re-enacted Boccaccio's famous collection of bawdy
stories called the *Decameron* at the Burgundian court, by exchanging salacious anecdotes among themselves. Duke Philip
had this museum of Burgundian ribaldry written down by an
editor who displays distinct literary talent though he has
remained anonymous. It was given the title of *Cent nouvelles
nouvelles, The Hundred New Stories*. Well over half of these tales can
be shown to be more or less historical; over half of them are
set on Burgundian territory, usually in the Low Countries.
Their subject-matter is similar to that of the *Decameron*. Wicked
or lustful innkeepers rob or cuckold unsuspecting travellers;
noblemen pursue seductive chambermaids; monks and priests
indulge in their time-honoured erotic adventures; and, over

and over again, spouses are unfaithful. Though the *Cent nouvelles nouvelles* is a very minor work when compared to its model the *Decameron*, nevertheless it does stand out, among Burgundian courtly literature, as a distinct and even somewhat original, or at least unusual, work.

It was not only the Burgundian dukes who inspired literary works; Burgundian events did the same. Literature and real life were never far apart at the Burgundian court. The disaster of Nicopolis prompted the crusading publicist and French royal councillor Philippe de Mézières to address his *Epistre lamentable et consolatoire* or *Woeful and consoling letter* to Duke Philip the Bold. The battle of Othée was celebrated by an anonymous poet in 500 lines of mediocre verse. In 1468 Charles the Bold's wedding to Margaret of York was described in Flemish by the local writer and poet Anton de Rovere, and Charles's campaigns against Liège gave rise to a whole crop of poems.

Other writers besides those so far mentioned were Burgundian at least in the sense that they were attached to the dukes or their court. Anthoine de la Sale wrote the popular romance *Petit Jehan de Saintré* and two works with titles playing on his name called *La Salade* and *La Salle*. Bertrandon de la Broquière, sent by Philip the Good to the Holy Land in 1432, wrote a *Voyage d'Outremer* or *Journey Overseas*. The bishops and ducal councillors Jehan Germain and Guillaume Fillastre were well-known authors. Guillaume Fillastre wrote a book on the Order of the Golden Fleece and became the Order's second chancellor in 1461. Guillebert de Lannoy has left an interesting account of the embassies and journeys he undertook for Duke Philip the Good; his brother Hue submitted several lengthy memoranda to the duke on affairs of state which make up for their slender literary merit by their unique historical value.

Poetry was not at all neglected at the Burgundian court. The courtier-chroniclers Chastellain, de la Marche and Molinet all wrote in verse as well as prose. The poet Pierre Michault was a secretary of Charles the Bold in 1466 when he was still count of Charolais. Michault de Caron, or Taillevent, sometimes confused with him, who has been described as a link between Chartier and Villon and as one of the best poets of his age, was Philip the Good's *valet de chambre* and *joueur des farces*. He wrote numerous poems in praise of his duke and some of more personal inspiration, in particular *Le Passe-Temps Michault*.

The court title, or post, of *valet de chambre*, was more often conferred on artists and craftsmen than on poets. The two most famous Burgundian *valets de chambre* were the sculptor Claus Sluter and the painter Jan van Eyck. The painter, in this period of history, was still very much a craftsman–decorator and his services were absolutely vital to the life of the court. Far more than painting pictures, he busied himself in the normal course of his duties decorating banners, painting the ducal motto on furniture and cannon, and colouring carvings. Naturally the Valois dukes of Burgundy employed the very finest masters available whether for painting their portraits or for painting their coat-of-arms on carriages. Jehan de Beaumetz decorated the chapel of the ducal château at Argilly in the 1380s; later he worked at the Charterhouse of Champmol outside Dijon. In 1397 he was succeeded as principal court painter by Jehan Malouel, who continued his work at the Charterhouse. The Flemish painter Melchior Broederlam, of Ypres, was the most famous and skilful of the Burgundian court artists around the year 1400. It was he who painted the shutters for the two magnificent altarpieces which still survive at Dijon, after they had been constructed, and their central retables carved, by Jaques de Baerze of Termonde in Flanders.

John the Fearless maintained Jehan Malouel in office and employed him in decorating armour and in colouring the funeral effigies of his parents. In 1412 he was required to paint a portrait of the duke for dispatch to King John I of Portugal. Some sixteen years later another Burgundian embassy was sent to Portugal, this time by Philip the Good, who was investigating the possibility of his marriage to King John's daughter Elizabeth, or Isabel, as she became known in Burgundy. The ambassadors took with them 'a *valet de chambre* of my lord of Burgundy named Jan van Eyck, who was an exquisite master of the art of painting, to paint my lady the infanta Elizabeth from life'. Born probably at Maaseik in the extreme east of the present-day Belgian province of Limbourg, Jan was taken over by Philip the Good when his first employer, the ruler of Holland John of Bavaria, died in 1425. That summer he was brought to Lille and set to work as official court painter 'because of the excellence of his artistic work', at an annual salary of £100 of Paris. The duke recognized Jan van Eyck as an artistic genius of the first rank. He actually went to his studio to see him at work and, in 1434, he stood as godfather to his son and sent six silver cups for the christening. When economies caused the temporary withholding of salaries, Philip the Good made an exception for Jan van Eyck 'for we should never find his equal in artistic skill'. How right the good duke was! Jan van Eyck has been accepted ever since as one of the greatest artists of all time.

The only other fifteenth-century Low Countries master who is generally considered the equal of van Eyck is Roger van der Weyden. Unfortunately, little is known for sure about this most elusive figure except that he was a native of Tournai who worked in Brussels as official civic painter and died there in 1464. Unlike Jan van Eyck, who for example carefully identified his famous painting of the Italian merchant Giovanni Arnolfini and his wife now in the National Gallery, London, by signing it with the words '*Johannes de Eyck fuit hic*' – 'Jan van Eyck was here', Roger does not seem to have signed his works. Certainly, not a single existing painting bears his signature; nor has any painting stated to be by him in a contemporary document survived. In spite of this, art historians have had little difficulty in establishing a number of paintings as indubitably by him, and some have even claimed that he was an official or titular Burgundian court painter. On the flimsiest of evidence they have almost unanimously attributed to him the famous portrait of Charles the Bold as a young man in the Dahlem Museum at Berlin; and they are nearly all agreed that the lost original portrait of Philip the Good which is duplicated in several early surviving copies was also the work of Roger van der Weyden. If they are right, van der Weyden was, like van Eyck, directly patronized and employed by the dukes of Burgundy.

Like painters, musicians were needed at court, above all to staff the dukes' musical chapel. And, as with artists, so with musicians, some of the foremost masters of the day found employment at the court of Burgundy. Among their chaplains the last two Valois dukes could proudly number composers like Gille Binchois, Anthoine Busnois and Hayne van Ghijzeghem. Philip the Good learned to play the harp, and is said to have personally heard and assessed the voices of potential new recruits to his chapel. Charles the Bold was widely known for his musical interests and aptitudes; he had taken lessons in music from the Englishman Robert Morton, who was a member of the ducal chapel towards the end of Philip the Good's reign. According to Chastellain, Charles 'had a fine clear voice, except for singing, and he was well versed in music', and Wielant echoes this: 'He also took pleasure in music and was himself a musician.

He could compose and sing willingly though he by no means had a good voice.' The Milanese ambassador Panigarola wrote of Duke Charles in one of his dispatches of May 1475 sent from the siege of Neuss: 'Even though he is in camp, every evening he has something new sung in his quarters and sometimes his lordship sings, though he does not have a good voice. But he is skilled in music – *perfecto musico*.' The Burgundian court provides a nearly unique example of a musical event finding its way into a chronicle. The author of the Dutch *Divisie-chronijk* records that, at Aachen in August 1473, Duke Charles was accompanied by 'his entire musical chapel and his mastersingers, who performed a beautiful musical service and office all day long in honour of the Mother of God'.

Besides the thirty or so chaplains, all skilled musicians or singers, of the ducal chapel under the last two Valois dukes, instrumentalists were employed at court for all kinds of musical entertainment. Philip the Good's twelve trumpeters sometimes formed up below his window and played a fanfare to wake him in the morning. Charles had them blow a fanfare when he formally set out on the campaign against Liège on 19 October 1467. His ordinance of 1469 mentions five *trompettes de guerre*, six *trompettes de menestrels* and three *joueurs des instrumens bas* on the permanent strength of the court. Bagpipes, cornets, organs and many other instruments are mentioned in the documents.

On the whole, the Valois dukes of Burgundy were not great builders. They maintained and enlarged their various palaces, at Dijon, Brussels and elsewhere, but these ducal building works cannot compare with the splendid contemporary efforts of some civic authorities. The town halls of Brussels, Louvain and Middelburg, for example, were all constructed in Philip the Good's reign. On the other hand the first Valois duke, Philip the Bold, was responsible for a great deal of military building in Flanders, especially the Tower of Burgundy at Sluis; for substantial restorations to ducal residences in Burgundy, especially at the château of Germolles; and, above all, for the foundation and construction of a magnificent new Charterhouse, for twenty-four instead of the usual twelve Carthusian monks, at Champmol just outside Dijon. Almost all its buildings were destroyed in 1793, and since then the Departmental lunatic asylum has been built on the site of this Burgundian St Denis. All that remains *in situ* is the main doorway or portal of the convent church and the so-called Well of Moses, which was originally a monumental Crucifixion towering some twenty-five feet above the pool of water in which it stood in the centre of the main cloister of the Charterhouse. But the carving which survives, five statues on the portal, one of them a superb likeness of Duke Philip the Bold, six full-size figures of Old Testament prophets round the pedestal of the Crucifixion, and the magnificent tomb of Philip the Bold now in the Dijon Museum, is substantially the work of the greatest sculptor then living north of the Alps, Claus Sluter of Haarlem in Holland. Most of this monumental statuary was created between Sluter's appointment as ducal *imagier* or sculptor and *valet de chambre* on 23 July 1389 and his death in 1405. It was completed by his nephew Claus de Werve.

What then was the contribution of the dukes of Burgundy to the literature and art of western Europe? A wide and influential sector of French fifteenth-century literature became specifically Burgundian; something which is particularly noticeable in historiography and in the many new versions of old romances of chivalry. Here the Burgundian impact was important at the time but, in a sense, temporary, for Burgundian literature was conservative and traditional. In the history of music the reverse is the case; the impact of Burgundy was a long-term one. The Burgundian musical chapel was only one among several, comparable perhaps in size and importance to those of the kings of France and the popes. Its chaplains came from famous choir schools like those of Liège and Cambrai, which incidentally were both of them enclaves in ducal territory. The Burgundian chapel made no vital impact on the European musical scene at the time, but this Burgundian musical tradition, which was Netherlandish in character, was transformed at the end of the fifteenth century by Maximilian into a new native German tradition of very real significance for the whole future of European music. In painting, the dukes were generous patrons, but Roger van der Weyden certainly and Jan van Eyck probably would have achieved fame and secured their position in the history of art without Burgundian ducal interventions. But this is not true of sculpture. Claus Sluter owed everything to Philip the Bold, as did the tradition of monumental funerary sculpture which Sluter helped to inaugurate. Sculpture and music were the two major arts to be most significantly enriched by the Valois dukes of Burgundy.

So much for the great living arts of literature, music, painting and sculpture. When we turn to lesser arts and crafts, some of which, like manuscript illumination, are no longer significantly living, we find them all superbly represented at the Burgundian court. The Burgundian ducal library, about a quarter of which still survives in the Royal Library at Brussels, was one of the finest ever put together up to that time. Philip the Good's scribe and editor, David Aubert, called him 'the Christian prince without any reservation best provided with a rich and authentic library'. By the time of his death in 1467 the library contained nearly 1,000 books and was certainly one of the finest in Europe. Yet in this as in nearly every other significant respect Philip the Good owed a great deal to his predecessors, for his father and grandfather had between them assembled at least 250 books, many of them superbly illuminated.

Europe's first two important princely libraries were installed in the 1360s, one in the Louvre at Paris by King Charles V; the other at Pavia by Galeazzo Visconti. By the end of the century each contained close on 1,000 volumes, while Philip the Bold and his wife together possessed a mere 200. His brother Duke John of Berry, who collected works of art instead of territories, had 300 books, among them some of the finest illuminated manuscripts ever produced, notably the *Très Riches Heures* of the brothers Limbourg. Philip the Bold's library was certainly less important than his brother's but it was still among the foremost princely collections of the time. He knew no Latin, and his only Latin books were liturgical and devotional. He possessed a fine series of bibles, 'hours', missals and psalters; he had *chansons de geste* like *Ogier of Denmark* and *Aymeri of Narbonne*; he had half-a-dozen Arthurian romances, including three works of Chrétien de Troyes; the usual tales of eastern travels, some chronicles, Bonet's *Tree of Battles*, a book on chess and the French translation, with illustrations, of the Emperor Frederick II's *On the Art of Hunting with Birds*. Many of his books were given to him; John of Berry gave him a book of hours in 1402. Others he bought; an illuminated Livy from Dino Rapondi in 1398 and three illumin-ated copies of Hayton's *Flower of Histories of the Orient* in Paris in 1403, two to give away. He also commissioned illuminated manuscripts, setting two of the Limbourg brothers to work on a magnificently illustrated bible in 1402. Indeed Philip the Bold seems to have discovered these illuminators and then passed them on to his brother of Berry.

It was mainly in the second half of his long reign, more

especially after 1445, that Philip the Good began to commission numerous manuscripts to add to the remarkable library he had inherited from Philip the Bold and John the Fearless. Many of them were illustrated large-format volumes, often of enormous size. Soon groups of scribes and illuminators were at work at Mons, Valenciennes, Hesdin, Lille, Oudenaarde, Bruges, Brussels and Ghent producing these lavishly illustrated books for the Burgundian ducal library and for other princely patrons. And of course the courtiers followed suit. Anthony, the bastard of Burgundy, assembled an admirable collection of his own which included the Breslau Froissart. So did Jehan de Bourgogne, count of Étampes and Nevers, the chronicler Jehan de Wavrin, Jehan de Croy and others.

Three men were chiefly responsible for providing Philip the Good with the books he wanted, and they employed the illuminators and other craftsmen needed to produce them. At Mons in Hainault Jehan Wauquelin acted as translator and scribe, but he contracted for the illustrations with miniaturists like Guillaume Vrelant and Loyset Liédet. The *Chronicles of Hainault*, translated from the Latin and beautifully illustrated, was a famous product of this atelier. At Lille, a canon of St Peter's, Jehan Miélot, was responsible for translating books and sometimes acted as scribe too. It was he who employed the exquisite illuminator Jehan le Tavernier of Oudenaarde. David Aubert, working at Bruges and Brussels, was more a scribe than anything else; he too provided illuminations by contracting with the artists.

What were these new books which Philip the Good had specially made for his library? Wauquelin provided a *Girart of Roussillon* and a *History of Alexander* besides the *Chronicles of Hainault* already mentioned. Aubert produced a three-volume *Chronicles and Conquests of Charlemagne* and a four-volume *History of Charles Martel*; his *Renaud of Montauban* filled five large tomes. Most of these, and others, are in fact prose versions of earlier medieval epic poems and romances. We see the duke's literary interests closely reflected in the new acquisitions to his library. Several of these massive works were only completed after Philip the Good's death, by Charles the Bold. He added only a few more books to the library, but he employed some of the finest scribes and illuminators available making *de luxe* copies of his household and military ordinances.

A prince's books were still in the fifteenth century often

regarded as a part of his *trésor* or treasure, that is, his personal valuables. At the court of Burgundy the books were already in Philip the Bold's reign under the separate care of a librarian or *garde des livres*, keeper of the books. As a matter of fact the librarian was at that time also the court hairdresser, but that is beside the point. Another important part of the *trésor* was the jewellery and plate. Here too, Philip the Bold laid down foundations on which his successors could build. He possessed nine gold or silver-gilt crosses for use in chapel; gold and silver-gilt statuettes, mostly of saints, one of them a 'St' Charlemagne, reliquaries and plate, including an ancient silver-gilt cup which was supposed to have belonged to Julius Caesar; however, this had not deterred Philip the Bold from engraving his coat-of-arms on the cover. Among these valuables was an unusually large boar's tooth. John the Fearless seems not to have added much to this ducal treasure, but he commissioned precious objects in quantity. In 1406 he gave away 315 gold carpenter's planes, many of them studded with diamonds and engraved with his motto. He had chosen the plane as his emblem to symbolically plane away the knotty club which was his rival the duke of Orleans's favourite emblem. A few years later there was another distribution of planes: 200 gold ones for John the Fearless's courtiers and 300 in silver for his servants. At the start of Philip the Good's reign, in 1420, the Burgundian ducal treasury contained sixteen pieces of plate in solid gold, fifty-three of silver-gilt or silver, and hundreds of jewels. Charles the Bold was a great lover of jewellery, and he liked to put the ducal plate on exhibition on court occasions. When he entertained the Emperor Frederick III to a banquet at St Maximin's Abbey outside Trier on 7 October 1473 his plate was set out on a raised sideboard at one end of the hall. There were 'thirty-three gold and silver vessels of many kinds, seventy jugs, large and small, a hundred dishes and cups decorated with pearls and precious stones, six large silver ladles and twelve gold and silver basins for washing hands, six unicorns' horns, etc.'.

Tapestries too are described in the inventories of the Burgundian ducal *trésor*. Philip the Bold had tapestries with religious subjects such as the Coronation of the Virgin, the Creed, and the Prophets; he also had recent history: Bertrand du Guesclin, a famous French captain of his own lifetime, and the battle of Roosebeke, specially commissioned by himself. Jason and the Golden Fleece, the Nine Worthies, the *Romance of the Rose* and the Twelve Peers of France also figured on his tapestries. John the Fearless added to his father's collection a tapestry representing his victory at Othée against Liège. Philip the Good, besides the above-mentioned pieces and Renaud de Montauban, Godefroi de Bouillon and other heroes of chivalry, possessed 'nine large tapestries and two smaller ones, worked in gold, showing plovers, partridges and other birds, with the figures of the late Duke John and my lady the Duchess his wife, both on foot and on horseback'. That the duke took a personal interest in his tapestries is shown by an entry in the ducal accounts recording part of the payment of 8,960 crowns to some tapestry merchants of Tournai for eight large pieces of tapestry illustrating the History of Gideon and the Golden Fleece. They had agreed 'to have the cartoons, with the figures and emblems decided on and explained to them by my lord the duke, made by Baudouin de Bailleul or the best artist they can find'.

The chronicler Jehan de Haynin was so impressed by the tapestries adorning the great hall set up at Bruges for Charles the Bold's wedding in 1468 that he wrote down a lengthy description of them. 'The ceiling of the great hall was lined with white or blue silk or cloth and the walls were hung with fine and rich tapestries of embroidered serge, depicting the story and mystery of Gideon and the Fleece.' Near the sideboard were the tapestries 'of the great battle of Liège, where Duke John of Burgundy and Duke William of Bavaria, count of [Holland and] Hainault, defeated the Liègeois near Othée in the year 1408, on a Sunday, 23 November'. He also noted tapestries of King Clovis of France and King Gundobad of Burgundy and another of 'King Ahasuerus, who governed 127 provinces'. In 1473 at Trier the 'story of how Jason got the Golden Fleece in the land of Colchis' was on show, also a set of tapestries of Alexander the Great.

The Burgundian ducal wardrobe was one of the finest in existence. Philip the Bold possessed thirty-six *houppelandes* or robes of satin, velvet or cloth-of-gold, and the skins of 9,408 ermines, sufficient to line eleven more *houppelandes* and a mantle. Two of his best *houppelandes* were of crimson velvet with sleeves covered with pearls and precious stones. He appeared at one court festivity with his eldest son and a retinue of 130 knights and squires, all dressed in green velvet embroidered with the ducal coat-of-arms; for another he had four velvet doublets specially made, one of which was sewn all over with sheep and swans, each with a bell in its beak or round its neck, picked out in pearls. John the Fearless followed in his father's footsteps. He appears in illuminated manuscripts wearing a high-fronted black velvet cap and with planes embroidered all over his robes. Of Philip the Good, Olivier de la Marche wrote that 'he liked clothes and adornments and the way he wore them suited him so well and agreeably that he had no equals in this', and Chastellain says 'he dressed smartly in rich array and was always changing his clothes'.

As in most things, so sartorially, Charles the Bold simply followed the pattern set by his predecessors. For his ceremonial meeting with Frederick III at Trier he spent £38,830 on a special issue of materials to clothe the thousand courtiers and attendants he took with him. Each was provided with sufficient for a short or long robe and a pourpoint. The cloth was graded according to rank: twenty-five leading courtiers received cloth-of-gold, many others had velvet or satin, still others were given camlet or damask, and two hundred menials were clothed in wool. Every conceivable colour was represented, some wore black and crimson, some wore blue, white and black, the kings-of-arms wore crimson and violet, the duke's fool wore green and crimson, twelve officers of the guard wore silver brocade robes and crimson pourpoints. Contemporaries were staggered by Duke Charles's personal turn-out on the various ceremonial occasions at Trier. More than once he visited the emperor in an ermine-lined open-fronted cloth-of-gold mantle reaching to the ground, with a collar or cape reaching half-way down his back – longer than the capes worn by the electoral princes of the Empire. Underneath this mantle his black cloth-of-gold coat bordered with pearls was studded all over with diamonds, sapphires and rubies 'which stood out and twinkled like stars'.

Duke Charles's splendid plumed and jewelled hat was a source of wonder and curiosity. Was it a ducal or an archducal hat? One Italian observer described it as 'an extraordinarily splendid crown, with rubies and pearls, diamonds and sapphires . . . to me it looked like the crown of a king'. One such hat, described in detail in the accounts, cost close on £500. It or another was left behind on the field of Grandson and formed part of the booty captured there by the victorious Swiss and their allies. It was sold in the sixteenth century by the civic authorities of Basel to the famous German merchant and banker Johann Jakob Fugger. Unfortunately only a drawing of it has survived.

The books, paintings, music, jewellery and other trappings of the court so far described were an intrinsic part of its day-to-day existence, but only on special occasions was this aristocratic paraphernalia really displayed and used to the best possible effect. Traditionally, these ceremonial events were weddings, tournaments, banquets, funerals, receptions of distinguished guests, and the dukes' first visits as duke or count to their various lands. Often several events happened at once – tournaments and banquets invariably accompanied weddings. Charles the Bold seems to have added to the list by turning the publication of treaties and ordinances and the reception of ambassadors into ceremonial court occasions. The function of these lavish and elaborate ceremonies was to enhance the duke's prestige by impressing his power and wealth on all and sundry. They were public, not private, functions. At the famous Feast of the Pheasant, held in Lille by Philip the Good in February 1454, there was a public gallery.

For the very first of the great Burgundian court spectacles, Philip the Bold's wedding in Ghent in April 1369, wagon-loads of plate and jewels, as well as musicians, heralds and jousting horses, were brought to Ghent, some of them borrowed from the king of France, to impress the Flemings with the wealth and generosity of their future ruler. The Flemish nobility received a shower of expensive gifts, and special banquets were given for them and for the citizens of Bruges. Another splendid Burgundian wedding ceremony was arranged at Cambrai by Philip the Bold on 12 April 1385. It was a double event: the duke's son John married Margaret of Bavaria and her brother William of Bavaria married John's sister Margaret of Burgundy. Just as he had exploited his French connection – he was King Charles VI's uncle – militarily in the war he had to fight for his Flemish inheritance against the rebels of Ghent and financially as well, so now Philip the Bold used it to add to the magnificence and solemnity of his court. Besides the loan of the French crown jewels, or a large part of them, for his own adornment, Duke Philip actually brought his royal uncle to Cambrai in person to take part in the ceremonies. Philip the Bold's livery and that of his retinue was of red and green velvet, and its total cost was £34,000 – nearly the same as what was paid by Charles the Bold for his court livery at Trier nearly ninety years later. In the market-place at Cambrai after the weddings knights from France, the Low Countries, Spain, Scotland and Germany competed, using some of the 1,000 lances provided by the duke of Burgundy, for a jewelled clasp which, in the event, was removed from the bosom of the duchess of Burgundy and presented to a young knight from Hainault.

Spouses brought from overseas to wed Burgundian dukes were married at or near Bruges: Isabel of Portugal to Philip the Good in January 1430 and Margaret of York to Charles the Bold in 1468. Naturally both of them landed at Sluis. In both cases the wedding banquet was held in a wooden hall specially erected in the courtyard of the ducal palace in Bruges, which was normally used for tennis. Whereas Philip married Isabel at Sluis, Charles was married to Margaret in the church of Notre-Dame at Damme.

Philip the Good's accounts record the cost of bringing fifteen cart-loads of tapestries, one hundred loads of Burgundian wine, fifty loads of furnishings and jewels, and fifteen cart-loads of arms and armour for tournaments, from Dijon and Lille to Bruges for his wedding. His punctilious herald, Jehan Lefèvre, wrote a detailed account of the proceedings which might serve as a sort of official record. He noted the painted wooden lion set up on the palace façade which poured wine from its paw into a basin below; the stag and the unicorn in the courtyard which dispensed hippocras and rose-water in the same way; the minstrels' gallery inside the hall for sixty heralds, trumpets and musicians; the coats-of-arms of the duke's lands and leading gentry decorating a gilded tree. He described the tableaux or spectacles which accompanied each dish served at the banquet: men got up as savages riding on roast pigs, a castle with men and women in it holding pennons, and a huge pie containing a live sheep dyed blue, with gilded horns.

Charles the Bold's wedding festivities in July 1468, which seem to have been even more lavish and bizarre, are noteworthy for the abundant source material concerning them. A ducal official called Fastre Hollet kept a special account of 'the works and also the entremets and decoration carried out at Bruges for the wedding of my lord Duke Charles'. Chroniclers, most notably Jehan de Haynin, wrote lengthy eye-witness reports. Other contemporary descriptions found their way in Latin into an encomium of Duke Charles by an ecclesiastic called Symon Mulart; in German into the town chronicle of Strasbourg; in Flemish to the burgomaster of Lübeck; in English into England; and in French into a report written by Olivier de la Marche, who was a member of the committee entrusted with preparing the entremets at the banquet. Some of these reports give ridiculously exaggerated descriptions of the exact quantities of food consumed at the banquets: '200 fat oxen, 63 fat pigs, 1,000 pounds of lard, 2,500 calves, 2,500 fat sheep, 3,600 shoulders of mutton . . . 11,800 small chickens, 18,640 pigeons, 3,640 swans, 2,100 peacocks, 1,668 cranes', and so on. Nearly all the accounts describe how, in the procession on 3 July, behind the town councillors of Bruges in their flowing black silk robes came deputations of the foreign merchants resident in Bruges: the Hansards, the Spaniards, fifty Venetians with a figure of St Mark, the Genoese with their patron saint George, and fifty Florentines on foot and nearly that number mounted, all carrying lighted torches. One observer also noticed merchants of Lucca and Scotsmen, but it rained so hard at that point that he could not note down anything further.

Nine tableaux or pageants were presented to the bride at the street corners as she made her way through Bruges. The first was of Adam and Eve; 'it was so marvellously well done, for it was not in imagery, but it was acted by real living people'. The other pageants that followed all represented episodes from the Bible – the Song of Songs, Moses, the Crucifixion and so on – except for the second which, incongruously but typically, was 'Alexander the great conqueror', and the eighth, which was 'a maiden sitting between a lion and a leopard, bearing the arms of Burgundy, which Hercules conquered from the beasts'. On either side of the palace gateway the figure of an archer, one drawing a crossbow and the other a longbow, poured out red and white wine. Inside the courtyard a golden pelican poured hippocras out of its breast. All accounts of the banquet give space to the remarkable 'working' model of the castle which Charles the Bold had built at Gorinchem in Holland. According to the above-quoted English account, at each of its four windows there appeared, first, a bear with 'a trumpet with a banner of the duke's arms and he held it cleverly with his fore-paw and each one of them blew stoutly well'; next goats appeared 'with long pipes and piped'; then wolves, and lastly asses. But Fastre Hollet has it differently in his account. He says that four wolves appeared first to sing a ballad about the festivities, then four hares playing on flutes, four boars blowing trumpets and, lastly, four reed-playing donkeys.

For a week after the wedding jousts were held daily in the

market-place at Bruges. The champion defending the Tree of Gold against all comers was Anthony, bastard of Burgundy, who had been commanded by the Lady of the Secret Island to hold a joust at which 101 lances had to be broken either against him or by him against others, and 101 sword blows had to be exchanged. The bastard Anthony set about achieving this to the best of his ability from the Sunday to the Friday, when he was unfortunately put out of action by a kick from a horse which broke his knee.

Tournaments always went with weddings, but some famous ones were held separately, in their own right as it were. These *pas d'armes* or passages of arms have already been discussed in connection with Jaques de Lalaing and literature at the Burgundian court. There were a good many other jousts like his *pas d'armes* of the Fountain of Tears and the *pas d'armes* of the Tree of Gold just described. For example in 1443 Pierre de Bauffremont, lord of Charny, and twelve companions had set up a pavilion at the Tree of Charlemagne a mile outside Dijon and challenged all comers. But single combats, between two individuals or two groups, were perhaps more usual. Some of them took on the character of judicial duels, others were more like miniature battles. At Arras in 1430 five French knights fought for five days against five Burgundian knights. In 1423 at the same place the two contestants tilted on horseback with lances on the first day but could not break the required three lances because one of them was slightly wounded. Next day they fought with axes on foot and one of them was accused of cheating because he raised the other's visor during the combat and struck him in the face with his gauntlet. At both these tourneys and many others Philip the Good acted as judge.

Arras was a favourite spot for Burgundian jousting. One of the 'hardest fought and most hazardous' feats of arms took place in the main square there, under the presidency of Duke Philip, in April 1446. It was a protracted duel between a Castilian squire in the service of the duke of Milan called Galiot Balthazar, and Philippe, lord of Ternant, a ducal councillor-chamberlain and Knight of the Golden Fleece. Galiot had left Milan 'to travel and see the world and to perform bodily feats of arms in order to acquire renown, which is and should be the terrestrial paradise of noble young courage'. He was challenged by the lord of Ternant. The lists, and the pavilions of the contestants, Philippe's of blue and black damask, were duly set up, and the proceedings opened by the duke at precisely 3 o'clock. First, Galiot and Philippe fought on foot with lances. As they approached one another Galiot sprang into the air as if his armour meant nothing to him, handling his lance as if it were merely an arrow. After each encounter the contestants had to withdraw seven paces, which were carefully measured out by a herald with a knotted cord; a pace being two and a half feet 'as measured by the hand of a knight or at least a nobleman'. Next, they fought, or rather exchanged eleven blows, with jousting swords, this time withdrawing only five paces between encounters. Then the marshal of the lists brought out two battle-axes and offered the choice to Galiot who again showed his spirit by leaping in the air before rushing at his opponent. This time Philippe de Ternant jumped aside and dealt Galiot a tremendous blow on the basinet as he lumbered past. Any ordinary man would have been felled to the ground, but Galiot only staggered a little, then recovered, and the fifteen axe blows laid down beforehand were accomplished. A few days later the mounted combat took place, but not till Galiot had been ordered by the duke to remove some steel spikes from his horse's trappings. As often happened, the duke stopped the contest by throwing down his white baton before the stipulated thirty-one encounters had taken place.

The other inevitable accompaniment of a wedding was feasting, and this likewise often continued for several days. Banquets were organized on other occasions too. In 1435 Philip the Good gave one at Lille in honour of some visiting dignitaries. The table decorations were painted by the ducal artist and *valet de chambre* Hue de Boulogne: the arms of the leading guests were displayed on banners hanging from hawthorn trees covered in gold and silver blossom; a live peacock on a dish was surrounded by ten gilt lions each holding a banner emblazoned with the arms of all Philip the Good's lands. Hue de Boulogne also had to paint the fifty-six wooden plates specially made for this feast – in grey and black, with the duke's favourite emblem, a flint and steel with sparks and flames, on them.

Rather than describe once again here the best-known of all Burgundian banquets, the Feast of the Pheasant, held at Lille on 17 February 1454 and mentioned several times already, it seems desirable to point out something which is often forgotten, that exactly the same kind of entertainment, or spectacle, was provided at the courts of the other European rulers. There was nothing exceptional about Burgundy, at any rate in this respect. Witness, for example, the feasting at Chambéry in Savoy which accompanied the wedding of the duke of Savoy's son Louis in February 1434. At supper on the day before the wedding swans were brought in carrying the coats-of-arms of the guests, followed by two of the duke of Savoy's heralds displaying the arms of Savoy. Afterwards twenty-six knights, squires and ladies dressed in vermilion silk bordered with fur danced together in couples. Next day mass was sung by the duke of Savoy's chaplains 'so melodiously that it was beautiful to hear, for at that time the duke's chapel was held to be the finest in the world'. At the wedding banquet that day one of the entremets was 'a ship with a sail, mast and crow's nest with a man in it, and with the captain in the poop'. It was loaded with fish and was brought in between rows of singing sirens. Music was provided by trumpets and minstrels, and dancing again followed. At supper a horse got up like an elephant was led in by two valets, and a gentleman wearing wings of peacock's feathers in a wooden castle strapped to its back shot red and white roses among the guests with a bow. He was supposed to represent the god of love. That night the dancers wore white. At another feast four men masquerading as wild men or savages brought in a live goat or ibex in a leafy garden full of roses; at another the entremets was a huge pie which, when opened, revealed a man dressed as an eagle with very realistic beak, head, wings and body. When he flapped his wings a flock of white doves flew up and fluttered over the tables. The Burgundian herald Jehan Lefèvre, who wrote a description of the proceedings, was present with Duke Philip the Good. He says that 'the festivities were as fine as any to be seen and because of their beauty I have set them down in writing'. Evidently the court of Savoy stood on an equal footing with that of Burgundy.

Naturally, funerals were among the most solemn of court occasions. That of Philip the Bold, who died in the Stag Inn at Hal near Brussels on 27 April 1404, was unusually elaborate because of the decision to bury him in the Charterhouse of Champmol outside Dijon, some 250 miles from Hal as the crow flies. A special account was kept of the cost of this operation on a parchment roll eight feet long and one foot wide which is still fortunately preserved in the archives at Dijon. The corpse was first opened and embalmed. The entrails were buried on the spot, in the church of Notre-Dame at Hal. The heart was sent to the French abbey of St Denis outside Paris to be placed next to the mortal remains of the duke's royal ancestors. The body was clothed in the habit of a Carthusian monk, wrapped in thirty-two ells of waxed cloth and three cowhides, and placed in a leaden coffin weighing 700 lb. The funeral cortège left Hal on 1 May and the dead duke was finally interred at Dijon on 16 June. Along much of the route, through Burgundian territory, the hearse was accompanied by Philip the Bold's sons, by his sixteen chaplains, by leading members of the court and the administration, and by representatives of the Flemish nobility, all dressed in black at the duke's expense. The coffin was draped with a pall of cloth of gold edged with black, with a large crimson velvet cross in the centre. At each corner fluttered a blue banner emblazoned with the arms of Philip the Bold. The hearse was drawn by six horses caparisoned in black and followed by sixty mourners or *pleurants* dressed in black gowns. Outside Dijon the cortège was met by 100 burgesses and 100 poor men, also dressed in black, as well as by all the clergy of the town. Other Burgundian funerals followed a similar pattern. Philip the Good's body, heart and entrails were all buried at Bruges where he died. Later the body was transferred to Dijon for interment in the Charterhouse.

Solemn ceremonial was always laid on when the duke made a formal visit to one of his towns; all the more so if he was making his first visit, or joyous entry, to the capital of a territory. Traditionally the expenses and the responsibility for such functions lay with the municipality concerned, so that they were as much civic as court occasions. One of the most elaborate was staged when Charles the Bold entered Dijon on 23 January 1474. The usual platforms were set up at street corners with various personages on them, representing prophets, the three Estates of the duchy of Burgundy, Jesus Christ, and the inevitable Gideon. All were carefully identified by scrolls explaining who they were and what they were doing. A learned ecclesiastic of Dijon had searched through the scriptures to find texts appropriate to the lion on one of the stages, which held a sword in one of its paws and had Charles the Bold's coat-of-arms hanging from its neck. As if this identification of their duke with the lion was not enough, the good citizens of Dijon presented King Solomon on another stage, again with suitable quotations from the scriptures. The ducal procession passed all these representations on its way to and from the church of St Bénigne, where Charles was solemnly invested with his duchy of Burgundy by the symbolic placing of a ring on his finger by the abbot. Later the duke made a speech in which 'he did not forget to mention the kingdom of Burgundy, which the French had for a long time usurped by turning it into a duchy'.

Charles the Bold seldom missed an opportunity for speech-making. He liked to mark his solemn entry into one of his lands by appearing in state and haranguing the assembled company. At Nancy, on 18 December 1475, he celebrated his acquisition of the duchy of Lorraine – by military conquest as it happens – by calling a gathering of courtiers and representatives of the three Estates of the duchy. It was held two hours after dark because such ceremonies were more impressive by torchlight. Duke Charles mounted a dais at one end of the hall on which, at least six steps up, was set his throne, covered in brocade. He wore 'a long ducal robe of dark crimson velvet lined with ermine and beaver with a hat on his head, more or less in the form of a crown, richly adorned with the largest pearls, balas-rubies and carbuncles'. On the tribunal, but below the ducal throne, were seated ambassadors or representatives of the pope, the kings of Naples and France, and the duke of Milan. When his chancellor had finished, Duke Charles himself spoke, promising that he would hold Lorraine 'in the greatest affection, even more than his other territories, as commonly one prefers the works of one's own hands or things acquired by oneself'.

The visits of neighbouring rulers were also the occasion for displays of pageantry. When King Charles VI of France was received in Dijon by his uncle Duke Philip the Bold in February 1390 nearly 200 knights and squires were issued with the royal livery of vermilion and white velvet or satin in honour of the king. Dijon was carefully spruced up and the gardens of St Stephen's Abbey, requisitioned for the jousting, were cleared and partly levelled. The king was received in a pavilion set up in the courtyard behind the ducal palace, and a banquet inside the palace followed. Since it was Lent, salmon and other choice fish had to be specially brought from Basel. The king did not depart until the jousting had continued for three days and he had been shown round the Charterhouse of Champmol, then under construction, by a proud duke.

Charles the Bold's parading of the ambassadors of foreign powers at his court has already been mentioned. An event typical of many was staged on 13 June 1469, when ten ambassadors of the duke of Milan, two of them clad down to the ground in cloth-of-gold, with their thirty-six attendants, were formally received by the duke in the great hall of his castle at Ghent – the Castle of the Counts or the Gravensteen – which had been richly decorated for the purpose. 'The duke sat there in splendid majesty', wrote the local chronicler in Flemish, 'with the duke of Cleves on his left and the chancellor on his right, and all his noble officers and attendants stood in order along both sides of the hall.'

Duke Charles also turned the promulgation of his ordinances and the publication or ratification of treaties into court cere-monies. At the siege of Neuss he assembled his courtiers on 3 April 1475 in the church of the Oberkloster where he was lodged, in order solemnly to announce the conclusion of the League of Moncalieri between Burgundy, Savoy and Milan. When the church was full of people, the black silk curtains surrounding the duke's oratory were drawn aside, revealing Charles the Bold enthroned on a dais under a golden canopy embroidered with his arms. His cloth-of-gold robe was lined with sable and he wore 'a black velvet hat with a plume of gold loaded with the largest balas-rubies and diamonds'. While he sat there in solitary and almost regal majesty, nearly everyone else remained standing. After the speechifying he descended from the dais to a fanfare of eight trumpets.

The everyday life of the Burgundian court was not very much less splendid or solemn than were these special events. Pomp and ceremony continued daily, always with the same function, of projecting a favourable image of the great duke. Note the suitably awe-struck remark of some deputies from the city of Metz, sent on embassy to Charles the Bold in 1473: 'we went to see my lord of Burgundy at dinner, and we saw all the mystery and all the triumph which occurred when he dined'. The pomp was supported and regularized by a strict and well-developed etiquette which is described in a little book called *The Honours of the Court* written by the daughter of a Portuguese lady-in-waiting of Duchess Isabel of Burgundy, Alienor de Poitiers. We can learn from it that the duchess of Burgundy settled doubts about etiquette by consulting a reference work on the subject; also how to lay the table for a prince or a princess, who can kiss whom, how low to curtsy and who should precede whom. Both the last two Valois dukes were sticklers for etiquette. Philip the Good made himself look ridiculous when he played host to the Dauphin Louis of France (later King Louis XI) at Brussels in 1456. According to Chastellain, when they first met in the palace courtyard Philip remained kneeling in front of Louis for so long that the dauphin eventually exclaimed, "Pon my faith, good uncle, if you don't get up I shall go away and leave you.' Later, when Louis doffed his hat to Philip, the duke went down on one knee and remained like that until the dauphin replaced his hat. Charles the Bold was just the same. On 30 September 1473 he rode into Trier with the Emperor Frederick III in pouring rain. In the market-place difficulties of etiquette arose because Duke Charles 'wanted to accompany the emperor as far as his lodgings, and likewise the emperor wanted to accompany the duke to his lodgings, and they were a good half-hour in this dispute, each with his hat in his hand'.

Routine court life was to a large extent also dominated by religious devotion. In this respect all four dukes seem to have been identical, and their behaviour and beliefs were no different from everyone else's. Philip the Bold read a book of hours with the aid of a lantern and spectacles. He meditated alone in his oratory and went on pilgrimages to various places in France. He carried a rosary and reliquary with him wherever he went and gave alms liberally. He paid for candles and offered them at holy shrines. Once a year a statue of the Virgin in Tournai cathedral was adorned at his expense with a robe and mantle of cloth-of-gold lined with miniver and embroidered with his and his wife's coats-of-arms. Each year, too, he gave one fat pig for each living member of his family to the church of St Anthony at Pont-de-Norges. Before dawn on 22 November 1443 Duke Philip the Good, who was at Arlon five leagues away, had news of the conquest of Luxembourg by his troops. But instead of galloping off to share their triumph he went to mass, said his hours, and then dallied in his oratory saying prayers of thanksgiving. His soldiers were impatient, muttering that the duke was certainly taking his time; couldn't he make up for lost paternosters on some other occasion? When this was reported to Philip, his comment was that 'if God has given me victory he will keep it for me'. Philip the Good heard mass daily, but since he found it hard, towards the end of his life, to get up in the mornings, he took to the habit of attending mass in the afternoons. Like Louis XI of France, he obtained a papal dispensation to permit him to do this.

Of Charles the Bold the papal emissary at his court reported to the pope: 'He is very well resolved in our favour; steadfast, prudent, catholic and devout.' An Italian at his court described how 'about half an hour or sometimes an hour after his supper . . . certain legends of the saints are read for a space of two hours'. Before engaging the enemy outside Neuss on 23 May 1475 Charles the Bold 'went to the church near his pavilion to pray to our glorious Lady'. In June 1468 he sent knights with specified sums of money to burn candles for him in the churches of Notre-Dame at Liesse, St Martin at Tours, St Hubert in the Ardennes, St Nicholas at Varangéville and the Holy Spirit at Rue. These religious activities and attitudes were part and parcel of court life in Valois Burgundy.

One important function of the court was to provide sporting facilities for the duke. Philip the Good 'was skilful on horseback, liked the bow and shot very well, and was excellent at tennis. Out of doors, his chief pastime was hunting, and he spared no expense over it.' He wrote to his nephew Duke John I of Cleves in the winter of 1451–2 from Brussels: 'I do nothing save go hunting, but the wild boars are so thin that they run like the wind.' Philip the Bold, too, was a keen huntsman and falconer. The *vénerie* or ducal hunt and the *fauconnerie* were the two court offices responsible for the field sports of those days. Each comprised a staff of twenty or thirty persons. The headquarters of the hunt was the duchy of Burgundy; falconry was a sport for the northern territories. The hunt supplied the duke's table with venison when he was in the duchy. In 1427 the master huntsman Jehan de Foissy was allowed £2,000 per annum to cover all his expenses, which included the feeding, mainly with bread, of ninety-five hounds. The *fauconnerie* was staffed in 1463 by a master falconer, three falconers, three assistants to look after the sparrowhawks, and valets. Duke Philip the Good was trying to purchase a goshawk in 1442 and in 1446–7 he bought ten gyrfalcons from Norway. In November 1461 he lost one of his best falcons, a saker (*le grant sacre*), in Luxembourg, but it was recovered in Austria and returned to him in Brussels the following July. It seems that his falcons all carried on their bells or other fittings the name and arms of the duke of Burgundy.

The dukes of Burgundy were constantly on the move, though Philip the Bold and Philip the Good did settle down for long periods in one place, the former in Paris and the latter mainly in Brussels. A picture of the Burgundian court in transit was unwittingly painted by the clerk who kept the accounts of the

receipt-general of all finances. It had been in Burgundy throughout the winter of 1434-5, but in April it was transported from
Dijon to Arras and Lille. The move took almost a month, and
the hire of carts alone cost nearly 5,000 francs. Seventy-two
carts were used, most of them drawn by five or six horses. The
convoy was accompanied by two carpenters to make good the
breakages. Five carts were needed for the duke's jewels, four
for his tapestries, one for spices, one for the chapel furnishings,
one for the trumpeters' and minstrels' gear, and two for
artillery. The kitchen required five, the bread pantry and wine
pantry three each, and one was taken up with an enormous
marquee. The duchess's things occupied at least fifteen carts,
including two for her tapestries, one for her spices, two for her
jewels, and three for her trunks. Even the one-year-old Charles,
count of Charolais, required two carts for his toys and other
belongings. The move was supervised by an equerry specially
deputed for this purpose by the duke.

The traditions, the activities, the organization, of the Burgundian court all went back to its original creator Duke Philip the
Bold. In spite of the varying interests of the different Valois dukes,
not to mention the passing years, changes were slight. The same
literary concerns, the same religious attitudes, the same re-
creations are apparent throughout its century-long history.
There is no sign of the humanism that was sweeping through
Italy at this time; no sign that the Italian Renaissance, an intellectual and cultural movement which was broadly simultaneous
with the rise of Burgundy, was impinging on the dukes and their
court; no sign, that is, before Charles the Bold. How far was he
affected by the Italian Renaissance?

In January 1474 Louis XI gave Charles the Bold a book about
Charlemagne and other Frankish kings. It was written in
Italian, and the king explained to Charles that he gave it to him
'knowing that he was deeply devoted to the customs, ways of
life and methods of government of the Italians, so that he could
not delight in them more than he did'. Duke Charles certainly
knew Italian well enough to speak his mind in it at a public
audience he gave in May 1475 to the papal legate Alexander
Nani, bishop of Forlì, in the presence of the Neapolitan and
Milanese ambassadors. And at the chapter of the Order of the
Golden Fleece held at Valenciennes in May 1473 he replied to the
Venetian ambassador in Italian.

There had always been Italians at the Burgundian court. Dino

Rapondi of Lucca, resident at Bruges, was a ducal councillor
and *maître d'hôtel* in Philip the Bold's reign. In about 1444 a fifteen-
year-old Italian prince, the bastard son of the marquis of Ferrara
Lionello d'Este, was sent to be brought up at the Burgundian
court. He became the companion and probably the friend of
Charles the Bold, who was his junior by a few years only. Was
this association the origin of Charles's Italian awareness?
Francesco d'Este stayed on at court; indeed he remained for at
least thirty years in the service of Burgundy. In 1469 he was
joined at court by another Italian prince, a cousin of his, Rodolfo
Gonzaga, who was a younger son of the marquis of Mantua.
He certainly brought a retinue of Italians with him, as did another
Italian visitor, Federico, younger son of King Ferrante of Naples,
who stayed with Duke Charles from September 1475 until 21 June
1476. One of his attendants was a famous Neapolitan physician
who later treated Louis XI for apoplexy, Angelo Cato.

Besides princes, other Italians flocked to the Burgundian court
under Charles the Bold. Among the courtiers who were issued
with materials for their robes for the meeting of Duke Charles
with the emperor at Trier in 1473 were the Florentine merchant
and ducal councillor Tommaso Portinari, who was the manager
of the Bruges branch of the Medici bank; Angelo and Johanne
de Monforte, sons of Charles the Bold's Neapolitan *condottiere*
Cola de Monforte, count of Campobasso; Johanne de Candida,
ducal secretary and a famous engraver of medallions; and
Giuliano de Padua, 'a Venetian who brought news of the new
doge of Venice'.

Charles the Bold was on intimate terms with several of the
Italian ambassadors at his court. He discussed his health, his
political prospects and plans, his military projects, and many
other matters, freely with them, and he often sought their
advice. One of them was Bernardo Bembo, Venetian ambassador
from 1470 to 1474. Like so many Italians, Bembo admired Charles
the Bold, noting sadly in 1477: 'So did a cruel death carry away
the most mighty duke of Burgundy.' Another was Johanne
Petro Panigarola, who stuck to Duke Charles like a leech from
13 March 1475 until 7 August 1476. There were papal envoys too,
like Onofrio de Santa Croce, bishop of Tricarico, who was sent
to sort out the affairs of Liège, and Petro Aliprandi, who stayed
at the Burgundian court while waiting to undertake a mission
to England.

The recruitment of Italian *condottieri* for the Burgundian army has already been mentioned. Charles the Bold greatly admired these men and their contribution to the Italian element at court should not be overlooked. He had brought them 'to instruct his own people, who had become clumsy and block-headed in the art of war because they had been maintained in peace by his father for twenty years'.

It is easy enough to identify and enumerate this Italian influx at Charles the Bold's court, but difficult to show how it bore fruit. Charles may have worn Italian-style hats, but he continued to write a crabbed, untidy, gothic hand even though he admired the italic script of Duke Galeazzo Maria Sforza of Milan, who took the trouble to write him an autograph letter. He may have been cruel and unscrupulous; he certainly displayed arbitrary and absolutist tendencies as a ruler, but were these attributes in any conceivable sense Italian? He commissioned French translations of classical works – Quintus Curtius's *Alexander the Great*, Xenophon's *Cyropaedia*, Caesar's *Gallic War* – but does this make him a humanist? When the Flemish lawyer–chronicler Philippe Wielant says that Duke Charles 'took pleasure in the deeds of Julius Caesar, of Pompey, of Hannibal, of Alexander the Great and of other great and famous men, whom he wished to follow and imitate', he is certainly not implying that the duke was interested in classical literature as such. Nonetheless it would be less than fair to suggest that the Burgundian court did not change under Charles the Bold. It did. A fresh wind was blowing from Italy and Duke Charles opened windows to it. He surrounded himself with Italians and spoke the language. But, if ever there was such a thing as a Renaissance prince, it certainly was not Charles the Bold.

The material remains of Burgundian civilization which actually survive to this day are probably unique for the period both in quantity and quality. Architecturally, however, Burgundy has fared badly. The ducal splendour of the once magnificent palace of the Coudenberg in Brussels, created in the main by Philip the Good, has had to make way for royalty. The Cour des Princes or Prinsenhof at Bruges has also disappeared completely, as has the castle of Hesdin in Artois, though this favourite residence of the Valois dukes was not substantially altered or improved by them. At Dijon the Charterhouse of Champmol was almost wholly destroyed at the end of the eighteenth century and the ducal Sainte-Chapelle, once the finest Gothic church in Dijon and the headquarters of the Order of the Golden Fleece, was blown up in 1802. Already in the late seventeenth century the ducal palace at Dijon, which had been much enlarged by Philip the Good, was almost entirely replaced by a brand new palace to house the civic administration of Dijon and the Estates of the duchy of Burgundy. This combined Hôtel de Ville and Palais des États, which now houses the Dijon Museum, has obliterated all but a few fragments of the ducal palace – a hall called the Salle des Gardes, the kitchens, and two towers. In Paris the Valois dukes of Burgundy took over from their predecessors a fine palace called the Hôtel d'Artois in which the first two dukes often resided. It was demolished in 1543 by royal command, but one small part was spared and still survives, the Tower of John the Fearless. Designed for that suspicious duke's personal safety, it was a sort of fortified bedroom with a private bathroom below it. Inevitably, it was adorned with Duke John's personal emblem, the carpenter's plane. This 'strong tower built of masonry in which the duke slept at night', as the chronicler Monstrelet put it, was built between 1408 and 1411 at a cost of over 14,000 francs. The architect and builder was the royal *maître des œuvres* Robert de Hellebuterne. It and the remains of the ducal palace at Dijon are virtually all that is left of the buildings erected or used by the Valois dukes of Burgundy.

Fortunately a very different story can be told of the magnificent collection of books, many of them superbly illustrated, which the Valois dukes collected or commissioned. At its largest, the ducal library contained almost 1,000 volumes, and 247 of these are still preserved in Brussels, where many of them were originally housed by the dukes, in the Royal Library of Belgium, which was established by Philip II in 1559. Over a hundred other Burgundian ducal books have been dispersed far and wide, but still survive, the majority in the French national library in Paris. Others have reached Austria and Russia, England and the United States of America. Furthermore we still have several quite detailed contemporary catalogues of the ducal library, the most important dating from 1404 to 1405, 1420, about 1467, and 1485 to 1487. These contain much of the history of its formation.

Apart from the books, only a few major works of art, mostly paintings, commissioned by the Burgundian dukes or their courtiers have come down to us or been identified. The Dijon Museum is indeed fortunate to have recovered as it were from the ruins of the Charterhouse of Champmol some of Claus Sluter's finest carvings and other sculpture, including the tombs – albeit battered and incomplete – of the first two dukes, as well as the superbly preserved wooden altarpieces carved by Jaques de Baerze and painted by Melchior Broederlam, two of the finest Flemish artists of the late fourteenth century. All the surviving portraits of the dukes are copies, unless indeed the Berlin portrait of Charles really is an original van der Weyden. One famous painting, by Jan van Eyck, the Virgin and Child 'of Autun' in the Louvre, was long supposed to portray Philip the Good's chancellor Nicolas Rolin kneeling opposite the Virgin and Child. Indeed this alleged portrait of him was reproduced as one of the illustrations in my *Philip the Good*. Even before that work was published, however, the Belgian historian Professor Jean Lejeune had identified the city in the background of the picture as Liège and shown that the kneeling figure must in fact be the known employer of Jan van Eyck, John of Bavaria, bishop of Liège, and not the Burgundian chancellor. Two works of art, indubitably commissioned by the duke of Burgundy and not paintings, deserve separate mention. Both were executed for Charles the Bold. In 1472 the city and castellany or Franc of Bruges commissioned a set of eleven tapestries showing 'the story of the destruction of Troy' to give 'to our much feared lord and prince upon his instant prayer and desire'. They were executed by Pasquier Grenier, the most famous tapestry-maker in the most famous tapestry-making town of those days, Tournai. When assembled together they would have measured some 310 feet in length and fifteen feet in height. One quarter of one of the eleven pieces showing Hector and Andromache, in excellent condition, is in the Metropolitan Museum of Art, New York; there are a few fragments elsewhere. The other memorable work of art is the extraordinarily beautiful gold reliquary in the diocesan museum of Liège. It consists of a kneeling statuette of Charles the Bold holding a small crystal reliquary, which is an excellent likeness of the duke; behind him is the figure of St George in armour, standing and doffing his helmet. Both figures are attached to a base on which the duke's motto is engraved. This superb example of the fifteenth-century goldsmith's art was ordered by Charles the Bold in 1467 from his goldsmith and *valet de chambre* Gerard Loyet and presented by the duke to the cathedral of St Lambert at Liège in 1471.

So far no mention has been made of the priceless booty which fell to the victorious Swiss after the battles of Grandson, Murten and Nancy in 1476-7. There is little comparable in all history to this astonishing *Burgunderbeute*. It makes one think of the riches which came into the hands of Alexander the Great when he defeated Darius III in 334 and 333 B.C., or the booty after the near annihilation of the Ottoman Turkish army in August 1691 at Zalankemen not far from Belgrade. The exceptional value and quantity of the booty of Grandson was apparently due to the suddenness and completeness of the Burgundian defeat and their very rapid flight at the very moment when the duke's bags had been packed and he was in the middle of moving camp. It included personal valuables of the duke and his courtiers, such as his privy or secret seal, of gold, and the seal of his half-brother the bastard Anthony, of silver-gilt, both of which still exist; the duke's ceremonial sword, his sceptre, throne and hat, which have perished; and some superb jewels and precious stones, including two famous diamonds. There was a good deal of plate: goblets, basins and spoons of silver and silver-gilt. In the booty too were the furnishings and fittings of the ducal chapel, including gold and silver chalices and reliquaries and costly vestments; some fine tapestries, in particular the famous Millefleurs tapestry made in Brussels in 1466; standards, banners, pennons, some elaborately painted; and various other embroidered textiles, including pieces of brocade as well as clothing; arms, armour, artillery in quantity; numerous tents and pavilions; and of course wine and provisions of all kinds.

Although this marvellously rich booty was supposed to be taken and held in common by the Swiss and their allies, so that it, or the proceeds of anything that was sold, could subsequently be divided among them in proportion to the number of troops each ally provided, much of it was privately appropriated, and a black market soon developed behind the authorities' backs. The goldsmiths, especially those of Basel, were among the leading purchasers. Inevitably there were quarrels among the victors over the distribution of the booty, and these continued for years afterwards. What is left of this priceless stuff, now carefully restored and tastefully exhibited, is preserved in the museums of Basel, Bern, Fribourg, Gruyères, La Neuveville, Luzern, Murten, St Gall, Solothurn, Thun, Zürich and others. One famous diamond, the Sancy stone of 106 carats, was bought in 1875 by the maharajah of Patiala and is now at Guttiola in India. A great deal of the *Burgunderbeute* was brought together for a special exhibition at the Historical Museum in Bern in 1969 and lavishly catalogued.

In the evolution of the courtly life of early modern Europe the Valois dukes of Burgundy were of some importance. Their model was France, but they held court for a century in considerable splendour at a time when the royal French court was at a low ebb. Burgundian court traditions (and Burgundian sentiment) survived to be transferred in significant measure to the Habsburg court of Maximilian and to the Spanish court under Charles V, while at the same time the court life of sixteenth-century France owed much to Burgundy.

CHAPTER NINE

The Fall of Valois Burgundy

Burgundy fell with Charles the Bold on the battlefield of Nancy on 5 January 1477. Its collapse was his personal political and military tragedy. But, although Valois Burgundy appears to have been stable and secure until Duke Charles over-reached himself and wrecked it, in fact the fabric which Philip the Good had enthusiastically completed in the first part of his long ducal reign had been subsequently neglected. In the late 1450s and early 1460s serious weaknesses appeared, important inadequacies remained, and the whole proud structure, with its resplendent duke and court, its Order of chivalry, its grand council and chancellor, its ample revenues, and its extensive territories, seemed in danger of internal disruption or conquest by France. In this final chapter we shall show how Duke Charles was trying energetically and not without success to rectify these deficiencies when his political ambitions, his military blunders, his excessive vanity and the aggressive determination of his formidable enemies combined to bring about his downfall.

What was wrong with the Burgundian state in those years after the fall of Constantinople to the Ottoman Turks in 1453 when 'the great duke of the West' seemed at the height of his power? In that very year Duke Philip the Good had decisively stamped out the revolt of Ghent by a resounding military victory. In 1454 he had held the Feast of the Pheasant, one of the most elaborate banquets of all time, at Lille, and then made a sort of triumphal progress through Germany. In 1456 his prestige was enhanced when the dauphin of France, heir to the royal throne of Charles VII, sought political asylum from his father at the Burgundian court. But the good duke was ageing: he was four years older than the century and he was losing interest in war and politics. He stayed up till the early hours 'to watch dances, entertainments and other amusements', dallying with his mistresses and exchanging bawdy stories with his courtiers instead of attending to affairs of state. He was distracted by a senile, or puerile, craze for handicrafts. 'In his old age he often spent his time in a work-room filled with gadgets which he took with him wherever he went, amusing himself at times by threading needles, making clogs, soldering broken knives, repairing broken glasses, and so on.'

Long before the Burgundian head of state began to lose his grasp important shortcomings were increasingly apparent in the body politic over which he ruled. The duke's territories remained divided into two blocks which, in spite of his conquest of Luxembourg in 1443, were still some 125 miles apart. They were separated by the duchies of Bar and Lorraine, but the shortest and most practicable route between them was through the French royal county of Champagne. No serious attempts at territorial 'rounding off' or at reducing this dependence on French territory were made by Philip the Good after 1443.

The north–south geographical bisection of the Burgundian state was matched by an east–west territorial bisection. Nor was there any prospect at all that Philip the Good could somehow do away with or alter this situation, which was caused by the fact that the frontier between France and the Empire ran right through both blocks of territory. But he could have tried harder to legitimize and secure the Burgundian possessions on either side of it. Perhaps he thought that the French problem had been solved and French hostility allayed by the treaty of Arras of 1435, but this was far from the case. Neither King Charles VII nor his son Louis XI who succeeded him in 1461 were in the least bit prepared to sit back and allow Burgundian power to grow along their eastern frontier. To them the dukes of Burgundy were usurpers. King Charles tried to wrest Luxembourg from Duke Philip, and King Louis succeeded in 1463 in recovering for France the strategically invaluable Somme towns. At the end of Charles VII's reign a French invasion of Burgundy was imminent, and the French royal council formally decided on 28 July 1460 that 'there is sufficient and just cause to proceed by force of arms to ensure obedience, in all of my lord of Burgundy's lands in the kingdom of France, to the king's letters, commands and ordinances and to the judgements of his court of Parlement'. And just as the French crown regarded the duke of Burgundy as a usurper of French territory and French rights, so the emperor could object that he had never authorized the annexation by Philip the Good of his lands on the imperial side of the frontier, notably Holland, Brabant and Luxembourg.

If Philip the Good did little, in his declining years, to improve

Burgundy's territorial security, he likewise failed to promote its legislative and judicial unity. Ordinances applied only to a single territory or to a group of territories: virtually no laws were universally applicable in all the duke of Burgundy's lands. The courts of law were split into separate hierarchies or sections, one in the two Burgundies and several in the Low Countries. Though an attempt was made to provide a supreme court in each territory in the shape of a ducal council, and to arrange for appeals from these councils to go to the *grand conseil* or great council at court, this system never replaced the existing muddle and mixture of jurisdictions. On either side of the Franco-imperial border appeals often went outside the duke's territories altogether, especially, on the French side, to the Paris Parlement. In 1454 the chief ducal official in Hainault was summoned to appear before the judicial tribunal of the University of Paris. Naturally, he refused, for Hainault 'which is part of the Empire, is in no way subject to the kingdom of France'. His recalcitrance was punished by a solemn notice of excommunication nailed to the doors of Tournai cathedral. Even though, at the duke of Burgundy's request, the king of France in 1445 and 1455 prohibited appeals from certain Flemish courts to the Paris Parlement, they continued. In 1447 the civic authorities at Dijon took the duke's financial officials there, the *gens des comptes*, to the Paris Parlement, in a dispute over their liability to pay rates. In sum, the dukes had no law and no law courts that were truly their own, and Philip the Good did little or nothing to rectify the situation.

The territorial and judicial fragmentation of Valois Burgundy was matched by its lack of central or even quasi-central administrative institutions. Here again, Philip the Good did little to supply the deficiency. He established a sort of personal savings bank for the duke, called the *épargne*; he regularized the composition and powers of the great council in an ordinance of 1446; in 1447 he set up a central financial committee; and at the end of his reign he played some part in the creation of the States General of his northern lands. But a great deal was left to be done. Philip the Good was by no means an administrative reformer.

One of the most characteristic shortcomings of the Burgundian state was that its ruler had no single title by right of which he could rule. Instead he was duke of Burgundy in Dijon, count of Burgundy in Dole, count of Flanders in Ghent, a duke in Brabant, a count only in Holland, a mere lord in Malines. In these circumstances, quite apart from the prestige attached to it, a crown and the royal title that went with it were evidently much to be desired, and from 1444 onwards Philip the Good made several attempts to obtain them. But it was not at all clear how his proposed kingdom would be constituted. After all, the kings of France could hardly be expected to permit part of royal France to be transformed into a separate kingdom. This meant that the Burgundian kingdom would in practice have to be limited in extent to the Burgundian lands within the Empire. In the 1440s and again after 1459 Philip the Good was involved in negotiations with the emperor with a view to his coronation but, while the duke wanted a kingdom feudally independent of the empire, Frederick III could only agree to offer him a dependent kingdom of Brabant which would be an imperial fief. So Philip the Good failed to obtain his crown. He also failed to have himself appointed an imperial vicar in his imperial lands, a possibility that was several times mooted.

Is it fair also to accuse Philip the Good of failing to cultivate the loyalty and support of his subjects? His policies towards the towns only provoked their opposition, and armed revolts had to be violently suppressed at Bruges in 1437, at Ghent in 1453, and at Dinant and Liège in 1466. No wonder Duke Charles's reign started with a rebellion in Ghent and a serious war against Liège. But Philip the Good provoked others besides the citizens of his towns. He even fell out with his own son, and a first serious quarrel between him and Charles, then count of Charolais, in 1457 was followed by a growing estrangement which came to a climax in 1462–5.

The main cause of the quarrel between father and son was Philip the Good's support of the Picard family of Croy, which became powerfully entrenched at the Burgundian court from John the Fearless's time onwards. They, and the court faction they gathered around them, had sympathies and lands in France as well as in Burgundy. They allowed themselves to be bribed in 1435 by the king of France in return for persuading Philip the Good to subscribe in the interests of France to the peace treaty of Arras. Besides nourishing a French sentiment which some thought bordered on treason, the Croys consulted their own interests and built up a power of their own inside the administrative framework of the Burgundian state. By 1456 Anthoine, lord of Croy, was governor of Luxembourg, of Namur and of Boulogne, and captain of St Omer. His son Philippe became a ducal chamberlain in 1458; his brother Jehan was bailiff and captain-general of Hainault until in that year he was succeeded by his nephew, Philippe, lord of Sempy. Soon the Croys were fighting wars of their own and manipulating the Burgundian administrative machinery in their own interests. It was not long before they trod on the rather sensitive toes of the count of Charolais, and the serene life of the Burgundian court was disturbed by the struggle of factions, as well as by family quarrels. In 1457 Duchess Isabel and the chancellor Nicolas Rolin retired in disgrace or disgust after many years of loyal service, and the count of Charolais more or less withdrew from court at the same time. This internal disintegration coincided with increasing pressure from France, and it seems probable that Louis XI and the Croys had at least exchanged ideas on the subject of dismantling the Burgundian state and dividing parts of it between them as soon as the old duke Philip the Good was dead and gone.

It was from about 1463-4 onwards, rather than after he became duke on 15 June 1467, that Charles the Bold, at the age of thirty or so, began to assert his personal authority and at the same time to restore the integrity of the Burgundian state. From then onwards he made a succession of vigorous attempts to crush his rivals at court, to resist and repel the threat from France, and to strengthen the Burgundian system of alliances in Europe at large. He had achieved all this by the time he became duke; thereafter he went further, and set about trying to rectify those permanent weaknesses of the Burgundian state which his father had disregarded. Against France he tried to insist in 1468 in the treaty of Péronne (which however Louis XI never approved and soon renounced) on the severance of all juridical connections which maintained the subordinacy of the duke of Burgundy to the king. On 12 November 1471 he issued an ordinance prohibiting appeals to any French court from his southern territories. These juridical moves were accompanied by military measures which were more realistic and effective: Charles the Bold set up a standing army of 'companies of ordinance' to be permanently ready to repel a French attack. Admittedly, no settlement with France was achieved, but at least Charles showed himself to be conscious of the French threat. On the imperial side, his policies were forceful enough. He tried much harder than his father had done to squeeze a crown out of the rather tight-fisted Frederick III. This time a kingdom of Burgundy or of Frisia was to be established for the duke of Burgundy. But Frederick is on record as saying that there were only four crowns in his Empire, those of Aachen, Arles, Milan and Rome – and they all belonged on his own head. Nothing came of these Burgundian initiatives with Frederick, but the Burgundian connection with the Empire was considerably strengthened by the matrimonial alliance between Charles's only child Mary of Burgundy and Frederick's son Maximilian of Austria which Charles the Bold managed to bring himself to sign but which he never saw consummated.

While Charles the Bold contributed in these ways to buttressing Burgundy against her potentially hostile French and German neighbours, he also made a determined effort to continue the work, dropped by his father after the conquest of Luxembourg in 1443, of rounding off and enlarging Burgundian territory. In the north he extended Burgundian influence still further in Liège and virtually completed the unification of the Low Countries – except for Frisia, which eluded his grasp – by conquering Guelders in 1473. Further south he temporarily acquired Upper Alsace, a frontier region long subject to Burgundian influences, and in 1473-5 he almost linked up the northern and southern blocks of territory by the conquest of Lorraine and by means of an alliance with the bishop of Metz which allowed free passage of Burgundian troops through that bishop's lands. These territorial acquisitions were, however, impermanent: the rightful ruler of Guelders was still alive, though in a Burgundian prison; and Charles had lost most of Lorraine within a year.

Charles the Bold's attempts to consolidate and unify the Burgundian state internally were extraordinarily far-reaching, though most of his reforms did not survive his death. The structure of the court was modernized; the army was revolutionized; the financial administration was pruned and rationalized. Then, at the end of 1473, as described above in Chapter 6, new institutions were set up at Malines which were central at least to the northern Burgundian territories, for their competence included all the Burgundian Low Countries but not the two Burgundies. These were a Parlement, to become a new supreme court to hear the appeals which had been going to Paris and to the Empire, and an accounting office or *chambre des comptes* to take over and centralize the work being done by the *chambres des comptes* at Lille and Brussels, which were now abolished.

At about the same time the voting of *aides* or taxes in the northern territories was centralized and placed in the hands of the States General. It is generally conceded that Charles the Bold went too far, too fast, with these reforms. They did however constitute a serious attempt to modernize the Burgundian state. Admittedly most of them were abolished in the critical times which followed his death, but many were resuscitated later by his grandson Philip the Fair, and in their general spirit and in the attitudes and motives that lay behind them they inspired and served as a model for the rulers of the early modern states of sixteenth-century Europe.

As a matter of fact Duke Charles's military tragedies never gave his administrative experiments opportunity to stand the test of time. Although his reforms, especially the Parlement of Malines, were criticized, there is little evidence of accumulating opposition and unpopularity to Charles the Bold. Most of his courtiers, captains and officials remained dutiful and loyal to the end. Even as late as the second half of 1476, after his two defeats at the hands of the Swiss, there is no sign of a serious crisis of confidence in him. Isolated incidents occurred, such as trouble at Ghent, an administrative blunder in Hainault, pillaging in some areas, the mutiny of the Flemish garrison of Abbeville, and some desertion from the army, but the machinery of state continued to work. True, the local authorities in Franche-Comté did try to arrange an unauthorized truce with the Swiss, but they were by no means acting in defiance of the duke. Nor should the determined stand made by the clergy of Holland against Charles the Bold's taxation of ecclesiastics be construed as a rebellion. Militarily, Charles was still a power to be reckoned with even after his twofold defeat by the Swiss. In the early autumn of 1476 he still had some 10,000 men with him in the field, and a body of 8,000 recruits set out on foot from the Low Countries in September and October 1476 to help in the recon-quest of Lorraine. They wore the blue and white ducal uniforms issued to them and had two months' pay in their pockets. The accounts show that Charles the Bold's expensive military operations had strained but certainly not exhausted his finances: he managed to extract a great deal more money from his subjects in taxes than had his father. In sum, it does not seem to have been internal disintegration which brought the history of Valois Burgundy to a sudden and dramatic end in 1476-7. Rather it was brought to a close because the policies and activities of Duke Charles, now to be recounted, led abruptly to his defeat and death.

It is difficult to say at precisely what point in time Charles the Bold reached the height of his power and when exactly decline, soon precipitated into collapse, set in. Perhaps it was at the end of 1475 that Burgundian power in Europe reached its zenith. Earlier that year Charles the Bold had remained at Neuss in spite of the emperor's attempt to relieve the town. He could boast that he had faced the imperial forces in open battle and continued his siege until a papal legate insisted on both sides making peace. At the same time his lands had been invaded by French royal troops which had, however, been withdrawn or repulsed. Since then the duke of Burgundy had made a satisfactory settlement on 13 September with the king of France in the truce of Soleuvre; he had made an alliance on 17 November with his late enemy Frederick III; and now he was spending Christmas at Nancy as the proud conqueror of that town and the duchy of Lorraine of which it was the capital, having entered it in triumph, after one of the gateways had been specially dismantled, like a Roman emperor or a Renaissance prince.

Potential enemies or victims of Burgundian power were everywhere fearful and dismayed at this time. It was in the autumn of 1475 that the great city of Strasbourg resolved to make preparations to withstand a Burgundian siege. A committee of eight leading citizens reported early in November that the city's extensive faubourgs would have to be systematically demolished to stop them being of use to the enemy. The work continued throughout that winter until five monasteries and 620 houses had been destroyed and a two-mile-wide belt of flat open ground surrounded the walls. A huge moat was dug to bring the Rhine waters right round the city walls; and powder and ammunition was laid in, with enough corn to last the inhabitants for ten years, and a three-year supply of wine and salt. But Charles had no intention of besieging Strasbourg; certain important events had already happened, long before Christmas 1475, which, though occurring on the outermost geographical fringe of the Burgundian sphere of influence, nevertheless impinged urgently on its future destiny and soon mesmerized the ambitious duke. In those events lay the origins of Burgundy's imminent downfall.

Everyone knows that Charles the Bold came to grief at the hands of 'the Swiss'. But who were the Swiss, and how did he come to be involved with them? The word Switzeri, Switzer, or Zwitsois, was only just coming into use in the fifteenth century as a synonym for the confederate cantons or *Eidgenossen*, literally 'oath companions'. The word was in fact a corruption of Schwyz, the name of one of the original three Forest Cantons (*Waldstätten*) that had joined together at the end of the thirteenth century to form the nucleus of the later Swiss Federation. The other two were Uri and Unterwalden. Later on two more rural communities, Zug and Glarus, joined, as well as the three towns of Luzern, Zürich and Bern. These confederate communities referred to themselves as the *Eidgenossen*; they called their organization 'the great league of Upper Germany'; they formed part of the Empire; and they thought of themselves as Germans, which indeed they were. In those days there was no such thing as Switzerland.

Burgundy under Charles the Bold had two important points of contact with the westernmost of the *Eidgenossen*, Bern, who had constructed a private empire of her own by persuading Solothurn, Biel, Murten, Fribourg, Valangin and Neuchâtel to become her allies and virtual satellites. The first point of contact was in Alsace, which Charles the Bold acquired on 9 May 1469 in mortgage from the impecunious Duke Sigmund of Austria, who needed money and soldiers to fight his traditional enemy Bern and her allies. By stepping into Duke Sigmund's shoes in this area, Charles entered into that duke's confrontation with Bern even though he resolutely refused the military intervention against her which Sigmund hoped for and demanded. Moreover, Charles took over the Austrian side of a serious dispute with one of the leading Alsace towns, Mulhouse, which was an ally of Bern and Solothurn and, within weeks of their entry into Alsace, Charles the Bold's officials there received complaints from Bern on behalf of this ally. Nor was it merely Bern who felt threatened and affronted by what she regarded as Burgundian aggression in Alsace; two other great towns, Basel and Strasbourg, felt affronted too – even more so when Charles the Bold's bluff bailiff of Alsace, Peter von Hagenbach, wrote to Strasbourg ordering the citizens not to proceed to the election of a new civic official; instead 'we will come in person to give you one, who will be neither a butcher nor a baker nor a ribbon merchant; you will have the honour of having for chief the noblest of princes, the duke of Burgundy'. The same bailiff annoyed Basel in the same way, threatening to conquer the

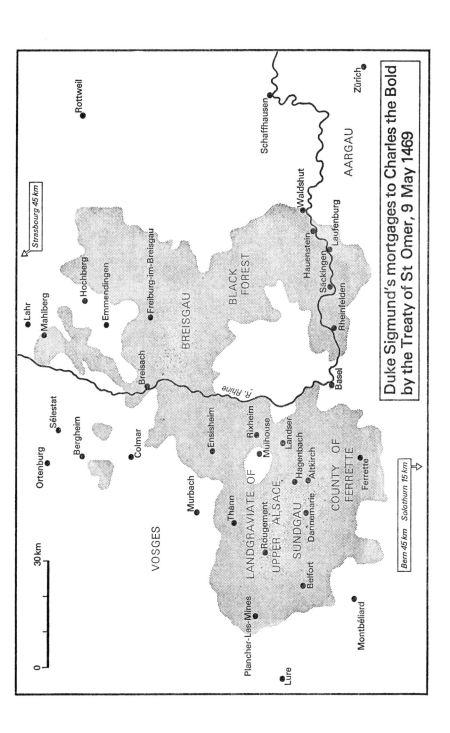

Duke Sigmund's mortgages to Charles the Bold by the Treaty of St Omer, 9 May 1469

town and flatten it just as Dinant had been flattened, and to decapitate or scalp some of its leading citizens. Thus in Alsace, from 1469 on, Charles the Bold, partly through the agency of his acrimonious and tactless bailiff Peter von Hagenbach, appeared to be on a collision course with the proud, independent and redoubtable German-speaking towns of Basel and Strasbourg, as well as with Bern.

The other point of contact between Burgundy and Bern was in what is now the Swiss canton of Vaud. In the fifteenth century this French-speaking area next door to Bern belonged to the dukes of Savoy. It was being thoroughly penetrated by expanding Bern, but it was also on the frontier of Franche-Comté and lay wide open to Burgundian infiltration. Thus the Burgundian family of Chalon possessed various lordships in the Vaud, including Orbe and Grandson; the baron of Vaud was Jaques de Savoie, count of Romont, who in May 1473 became Charles the Bold's lieutenant-general in all the Burgundian Low Countries; and the count of Neuchâtel, Rudolf, margrave of Hachberg or Hochberg, had become a Burgundian landowner, a chamberlain-councillor of Philip the Good and Charles the Bold's governor of Luxembourg, although he was at the same time an ally and co-burgess of Bern. When Charles the Bold established a kind of Burgundian protectorate over Savoy in 1473 at just the time when the Vaud seemed to be falling into Burgundian hands, and was certainly being brought into the Burgundian sphere of influence, Bern, once again, was deeply affronted. Thus, although Duke Charles himself probably had no aggressive or even provocative intentions against them, both in Alsace and in the Vaud the effect of his policies was to awaken the fears and hostility of Bern and her allies.

The situation was similar in Lorraine, but here Strasbourg was the town which felt itself most threatened. Charles the Bold had a long-standing agreement with the dukes of Lorraine to permit the free passage of Burgundian troops through their duchy, and this was renewed in 1473 by the new duke René II. But this alliance between the rulers of Burgundy and Lorraine gave way before long to hostility, perhaps because of the bad behaviour of Burgundian troops in the duchy, so that Duke René soon came to be numbered among the sworn enemies of Charles the Bold.

It was only slowly that those princes and towns who felt threatened by the far-reaching and apparently aggressive intentions and activities of Duke Charles the Bold in Lorraine,

The pays de Vaud and surrounding territories

Alsace and Savoy began to consider the formation of a general alliance against him. The first area of concern chronologically was Alsace. In June 1470 representatives of Strasbourg, Colmar, Sélestat, Basel and the *Eidgenossen* met in Basel to discuss measures that could be taken to counter Hagenbach's threats to take Mulhouse into the duke of Burgundy's 'protection'. A year later the expulsion of the Burgundians from Alsace was laid down by the Swiss as a condition for a peace settlement between themselves and Duke Sigmund, who was quite willing to do a deal with his old enemies the Swiss if his new friend the duke of Burgundy failed to help him resist them by force of arms. In the spring of 1473, at another Basel conference, a draft alliance was drawn up between the bishops of Strasbourg and Basel, the margrave of Baden, and the towns of Strasbourg, Basel, Colmar and Sélestat on the one side and the *Eidgenossen*, with Mulhouse, on the other. It was agreed that the money must be raised to redeem Sigmund's mortgage and so buy the Burgundians out of Alsace. To protect and encourage Mulhouse against the threatened Burgundian annexation it was solemnly declared that, if any 'foreign French-speaking people try unjustly by force to take away the liberties of or detach from the Holy Empire one or more members of this alliance, we others shall help and advise them truly in whatever way we and they consider necessary'.

The king of France was clearly a potential member of any projected alliance against Duke Charles. Would he not seek revenge for the Burgundian onslaught against him in the summer of 1472 when Charles the Bold had sacked Nesle and laid siege to Beauvais? In May 1473 the Milanese ambassador at the French court reported that 'the community of Strasbourg has sent an ambassador here to seek help from His Majesty against the duke of Burgundy'. But Louis XI did nothing, and he ignored a similar appeal made in the very same month by the *Eidgenossen*. It was not Louis XI or any other prince, but the towns, which took the initiatives which led at last, in April 1474, to the formation of the grand alliance against Charles the Bold. The necessary treaties were signed at a conference at Constance which, according to the Basel chaplain Johann Knebel, had been convoked 'to consider the peace of the land and how to extricate it from the tyranny of the duke of Burgundy and his wicked bailiff Peter von Hagenbach'. The league was based on the following elements: an alliance between Austria and the Swiss which was optimistically supposed to be everlasting; a ten-year defensive alliance between Duke Sigmund, the bishops of Strasbourg and Basel, and the towns of Strasbourg, Basel, Sélestat and Colmar, called the Lower Union in contradistinction to the *Eidgenossen* who called themselves the league of Upper Germany or Upper Union; the redemption of Sigmund's lands and rights in Alsace which he had mortgaged to Charles the Bold, the money for this to be found by the allied towns; and, finally, a ten-year defensive alliance between the Lower Union and the *Eidgenossen*.

This anti-Burgundian alliance was urban in character, loosely organized and geographically scattered in nature, and at first defensive in spirit. It was not through its cumbersome mechanism that the projected expulsion of the Burgundians from Alsace was brought about, but by sudden, unexpected, rebellion. On 10 April 1474, within days of the signing of the treaties of the League of Constance, Hagenbach's troops in Breisach mutinied and the townsmen rose in revolt, seized the unpopular bailiff and threw him into prison. Rough justice was meted out to this crude, somewhat tyrannical man who had acquired a sinister reputation, partly for acts of gross indecency which the Basel chaplain Johann Knebel evidently enjoyed enlarging upon in his diary in spite of his feelings of moral outrage. It is he who makes the bailiff boast at a public banquet that he had had the pubic hair of his wife and three noblewomen shaved off and given to his cook to pulverize and then sprinkle on the dishes served to the ladies. After being maimed by savage tortures, Peter von Hagenbach was given a summary trial at Breisach on 9 May 1474 and executed on the same day before a large crowd. That was the end of Burgundian rule in Alsace.

The successful revolt of Alsace encouraged the League of Constance to substitute an offensive campaign against Charles the Bold for their originally rather limited plan of peacefully buying him out of Alsace and otherwise merely defending themselves against him. Through the summer of 1474 an enthusiastic anti-Burgundian spirit was very evident. Strasbourg and Basel led the way: they declared war on the duke of Burgundy on 22 April 1474. The rest of the Lower Union supported them, but hesitated to act on a large scale without their Swiss allies. These hung back for a time, then, encouraged by French diplomacy and bribes and by their Lower Union allies, incited by a Burgundian retaliatory raid into Alsace on 18 August, and in obedience to the command of their natural lord the Emperor Frederick III, the *Eidgenossen* on 29 October 1474 sent a formal declaration of war against Duke Charles to Henry de Neuchâtel, who was the duke's 'lieutenant-general on the frontiers of Germany', at his castle of Blamont in Franche-Comté. It was carried there aloft on a cleft stick by a mounted messenger dressed in the town livery of Bern.

The *Eidgenossen* followed up their declaration of war by joining with their allies of the Lower Union in what was the only aggressive move successfully undertaken against Burgundy by the League of Constance as a whole. The allied target in the autumn of 1474 was the castle of Héricourt on the frontier of Franche-Comté between Belfort and Montbéliard, which belonged to the recipient of the Swiss challenge, Henry de Neuchâtel. The men of Bern set out on 28 October 'in the name of God and the heavenly queen maid Mary', with banners unfurled, and the allied army took up positions round the castle in cold wet weather from 5 November onwards. It was a massive army which encamped round the pink sandstone walls, partly still standing, of this remote and minor outpost of Burgundian power among the extensive deciduous forests along the valley of the River Lisaine. Strasbourg alone sent 2,000 infantry with 250 horse and 140 wagons, and the city's great gun *der Strauss*, 'the ostrich', was dragged to Héricourt by eighteen horses. The Strasbourg versifier who for many years successfully concealed his name, Conrad Pfettisheim, in the initial letters of the first eighteen verses of his poem about Peter von Hagenbach and the Burgundian wars (printed at Strasbourg in 1477 by Heinrich Knoblochzer), described this gun as buzzing and doing a wild dance. 'When it had a crop full of powder, then it laid hard eggs.' It actually achieved a rate of fire of fourteen shots per day and a hole was made in one of the castle's towers. But the siege of Héricourt was brought to a sudden end by the appearance of a Burgundian relieving force on 13 November, led by Henry de Neuchâtel. The allies, who must have easily outnumbered him, drove him back or followed his retreating troops northwards up the Lisaine valley which here forms a winding defile amid thick forests, and defeated them and overran their camp on the open grassy ground somewhere between Chenebier and Châtebier, about six miles north of Héricourt castle, which surrendered three or four days later. The Strasbourgers returned home 'fresh and joyful with all their folk and equipment' on 25 November, with five captured Burgundian banners to hang proudly in their cathedral. Eighteen unfortunate Italian mercenaries in the Burgundian army were taken prisoner, accused of sodomy, rape, sacrilege and any other frightful crimes their captors could think of, and burned alive at Basel on Christmas Eve 1474 as heretics – 'in honour of God Almighty, of our Christian faith, and of all Germans'.

The news of the Swiss declaration of war and of this allied raid on an obscure frontier castle probably made little impression on Charles the Bold besieging Neuss, surrounded by courtiers, captains and foreign ambassadors. Nor was the success at Héricourt followed up; no more incursions into Burgundian territory were jointly and officially made until between 12 July and 24 August 1475, when the Lower Union on its own initiative organized the conquest and demolition of a group of castles in Franche-Comté, notably that of Blamont. The *Eidgenossen* as a whole did not take part in this campaign, but Bern sent a strong contingent and some mercenaries were recruited among the Swiss by Basel. As a matter of fact, since the successful expulsion of the Burgundians from Alsace in April 1474, the attention of Bern had been diverted to the other area where her and Duke Charles's aggressive intentions seemed to clash: Savoy. Bern could claim to be especially threatened by the formation of the League of Moncalieri, between Burgundy, Savoy and Milan, a diplomatic triumph for Charles the Bold which had been brought off by his ambassador Guillaume de Rochefort, who later became famous as chancellor of France, on 30 January 1475. On 14 February she reported to her sister-town Fribourg the rumour of a vast alliance against the Swiss. 'And it is said in Geneva,' the letter ran, 'that these lords will make for our town, will conquer it first and then utterly destroy it, placing [on the site] an inscription saying "Here once there was a town called Bern".'

The great city was neither frightened nor cowed by the activities of Charles the Bold. She was simply using them as a pretext to gain the support of her friends for her own anti-Burgundian policies. She was concerned to prevent the passage of Charles the Bold's Italian recruits through Savoy and the Vaud, where they passed close to her frontiers on their way from Piedmont to Burgundy, and she was determined also to eradicate every element of Burgundian power from the Vaud, an area which she regarded as peculiarly destined for her own political and economic purposes. In January and April 1475 she seized and occupied or demolished all the Burgundian castles in the area, especially the group of strongpoints at the southern end of the Lake of Neuchâtel which controlled access to the most important passes through the Jura Mountains between Savoy and Burgundy: Grandson, Echallens, Jougne and Orbe. In August a force from Bern delivered a midnight attack on Aigle at the very moment when a contingent of Italian mercenaries was passing through; and by September she had made arrangements with Bishop Walter Supersax of Sion or Sitten in the Upper Valais for a combined attack on Savoy. Bishop Walter was only too pleased to help because some of his episcopal lands in the Lower Valais had been forcibly annexed by Savoy; here was a chance to recover them.

The mechanism of the Burgundian involvement in Savoy was in many respects similar to the way Charles had been drawn into a confrontation with Bern, Basel and Strasbourg in and after 1469 by taking Duke Sigmund into his protection and undertaking the administration of Austrian lands in Upper Alsace. But in Savoy the Burgundian 'take-over' was more gradual, less formal and more personal. Charles increased his influence and tightened his connections with the princely house of Savoy gradually, over the years 1468–73. There was no question of mortgaging territory but, whereas Charles and Sigmund seem to have disliked each other, Yolande, duchess of Savoy, appears to have admired Duke Charles and he may have esteemed her. The two were also brought together by their mutual dislike and distrust of Louis XI, who was Yolande's brother. In August 1473 Charles wrote to Yolande assuring her that 'in these affairs [with the Swiss] and in all others concerning yourself, my nephews your children, and your lands and lordships, I shall never abandon you whatever happens to me'. In January 1475 an Italian observer noted that Duchess Yolande of Savoy was 'entirely Burgundian' and that 'she conducted her affairs as the duke of Burgundy wished and not otherwise'.

It goes without saying that many contemporaries were convinced that Charles the Bold was determined to incorporate both Alsace and Savoy into his own territories. History confirms that he did consider these and many other prospects of annexation and conquest, but suggests that he showed no special determination either towards Alsace or in Savoy. Alsace was more of a nuisance and an expense to him than anything else;

Savoy was only important as a potential ally against Louis XI and as a route for his Italian troops. It was Lorraine which, more than either of these, excited his aspirations as a conqueror. As early as June 1474 he was thought to have 'something in mind' against the duke of Lorraine. In 1475 that youthful ruler was foolish enough to give the duke of Burgundy every possible pretext for invading Lorraine. While Charles seemed irretrievably transfixed at Neuss, René II allowed himself to be persuaded on 18 April to join the Lower Union and therefore the League of Constance, and on 9 May actually to declare war on Duke Charles the Bold. From early June at the latest the conquest of Lorraine was given first priority in Charles's future plans and it was effected at the earliest possible moment thereafter. It was on its successful conclusion that he now held state at Nancy, in all his conquering splendour, at Christmas 1475.

The foregoing pages will have shown that, although the Burgundian sun was shining brightly at the end of 1475, there were clouds on the horizon, though few would have dreamt that they could ever obscure it. One was caused by the so far unavenged injury Duke Charles had suffered in Alsace. Another was the existence of the dispossessed Duke René of Lorraine, determined to recover his duchy, the conquest of which by Duke Charles was a very serious affront and a standing threat to the League of Constance, whose members had tried to assist René in defending it. A third was the aggressively hostile attitude of Bern, especially towards Savoy. At the very time when Duke Charles was conquering Lorraine, Bern retaliated by invading and conquering the entire Vaud, while her ally the warlike Bishop Walter of Sion attacked and annexed the Lower Valais. These events, occurring between 14 October and the end of November 1475, completed the virtual closure of Charles the Bold's best line of communication with Italy. New recruits for his army could no longer pass freely from Aosta and the Great St Bernard Pass through Martigny, Aigle, Montreux and Pontarlier to Besançon, as they had been doing. Furthermore, the baron of Vaud was one of Charles's most trusted lieutenants, Jaques de Savoie, count of Romont, who had just been appointed the duke's 'governor and lieutenant-general' in all his southern territories. He was the brother-in-law of Charles's ally Yolande, duchess of Savoy, but it does not appear that Jaques and Yolande needed to persuade Charles the Bold to right their wrongs by taking revenge against Bern and her ally the bishop of Sion. He had probably decided on this course of action because of the raids on the county of Burgundy already described and because of the succession of minor unofficial raids which accompanied and followed them. As early as 28 November he wrote informing Jaques de Savoie that he had decided to take the field against 'the Germans and the Valaisans' who had been attacking both Burgundy and Savoy. Later, Dijon was informed that her duke hoped 'with the help of God and Monsieur St George, to deliver our lands and subjects of Burgundy and those of the house of Savoy from the Swiss, Valaisans and other Germans who, up to now, have interfered to cause them various injuries, oppressions and damages'. The Dijonnais, ducal subjects, were ordered to provide bread, wine, meat, fish and oats for the ducal army. Geneva was informed that Charles the Bold was about to attack 'the Bernese, Zürichers and their allies, your enemies and ours' for the 'glory and solace of the land of Savoy', and politely requested to sell him what provisions they could. On 11 January he left Nancy for Besançon to make final preparations for the campaign.

Charles the Bold's military campaigns were always conducted with due caution, and the one he now set out on was no exception. He tried to make sure, first of all, that he had a large enough army with him. He told the Milanese ambassador Panigarola that he had brought 11,000 combatants 'because it would not do to advance against the Swiss with insufficient forces'. Little did he know that the League of Constance could muster twice that number. Secondly, he made sure of depriving his enemy of their allies. Even though every single member of the League of Constance belonged to the Empire, and every one of them might reasonably have expected assistance from their emperor Frederick III, that ruler refused to help them: he had been carefully neutralized by Charles the Bold in the treaty of 17 November 1475. Even though the *Eidgenossen* were the special allies of Louis XI, who had promised to help them against the duke of Burgundy, that ruler did nothing. He too had been neutralized by Burgundian diplomacy – in the truce of Soleuvre of 13 September 1475. No wonder Charles the Bold was in a buoyant mood as he set out on campaign from Besançon on 6 February 1476 to make for Jougne. When one of his officers suggested that the mountains of Savoy might present them with difficulties, the duke referred him to Hasdrubal and told him that 'nothing was so harsh and difficult that it could not be conquered by the courage of men and by military discipline, and he would certainly attempt it'.

Who exactly were the enemies against whom the duke of Burgundy was now advancing? The word 'Swiss' is misleading, though not so much so as the ridiculous designation 'the mountaineers' beloved of some American biographers. In fact Charles's plan of campaign shows that he rightly understood that Bern was his prime enemy. His first objective was to recover the fortified places in the Vaud which she had seized and garrisoned in 1475. After that he would advance against Bern herself, but he cannot have seriously contemplated laying siege to that city; evidently he hoped to meet the enemy in a single decisive encounter. The powers of the League of Constance, who had been unwilling to help Bern conquer the Vaud in the previous autumn, were now ready to come to her assistance and they too fully intended to stake everything on one big battle. The army which they mustered against Charles the Bold in February 1476 was primarily urban in character. The rural *Eidgenossen* like Uri, Schwyz and Unterwalden sent contingents; the princely members of the Union – the bishops of Strasbourg and of Basel and Duke Sigmund of Austria-Tirol – sent theirs; but more than half the army was contributed by towns, some, like Zürich and Luzern, were *Eidgenossen*; others, like Basel and Strasbourg, belonged to the Lower Union. The leader of this alliance, its headquarters, its nucleus, was Bern, who provided one third of its army's numerical strength: on one calculation, 7,343 men of a total of 20,376.

The campaign of Grandson really opened when Charles the Bold left Jougne and crossed the frontier between the county of Burgundy and the Vaud on 12 February 1476. Two days before, in a letter to Luzern, Bern entreated her 'from the bottom of our hearts, on the strength of your brotherly love, to set out at once with all your power for our town to save our land, people, lives and belongings'. On 21 February Charles conquered the village of Grandson and thereafter siege was laid to the imposing rectangular castle with its round corner towers which rose, and still rises, above the shore of the Lake of Neuchâtel and the roofs of the houses, at the eastern end of the village. The several hundred Bernese soldiers garrisoning this castle unaccountably surrendered on 28 February, and Charles savagely ordered them to be drowned in the lake or hanged on the walnut trees in and around the village.

As soon as she had news of the Burgundian army's first attack (of 18 February) on Grandson, Bern had summoned her allies to Neuchâtel to be ready to go to the rescue of the castle's garrison. They began assembling south of Neuchâtel around Bevaix and Boudry on and soon after 28 February, and this explains why Charles, when he set out from his Grandson encampment early on 2 March, advanced north-eastwards along the northern shore of the lake instead of heading round its southern tip into the Vaud. He knew approximately where the enemy was and hoped to engage them. On 29 February (1476 was a leap year) he had carried out a personal reconnaissance along the lake shore and left a garrison of élite household troops in the castle of Vaumarcus, half-way along the shore between Grandson and Boudry. It was strategically situated to command the only difficult section of the route along this shore of the lake; difficult because at this point the wooded slopes of Mount Aubert came right to the lake shore. Each side now miscalculated or misunderstood the plans of the other. Charles advanced his army along the more or less level lake-shore plain with the intention of moving camp some five miles or so and establishing himself at the southern end of the above-mentioned defile. He was not expecting an enemy attack and evidently planned next day to move on through the defile ahead of him, protected as he was by the Vaumarcus garrison, which was still several miles in front of his new position.

On the same morning, 2 March, the allies set out to assault and conquer the castle of Vaumarcus. Although they seem to have had no concerted or official plans to do more than eliminate it and its garrison, one large contingent formed an unofficial van or advance party and marched on beyond it through the woods, emerging soon after midday quite high up the slopes of Mount Aubert somewhere near the farmhouse called Prise Gaulax. Below them they were suddenly confronted with the entire Burgundian army, moving up in three columns. Either because of their uncontrollable enthusiasm for battle or for some other reason, they charged downhill in a solid phalanx and were soon more or less surrounded and attacked on all sides by Burgundian infantry and cavalry. At this critical moment two things seem to have happened simultaneously which gave the day to the allies. A partial withdrawal of his leading troops, which was ordered by Duke Charles either to tempt this allied van still nearer or to facilitate the deployment of his artillery against it, was misinterpreted as a retreat by the rest of his army, which began to fall back. At the same time the whole of the rest of the allied army, which had abandoned its attack on Vaumarcus castle as soon as it realized fighting had begun ahead of it, emerged from the trees at several different points making blood-curdling noises with horns and other instruments. This precipitated the Burgundian flight. 'God gave us luck so that they fled,' wrote the Zürich chronicler laconically. The Burgundian retreat was so rapid that the Milanese ambassadors only just escaped with their lives, though they had been hovering well to the rear of Charles's army. Nearly all the baggage and valuables, including the duke's personal treasure, fell into the hands of the League, much of it still packed for transit from the Grandson encampment to the planned new encampment which Charles had hoped to establish near Concise.

The battle of Grandson was a serious defeat for Charles the Bold, but he suffered relatively few casualties. He raced back to Nozeroy in Franche-Comté, cautiously returning to Jougne, and then to Orbe, when he realized that the allies had no intention of following up their victory in spite of Bern's entreaties. They camped for the traditional three days on the battlefield collecting booty, cut down and buried the bodies of the Bernese soldiers which were still hanging from the nut trees at Grandson, and threw the thirty-odd Burgundians they found in the castle there to their deaths from the battlements. Then they were off home while Charles, resolving to continue the war at all costs, wrote off for reinforcements and made for the imperial city of Lausanne, where he established his headquarters on 14 March.

Charles the Bold remained encamped with his army outside Lausanne from 14 March until 27 May 1476. Just as in the previous year the eyes of Europe had been riveted on his camp at Neuss, so now the attention of everyone was directed to Lausanne. Ambassadors flocked there and, on 6 May, the treaty of engagement of Maximilian of Austria and Mary of Burgundy was signed there, clinching the alliance of Charles the Bold and Frederick III. Other European rulers wrote assuring Duke Charles of their friendship in spite of his mishap, and commiserating with him; some offered to mediate a peace settlement; one or two even dared to advise him not to risk another attack on the Swiss. But the star of Burgundy still seemed in the ascendant, especially after Charles recovered from a very

serious illness which caused him to be put into hospital in
Lausanne on 29 April during a freak snowstorm. While Bern and
some of the Lower Union powers kept up a desultory warfare
against the Burgundian forces stationed in the Vaud, her
fellow *Eidgenossen* withdrew their support and even refused to
assist her in the defence and garrisoning of Murten, a very
recent conquest of Bern from Savoy for which they rightly
rejected all responsibility. But the League of Constance stretched
a good way across Europe and, while one part of it was in
disarray, another was moving forward aggressively. On 14 April
René II of Lorraine inaugurated the reconquest of his duchy
from the Burgundians by the recovery of Vaudémont. Thus war
began, and continued, against the Burgundians in Lorraine
while their duke was preoccupied by the Vaud.

Starting out from Lausanne on 27 May and heading once more
towards Bern, Charles had first to conquer either Fribourg
or Murten. He chose Murten, which was smaller. Taking with
him an army which was essentially the same as the one that had
fled at Grandson, and roughly similar in size, the duke advanced
through the Vaud with the utmost caution. He confided to
Panigarola that 'he could not live with the disgrace of having
been defeated by these bestial people' the Swiss, even though he
was well aware that, by attacking them again, he was risking
'his state, his life, his everything'. He laid siege to Murten, well
fortified but a mere village, on 11 June.

A little less than a mile south of Murten is an isolated hillock
called Bois Domingue. Here Charles the Bold's personal pavilion
was erected, and the main part of his army camped on the
slopes and on other hillocks in the immediate neighbourhood.
While these contingents blocked the roads from Murten to
Fribourg and Bern, other army corps were posted at either end
of Murten near the lake, Jaques de Savoie with troops from the
two Burgundies and Savoy at the northern end, and the bastard
Anthony at the southern end, of the village. Trenches were
soon dug round it and a first, unsuccessful, general assault was
made on 18 June. The garrison, commanded by a famous Bern
captain Adrian von Bubenberg, held firm, ignoring messages
fired into the town on Burgundian crossbow-bolts which
announced that 'we shall shortly enter the town and take you
and kill you and hang you by your throats'. But Charles may
have been more concerned to provoke a general engagement
with the League of Constance – his only real hope of an

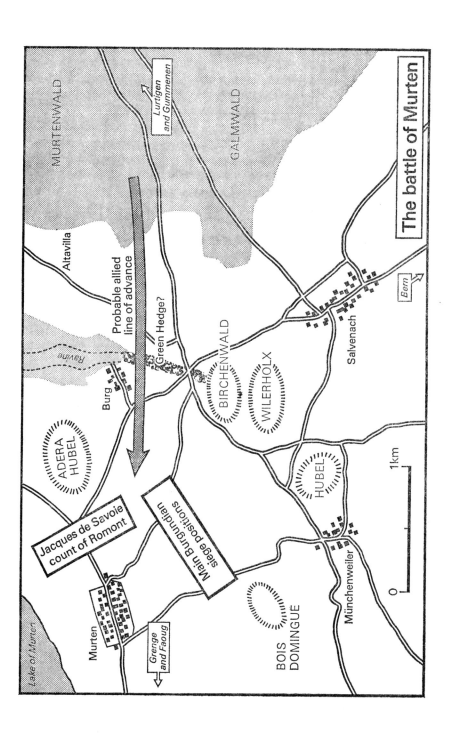

The battle of Murten

MURTENWALD

GALMWALD

Lurtigen and Gummenen

Altavilla

Probable allied line of advance

Ravine

Green Hedge?

Burg

ADERA HUBEL

BIRCHENWALD

WILERHOLX

Salvenach

Bern

Jacques de Savoie count of Romont

Main Burgundian siege positions

HUBEL

Lake of Murten

Murten

Grenge and Faoug

BOIS DOMINGUE

Münchenweiler

0   1km

outright victory – than to take Murten. On 12 June, only a day after his arrival at Murten, his men pushed on directly towards Bern and attacked the crossings over the Rivers Aare and Saane, defending Bern.

The effect of these attacks aimed at Bern was to provoke the immediate assembly of the military forces of the entire League of Constance because Bern, in contrast to Murten, was one of their own number. Charles must have known perfectly well that, once assembled, the allied army had a simple choice open to it: either march at once and give battle to the enemy or disband and return home. They were quite incapable of staying in the field. He expected an attack on 21 June and had his men drawn up all that day in battle order 'on elevated ground where there was a fine plain above the camp', that is, probably, on the plateau south of Burg. That night it poured with rain and Charles made the fatal blunder of assuming that the allies would not attack the next day, which opened dull and wet. Actually they were still assembling that very night, 21–2 June, somewhere near Ulmiz. Several thousand men from Zürich only arrived at Bern on the Friday afternoon, 21 June, having covered the 87 miles from Zürich on foot in three days. They left Bern at 10 o'clock in the evening and stopped for an hour or two to hear mass and rest in the rain at the Gümmenen bridge in the middle of the night before moving on to join their colleagues at Ulmiz. Duke René of Lorraine likewise only arrived in the nick of time. He reached Solothurn on the Friday morning after riding almost non-stop since leaving Strasbourg on the Wednesday. Early on 22 June, in spite of their fatigue, the allied troops began moving forward in three densely massed columns through the deciduous forest of the Murtenwald or Galmwald, heading directly towards Murten. The army was considerably larger than the one assembled before Grandson, where many of the men in it had also fought.

All accounts agree that Charles the Bold was taken completely by surprise when the attack came. He had had his troops paid that morning, and most of them were enjoying their dinner break and some welcome sunshine after the rain, when the enemy appeared on the scene. The duke had left a defensive screen along a hedge which crossed the plateau south of Burg in a north–south direction or nearly so. The English archers and other troops, with some artillery, posted here, would probably have seen the allied army emerging from the forest edge about a mile away from them across the open plain. They would have had about twenty minutes to give the alarm and get ready to defend themselves before the allied van was upon them. But they succeeded in holding the enemy for a short time only, not long enough, in spite of the twenty minutes, for the rest of the Burgundian army to arm and form up properly in defensive array. Very soon after the allies had fought their way through the hedge as they advanced towards Murten they could see ahead of them the Bois Domingue covered with Burgundian tents, and beleaguered Murten. While still on the plateau they encountered hastily mustered cavalry contingents, in one of which was the duke himself, who had only just managed to get into his armour in time. But these mounted forces arrived haphazardly and were forced back or overcome piecemeal by the well-disciplined, closely packed allied infantry, which soon advanced downhill and began to overrun the Burgundian camp and siege positions. Charles the Bold's army was put to general flight and, this time, it suffered heavy casualties. The only effective escape route, along the lake shore between Greng and Faoug, soon became hopelessly blocked, and Burgundian fugitives were shot as they waded and swam in the lake, like so many ducks, and even shot down like birds from the foliage of trees in which they had tried to hide. In conformity with battle orders issued by the federal diet on 18 March 1476 the *Eidgenossen* took no prisoners but killed all the enemy they could lay their hands on. Charles the Bold lost perhaps one third of his army. He was the victim of one of the most decisive and destructive battles in the military history of Europe up to that time.

Not all, however, was lost. The duke himself was by no means overwhelmed by his disaster. On 3 July the Milanese ambassador reported that Charles the Bold was busy with preparations for a third campaign against the Swiss. 'He laughs, jokes and makes good cheer' quite unlike someone who has been defeated. He gave the Estates of Burgundy, assembled at Salins on 8–12 July, an historical lecture on rulers who had been helped by their subjects to recover from defeats and setbacks. Nor was his military and political judgement entirely clouded by a passion for revenge against the 'Germans' as he often called the *Eidgenossen* and their allies. By 11 August he had decided, rightly, that his troops were needed in Lorraine. This switching of the theatre of war from Savoy to Lorraine did not mean facing an entirely new enemy, for Duke René of Lorraine was a member of the League of Constance and had fought in person on the field of Murten. But it did complete a process which Charles's defeat at Murten had begun – the collapse of Burgundian influence in Savoy. Had Charles won the battle of Murten, Savoy would have been his; because of his defeat, it slipped from his grasp, and King Louis XI of France was in firm control of it, with his sister the Duchess Yolande safely under his wing, before the end of 1476.

Even if we leave aside the duke's errors of judgement, excessive self-confidence, and repudiation of professional advice, the defeats of Charles the Bold at Grandson and Murten are not difficult to explain. Apart from anything else, almost everyone who ever had marched against the Swiss had been bloodily repulsed; for example the Austrians at Morgarten in 1315 and at Sempach in 1386. The powers of the League of Constance had at their disposal against Charles the Bold a very remarkable military machine, combining the traditional invincibility and admirable organization of the *Eidgenossen* with the well-armed and en-thusiastic forces of Basel, Strasbourg and other towns, and including cavalry elements supplied in particular by Dukes Sigmund and René. The allied army was linguistically homo-geneous – about 90 per cent German with small French elements from Fribourg and thereabouts and Lorraine – and about twice the size of Duke Charles's. It was made up in the main of infantry contingents (at Grandson it had no cavalry at all in action, hence the light Burgundian casualties) and it had little or no baggage train. It could be assembled with pinpoint accuracy at any chosen spot and the whole of it, moving and fighting in a dense mass, could be brought to bear at a single point. The men were volunteers, out for plunder, determined to defend their homes against the foreign invader. They knew the ground; theirs was the power and the glory.

By contrast the Burgundian army was weak and flabby. It was heterogeneous. There was a large French-speaking element of Burgundians and Picards; there was a large Italian element; and there were smaller English and Flemish–Dutch elements. Its cavalry contingents were on a *de luxe*, heavily armoured basis, needing a numerous and complicated support organization. It was full of non-combatants. Worst of all, it had with it the duke and his extravagant court, with its non-military paraphernalia. All this made it something less than a fighting machine. Inevitably, it was slow-moving and spread-out. It could offer no concentration of power comparable to the phalanxes of civic halberds the League could send into the attack. True, it had the best artillery in Europe; but the guns of those days only had time, usually, to fire one salvo before battle was joined hand to hand. Moreover their rate of fire was still far too slow to stop advancing infantry, nor were they accurate enough. The Burgundians, too, had to move through difficult terrain, quite unknown to them, without maps. Charles the Bold was quite right in admitting that he was risking everything in advancing against the Swiss and their allies.

Avoiding a pitched battle would have been military nonsense for either side. Duke Charles could only hope to punish and subdue his enemies in the League by defeating their combined forces decisively, all at once. As for the League, its army could stay in the field for only a week or ten days at the most. It simply had to find the enemy and destroy him as quickly as possible. Given these circumstances on either side head-on collisions were inevitable. At both Grandson and Murten the allies enjoyed overall numerical superiority. At Grandson the Burgundians were concentrated and the allies were separated into two bodies. Their superior numbers counted for little or nothing, but the element of surprise gave them their victory: the sudden on-slaught of the van followed, later, by the equally sudden emergence from the forest of the rest of their army. At Murten the allied numerical superiority was probably all-important. They marched their 25,000 men in concentrated columns into and through Burgundian positions in which a mere 12,000 or so men were extended over several miles. Here likewise they enjoyed and exploited the element of surprise. By sheer good luck they caught the duke with his trousers down.

While Charles the Bold was campaigning so unsuccessfully against the Swiss Duke René II of Lorraine was intermittently occupied between April and August 1476 in assisting his subjects to reconquer his and their duchy from the Burgundians. By the end of July, a month after Murten, virtually the whole of Lorraine was in their hands and they laid siege to Nancy, which was defended by Charles the Bold's governor and lieutenant-general Jehan de Rubempré, lord of Bièvres. He was forced to surrender on 6 October after the mutiny of his English archers. Charles the Bold had set out from La Rivière in Franche-Comté for Lorraine on 25 September at the head of his men. Too late to relieve Nancy, he soon harried Duke René's rather small army of League of Constance contingents into disintegration and dispersal in a series of marches and counter-marches. But instead of thereupon withdrawing northwards for the winter as his captains advised, Duke Charles marched south on 19 October from Pont-à-Mousson and established his siege round Nancy on 22 October; he was resolved to retake it as soon as possible.

The Burgundian siege of Nancy in the autumn of 1476 was a strategically risky enterprise. The duke's only line of communication – down the Moselle valley through the friendly bishopric of Metz to Thionville and Luxembourg – was tenuous and insecure. Furthermore his siege camp was open to attack from the enemy garrisons which had been left by Duke René in most of his important towns: Épinal, Vaudémont, Lunéville, Mirecourt, Arches, St Dié and other places were all strongly held. On the other hand Nancy was small and could scarcely hope to hold out against the Burgundian army for more than two months. Could Duke René bring a relieving force within that time? His prospects looked doubtful. Louis XI was unwilling to lend him any military assistance at all, appealing to his truce with Charles the Bold. Admittedly the Lower Union powers were willing and ready to help relieve Nancy, but the rest of the League of Constance, namely the *Eidgenossen*, were reluctant in the extreme. Yet past history had shown, and the Lower Union powers were perfectly well aware, that Swiss participation in the League's army was essential for military success. On 23 November René arrived at Luzern in person and harangued the federal diet, but still the *Eidgenossen* refused to turn out on his proposed expedition for the relief of Nancy. On 4 December Schwyz, Unterwalden and Glarus claimed that it was too cold for campaigning; Bern and Fribourg pretended that they needed to keep their forces at home against a possible attack from Franche-Comté; and Zürich, Luzern and Solothurn would only turn out if all the other *Eidgenossen* promised to turn out too. However, Duke René's efforts were not wholly fruitless, for he obtained leave to recruit volunteers from among the Swiss, to serve with him, unofficially as it were, as mercenaries. A legacy of £200,000 of Tours from his dying grandmother, and possibly a subvention from King Louis XI, enabled him to pay these troops, which were given orders to assemble at Basel on 15 December.

Meanwhile at Nancy, Charles the Bold's determination to take the town at all costs began, as winter advanced, to become increasingly irrational and almost despairing. More and more, he trusted in his own judgement, now evidently impaired, and rejected the advice, and even the information, proffered him. He discounted rumours that his leading Italian *condottiere*, Cola de Monforte, count of Campobasso, was contemplating treachery. He refused to believe that the Swiss would go to Duke René's assistance. He insisted that withdrawal northwards to the relative safety of Luxembourg was out of the question. Reinforcements continued to reach him till the first week of December; after that the enemy seems to have cut his lines of communication somewhere between Nancy and Thion- ville.

It was on Boxing Day 1476 that the main body of René's Swiss volunteers set out northwards from Basel down the Rhine. Naturally, most of them were veterans of Grandson and Murten, eager for yet more booty and supremely confident. Their captains were the same experienced leaders who had commanded them on these campaigns, including Hans Waldman of Zürich and Brandolf von Stein of Bern to name but two. These 6,000 or more seasoned Swiss troops formed the nucleus of Duke René's army, but it included also sizeable contingents from Basel and Strasbourg and the other Lower Union powers, not to mention René's own Lorrainers. The entire allied army was ordered to be at St Nicolas-du-Port, seven and a half miles south-east of Nancy, on 4 January, and the author of the *Chronicle of Lorraine* was given the task of galloping round the Lorraine towns to give word of this plan to the captains of René's garrisons, so that they could bring their forces along too. There is no reason to disbelieve Duke René's own statement, which he apparently dictated to a secretary, that he had some 19,000–20,000 men in the army which marched out of St Nicolas-du-Port on Sunday morning, 5 January 1477, in a snowstorm, and headed for Nancy.

This time Charles the Bold was probably outnumbered by three to one, but it is impossible to ascertain the size of his army with any exactitude. The last date on which his men were reviewed and paid was a month before, on 8 December. The numbers actually recorded then in the accounts were 1,136 mounted men-at-arms, 1,788 mounted archers and 2,463 infantry. But these 5,387 men certainly did not include the entire army at that time, for several well-known captains and their men were for some reason omitted. On the other hand there had been losses through desertion, disease and other causes since then: 400 Burgundian soldiers were said to have been frozen to death on Christmas Eve, and only a day or two before the battle of Nancy Cola de Monforte had defected to the enemy with his two sons and their entire contingent of Italian mercenaries, amounting to some 300 combatants at least. On the morning of 5 January, when Charles drew up his men in a defensive position across the road from St Nicolas along which his enemy would have to advance towards him, he must have left a substantial force to protect his siege lines and baggage round Nancy. His depleted army was thus probably only some 5,000–7,000 strong at most as it formed up behind the Jarville stream's narrow ravine and awaited events.

Just short of Jarville on their way along the main road to Nancy from St Nicolas and Lunéville the allies halted. Their response to the discovery that Charles, with his artillery, was barring the route in front of them, was to send a dense column of infantry through the forest on their left to outflank him. These men struggled with considerable difficulty and discomfort in snow and mist along forest paths, through thickets and across ice-cold streams, unseen by the Burgundians who were in any case out of their sight behind a low ridge which runs parallel to the Meurthe at this point. Once again Charles the Bold was taken by surprise as this allied vanguard emerged unexpectedly from the forest on his right flank, sounding three mournful blasts, each as long as the air in a man's lungs would allow, on their dreaded horns, and marched resolutely and rapidly against him. His artillery was pointing in the wrong direction and could not be used against this advancing infantry, which soon pushed back the Burgundian right wing. At the same time the rest of the allied army attacked the Burgundians frontally, scrambling across the Jarville stream. Soon the entire Burgundian army was in desperate flight, some of it escaping over the ford at Tomblaine, the rest attempting to retreat past Nancy, whose garrison now sallied forth to cut down these fugitives and burn and plunder the Burgundian camp. Charles the Bold's army, which had been only a remnant to start with, was more or less completely destroyed. It took two days of careful searching through the frozen and dismembered corpses littering the battlefield to find the body of the forty-four-year-old duke. Apparently his horse had failed to clear a stream in the general flight, and he had fallen, perhaps already wounded.

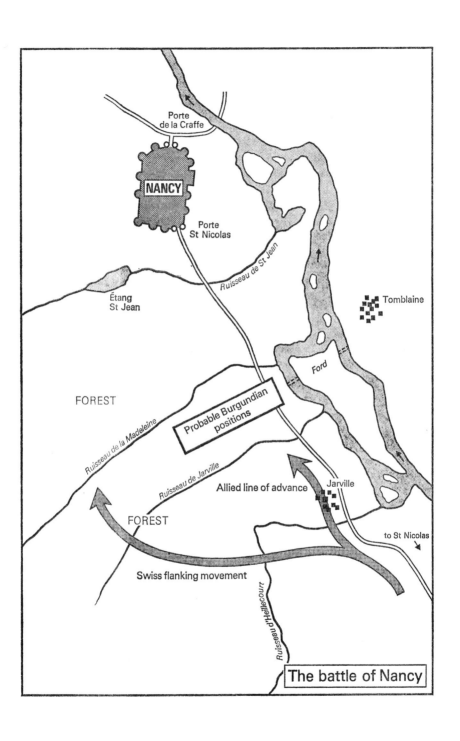

Porte
de la Craffe

NANCY

Porte
St Nicolas

Ruisseau de St Jean

Étang
St Jean

Tomblaine

Ford

FOREST

Ruisseau de la Madeleine

Probable Burgundian
positions

Ruisseau de Jarville

Allied line of advance

Jarville

FOREST

to St Nicolas

Swiss flanking movement

Ruisseau d'Heillecourt

The battle of Nancy

Someone then finished him off with a blow from a battle-axe which split his skull.

The Burgundian state, which had been put together by Dukes Philip the Bold and Philip the Good, fell apart on the death of Charles the Bold. He had betrothed his only child and heiress Mary to Maximilian of Austria, but that prince had been given no practical experience of Burgundian administration, and no one was immediately available, apart from Mary and Charles's widow Margaret of York, to take over from the fallen duke in circumstances made critical by the aggressive aspirations of King Louis XI of France and by the revolutionary activities of the Flemings and other dissatisfied townspeople in the Low Countries. Territorially and constitutionally the Burgundian state was so badly ravaged and undermined after Nancy that, long before the end of 1477, it had been crippled and dismembered. In any case after the wedding of Maximilian and Mary at Ghent on 19 August 1477 it was no longer Valois, it was Austrian or Habsburg.

Territorially, it was the permanent loss of the duchy of Burgundy to France, conquered by Louis XI within weeks of the battle of Nancy, which really altered the character of the polity which had been ruled over by the Valois dukes; for the loss of Guelders in 1492 was a minor affair, and Artois and Franche-Comté, lost for a time, were recovered in 1492–3. Constitutionally, the prince's powers, increased substantially by the successive Valois dukes, were diminished drastically at Mary of Burgundy's accession and afterwards. The recovery under Philip the Fair, who ruled most of the Low Countries from 1493 to 1506 as archduke of Austria just as Charles the Bold and his predecessors had ruled there as dukes of Burgundy, was significant but limited and in part temporary. It was this Philip who married Joanna, daughter of Ferdinand and Isabella of Spain, and fathered on her the prodigious Emperor Charles V, who maintained his Burgundian sentiments and loyalty till his death though without ever recovering what he regarded as his ancestral capital of Dijon. Of course Burgundy lived on in these remarkable Habsburg princes, Maximilian, Philip, Charles; but it was not the same Burgundy, not the Burgundy of the Valois dukes but a new Germanic, Renaissance, early modern Burgundy, soon part of a much wider Empire, the history of which is outside the scope of this book.

What has been the historical importance of Valois Burgundy

during the five hundred years since its demise? The loose federal structure of the seven United Provinces which formed the Dutch Republic was in its constitutional and administrative arrangements a legacy of Burgundian rule, and the same is true of the Spanish Netherlands. Indirectly both Holland and Belgium owe much to their distant Burgundian antecedent, and the presence of these two countries and Luxembourg on the present-day map of Europe is partly due to Burgundy. Belgium in particular, with its mixture and clash of French and Flemish traditions, still preserves a certain 'Burgundian' character, and the spell of the Burgundian dukes still exercises its power to this day in their homeland, the duchy of Burgundy, and in their original capital, Dijon. The flowering of Burgundian literary culture and the dukes' patronage of manuscript illumination were soon overwhelmed by the Italian Renaissance, and the fine buildings of the dukes were mostly neglected, but the courtly traditions and institutions of Valois Burgundy were in the main stream of European development: every subsequent European court owed something to Burgundy, and the Order of the Golden Fleece flourishes to this day. In the military history of Europe, too, the Burgundian dukes, especially Charles the Bold (the inventor of drill?), made a lasting contribution. In their love of chivalry and romance, in their extravagant court and lavish illuminated manuscripts, in their encouragement of the Estates, their use of heavy cavalry, their dreams of a crusade, the Valois dukes may be described as 'medieval', if that word in this context can mean drawing inspiration from the past. But, in their attempts to rationalize and improve their administrative institutions, in their encouragement of a new class of 'professional' civil servant, in their attempts to increase their authority and transform their status by the acquisition of a crown, and in other ways too, the dukes – and above all Charles the Bold – were looking forwards hopefully to a place for Burgundy in the modern sun which, however, the outcome of the battle of Nancy decisively denied it.

Select Reading List

A selective list of some of the more important books and articles on Valois Burgundy

Works relating to all four Valois dukes

C. A. J. Armstrong, 'La politique matrimoniale des ducs de Bourgogne de la maison de Valois', *Annales de Bourgogne* XL (1968), 5–58, 89–139

A. de Barante, *Histoire des ducs de Bourgogne de la maison de Valois*, ed. L. P. Gachard, 2 vols., Brussels, 1938

J. Calmette, *The Golden Age of Burgundy: The Magnificent Dukes and Their Courts*, 1962. Translated from *Les grands ducs de Bourgogne*, Paris, 1956

L. Febvre, 'Les ducs Valois de Bourgogne et les idées politiques de leur temps', *Revue bourguignonne* XXIII (1913), 27–50

P. Fredericq, *Essai sur le rôle politique et sociale des ducs de Bourgogne dans les Pays-Bas*, Ghent, 1875

M. Mollat, 'Recherches sur les finances des ducs Valois de Bourgogne', *Revue historique* CCXIX (1958), 285–321

H. Pirenne, 'The formation and constitution of the Burgundian state', *American Historical Review* XIV (1908–9), 477–502

W. R. Tyler, *Dijon and the Valois Dukes of Burgundy*, Oklahoma, 1971

Works relating to individual dukes

PHILIP THE BOLD

A. S. Atiya, *The Crusade of Nicopolis*, London, 1934

O. Cartellieri, *Geschichte der Herzöge von Burgund, 1363–1477*, vol. I, *Philipp der Kühne*, Leipzig, 1910

H. David, *Philippe le Hardi, duc de Bourgogne, protecteur des arts*, Dijon, 1937

H. Laurent and F. Quicke, *Les origines de l'État bourguignon: L'accession de la maison de Bourgogne aux duchés de Brabant et Limbourg (1383–1407)*, Brussels, 1939

E. Petit, *Ducs de Bourgogne de la Maison de Valois, I. Philippe le Hardi*, vol. I, *1363–1380*, Paris, 1909

R. Vaughan, *Philip the Bold: The Formation of the Burgundian State*, London, 1962

JOHN THE FEARLESS

J. d'Avout, *La querelle des Armagnacs et des Bourguignons*, Paris, 1943

A. Coville, *Jean Petit: La question du tyrannicide au commencement du XVᵉ siècle*, Paris, 1932

M. Nordberg, *Les ducs et la royauté*, Uppsala, 1964

J. Schoos, *Der Machtkampf zwischen Burgund und Orleans*, Luxembourg, 1956
R. Vaughan, *John the Fearless: The Growth of Burgundian Power*, London, 1966

PHILIP THE GOOD

P. Bonenfant, *Du meutre de Montereau au traité de Troyes*, Brussels, 1958
P. Bonenfant, *Philippe le Bon*, Brussels, 1955
A. Bossuat, *Perrinet Gressart et Françis de Surienne*, Paris, 1936
R. Vaughan, *Philip the Good: The Apogee of the Burgundian State*, London, 1970

CHARLES THE BOLD

J. Bartier, *Charles le Téméraire*, Brussels, 1944 and 1970
K. Bittmann, *Ludwig XI und Karl der Kühne. Die Memoiren des Philippe de Commynes als historische Quelle*, 2 vols., Göttingen, 1964, 1970
J. Foster Kirk, *History of Charles the Bold*, 3 vols., London, 1863–8
P. Frédérix, *La mort de Charles le Téméraire*, Paris, 1966
R. Putnam, *Charles the Bold*, 1908
E. Toutey, *Charles le Téméraire et la Ligue de Constance*, Paris, 1902
R. Vaughan, *Charles the Bold: The Last Valois Duke of Burgundy*, London, 1973

Biographies of ducal officals and courtiers

E. Bauer, *Négociations et campagnes de Rodolphe de Hochberg, 1427–87*, Neuchâtel, 1928
G. Blondeau, 'Guy Armenier, chef du conseil ducal', *Mémoires de la Société d'émulation du Doubs* 10, VIII (1938), 56–76, and 10, X (1940–42), 38–66
H. Brauer-Gramm, *Der Landvogt Peter von Hagenbach: Die burgundische Herrschaft am Oberrhein, 1469–74*, Göttingen, 1957
P. Champion and P. de Thoisy, *Bourgogne-France-Angleterre au traité de Troyes: Jean de Thoisy, évêque de Tournai*, Paris, 1943
F. de Coussemaker, *Thierry Gherbode*, Lille, 1902
G. Dumay, 'Guy de Pontailler', *Mémoires de la Société bourguignonne de géographie et d'histoire* XXIII (1907), 1–222
P. M. J. du Teil, *Guillaume Fillastre*, Paris, 1920
C. Fierville, *Le cardinal Jean Jouffroy et son temps, 1412–1473*, Paris, 1874
B. de Lannoy, *Hugues de Lannoy*, Brussels, 1957
P. de Lichtervelde, *Un grand commis des ducs de Bourgogne, Jaques de Lichtervelde*, Brussels, 1943
H. T. de Morembert, 'Jean Chevrot, évêque de Tournai et de Toul, vers 1395–1460', *Mémoires de l'Académie nationale de Metz* CXLV (1963–4), 171–220
W. Paravicini, *Guy de Brimeu: Der burgundische Staat und seine adlige Führungsschicht unter Karl dem Kühnen*, Bonn, 1973
J. Pot, *Histoire de Regnier Pot, conseiller des ducs de Bourgogne*, Paris, 1929

Burgundy's relations with her neighbours

B. Buser, *Die Beziehungen der Mediceer zu Frankreich, 1434–1494*, Leipzig, 1879
J. G. Dickinson, *The Congress of Arras, 1435*, Oxford, 1955
J. Faussemagne, *L'apanage ducal de Bourgogne dans ses rapports avec la monarchie française, 1363–1477*, Lyons, 1937
H. Grüneisen, 'Die westliche Reichstände in der Auseinandersetzung

zwischen dem Reich, Burgund und Frankreich bis 1473', *Rheinische Viertel-jahrsblätter* XXVI (1961), 22–77

P. M. Perret, *Histoire des relations de la France avec Venise*, 2 vols., Paris, 1896

B. A. Pocquet du Haut-Jussé, *Deux féodaux: Bourgogne et Bretagne*, Paris, 1935

M. R. Thielemans, *Bourgogne et Angleterre: Relations politiques et économiques entre les Pays-Bas bourguignons et l'Angleterre, 1435–1467*, Brussels, 1966

Chronicles

G. Chastellain, *Œuvres*, ed. Kervyn de Lettenhove, 8 vols., Académie royale de Belgique, Brussels, 1863–6

P. de Commynes, *Memoirs, Books 1–6*, transl. M. Jones, Penguin Books, Harmondsworth, 1972

J. Froissart, *Chronicles of England, France, Spain and the adjoining Countries*, transl. T. Johnes, 2 vols., London, 1849

O. de la Marche, *Mémoires*, ed. H. Beaune and J. d'Arbaumont, 4 vols., Société de l'histoire de France, Paris, 1883–8

J. Le Fèvre, lord of St. Rémy, *Chronique*, ed. F. Morand, 2 vols., Société de l'histoire de France, Paris, 1876, 1881

E. de Monstrelet, *The Chronicles of Enguerrand de Monstrelet*, transl. T. Johnes, 2 vols., London, 1840

D. Schilling, *Die Berner-Chronik, 1468–1484*, ed. G. Tobler, 2 vols., Bern, 1897, 1901

J. de Waurin, *Recueil des croniques*, ed. W. Hardy, Rolls Series, 5 vols., London, 1864–91

Estates

W. Jappe Alberts, *De Staten van Gelre en Zutphen*, 2 vols., Groningen, 1950, 1956

J. Billioud, *Les États de Bourgogne aux XIV e et XV e siècles*, Dijon, 1922

J. Gilissen, 'Les États Généraux des pays de par deça, 1464–1632', *Anciens pays et assemblées d'États* XXXIII (1965), 261–321

C. Hirschauer, *Les États d'Artois de leur origines à l'occupation française, 1340–1640*, 2 vols., Paris, 1923

F. H. J. Lemmink, *Het ontstaan van de Staten van Zeeland en hun geschiedenis tot het jaar 1555*, Rosendaal, 1951

W. Prevenier, *De Leden en de Staten van Vlaanderen, 1384–1405*, Brussels, 1961

Institutions and administrative history

E. Andt, *La chambre des comptes de Dijon à l'époque des ducs Valois*, vol. I, Paris, 1924

J. Bartier, *Légistes et gens de finances au XV e siècle. Les conseillers des ducs de Bourgogne*, Brussels, 1952

J. Bouault, 'Les bailliages au duché de Bourgogne aux XIV e et XV e siècles', *Annales de Bourgogne* II (1930), 7–22

P. Gorissen, *De Raadkamer van de hertog van Bourgondië te Maastricht, 1473–77*, Louvain and Paris, 1959

T. S. Jansma, *Raad en Rekenkamer in Holland en Zeeland tijdens Philips van Bourgondië*, Utrecht, 1932

E. Lameere, *Le grand conseil des ducs de Bourgogne de la maison de Valois*, Brussels, 1900

P. Renoz, *La chancellerie de Brabant sous Philippe le Bon, 1430–1467*, Brussels, 1955
J. van Rompaey, *Het grafelijk baljuwsambt in Vlaanderen tijdens de boergondische periode*, Brussels, 1967

Literature, the arts and the court

M. Beaulieu and J. Baylé, *Le costume un Bourgogne de Philippe le Hardi à Charles le Téméraire*, Paris, 1956
P. C. Boeren, *Twee Maaslandse dichters in dienst van Karel de Stoute*, The Hague, 1968
O. Cartellieri, *The Court of Burgundy*, London, 1929. Translated from *Am Hofe der Herzöge von Burgund*, Basel, 1926
L. M. J. Delaissé, *La miniature flamande: Le mécénat de Philippe le Bon*, Brussels, 1959
F. Deuchler, *Die Burgunderbeute*, Bern, 1963
G. Doutrepont, *La littérature française à la cour des ducs de Bourgogne*, Paris, 1909
P. Durrieu, *La miniature flamande au temps de la cour de Bourgogne*, Paris, 1931
C. Gaspar and F. Lyna, *Philippe le Bon et ses beaux libres*, Brussels, 1944
L. Hommel, *L'histoire du noble ordre de la Toison d'Or*, Brussels, 1947
J. Huizinga, *The Waning of the Middle Ages*, London, 1924. Translated from *Herfsttij der middeleeuwen*, Haarlem, 1919
A. Humbert, *La sculpture sous les ducs de Bourgogne, 1361–1483*, Paris, 1913
Inventaire de la 'librairie' de Philippe le Bon, 1420, ed. G. Doutrepont, Brussels, 1906
J. Marix, *Les musiciens de la cour de Bourgogne au XVe siècle*, Paris, 1937
C. Monget, *La Chartreuse de Dijon*, 3 vols., Montreuil-sur-Mer and Tournai, 1898–1905
Zuylen van Nyevelt, A. van, *Épisodes de la vie des ducs de Bourgogne à Bruges*, Bruges, 1937

Military history

C. Brusten, *L'armée bourguignonne de 1405 à 1468*, Brussels, n.d.
J. R. de Chevanne, *Les guerres en Bourgogne de 1470 à 1475*, Paris, 1934
J. Garnier, *L'artillerie des ducs de Bourgogne*, Paris, 1895
H. L. G. Guillaume, *Histoire de l'organisation militaire sous les ducs de Bourgogne*, Brussels, 1848
J. de la Chauvelays, 'Les armées des trois premiers ducs de Bourgogne de la maison de Valois', *Mémoires de l'Académie des sciences, arts et belles-lettres de Dijon* 3, VI (1880), 19–335
J. de la Chauvelays, *Les armées de Charles le Téméraire dans les deux Bourgognes*, Paris, 1879

Neighbours of Valois Burgundy

H. J. Cohn, *The Government of the Rhine Palatinate in the Fifteenth Century*, Oxford, 1965
M. José, *La maison de Savoie: Amédée VIII*, 2 vols., Paris, 1962
R. Lacour, *Le gouvernement de l'apanage de Jean, duc de Berry, 1360–1416*, Paris, 1934
A. Leguai, *De la seigneurie à l'État: Le Bourbonnais pendant la guerre de Cent Ans*, Paris, 1969
P. S. Lewis, *Later Medieval France: The Polity*, London, 1968
P. Tucoo-Chala, *Gaston Fébus et la vicomté de Béarn*, Bordeaux, 1959

Religion and the church

A. Hyma, *The Christian Renaissance: A History of the 'Devotio moderna'*, New York, 1924

A. G. Jongkees, *Staat en kerk in Holland en Zeeland onder de Bourgondische hertogen, 1425–1477*, Groningen, 1942

É. de Moreau, *Histoire de l'Église en Belgique*, vol. IV, *1378–1559*, Brussels, 1949

J. Toussaert, *Le sentiment religieux en Flandre à la fin du moyen âge*, Paris, 1960

J. Toussaint, *Les relations diplomatiques de Philippe le Bon avec le concile de Bâle, 1431–1449*, Louvain, 1942

Social and economic history

G. Bigwood, *Le régime juridique et économique du commerce de l'argent dans la Belgique au moyen âge*, 2 vols., Brussels, 1921, 1922

A. Bocquet, *Recherches sur la population rurale de l'Artois et du Boulonnais, 1384–1477*, Arras, 1969

J. Delumeau, *L'alun de Rome, XVe–XIXe siècle*, Paris, 1962

L. Lièvre, *La monnaie et le change en Bourgogne sous les ducs Valois*, Dijon, 1929

J. H. A. Munro, *Wool, Cloth and Gold: The Struggle for Bullion in Anglo-Burgundian Trade, 1340–1478*, Brussels and Toronto, 1974

P. Spufford, *Monetary Problems and Policies in the Burgundian Netherlands, 1433–1496*, Leiden, 1970

H. van der Wee, *The Growth of the Antwerp Market and the European Economy*, 3 vols., The Hague, 1963

Towns

Antwerp
F. Prims, *Geschiedenis van Antwerpen*, 11 vols., Brussels, etc., 1927–49
Basel
R. Wackernagel, *Geschichte der Stadt Basel*, 3 vols., Basel, 1907–24
Bern
R. Feller, *Geschichte Berns*, vol. I, Bern, 1946
Besançon
C. Fohlen and others, *Histoire de Besançon*, 2 vols., Paris, 1964, 1965
Bruges
J. A. van Houtte, *Bruges: Essai d'histoire urbaine*, Brussels, 1967
Brussels
P. Bonenfant and others, *Bruxelles au XVme siècle*, Brussels, 1953
Cologne
L. Ennen, *Geschichte der Stadt Köln*, 5 vols., Cologne and Neuss, 1863–80
Dijon
F. Humbert, *Les finances municipales de Dijon du milieu du XIVe siècle à 1477*, Paris, 1961
Ghent
V. Fris, *Histoire de Gand*, Bruxelles, 1913
Liège
G. Kurth, *La cité de Liège au moyen âge*, 3 vols., Brussels, 1910

Lille:

E. Marquant, *La vie économique à Lille sous Philippe le Bon*, Paris, 1940

L. Trenard and others, *Histoire de Lille*, vol. 1, Lille, 1970

Nancy

C. Pfister, *Histoire de Nancy*, vol. 1, 2nd edn, Paris, 1902

Supplementary Bibliography

The books and articles listed here have come to notice after the publication of the relevant volume of my *History of Valois Burgundy*.

PHILIP THE BOLD, published 1962

A. Buchet, 'La saisie du château et de la terre de Bolland par Philippe le Hardi, duc de Bourgogne, 1389–1402', *Bulletin de la Société verviétoise d'archéologie et d'histoire* XLIII (1956), 43–55

P. Cockshaw, 'A propos de la circulation monétaire entre la Flandre et le Brabant de 1384 à 1390', *Contributions à l'histoire économique et sociale* VI (1970–71), 105–42

P. Cockshaw, 'Le fonctionnement des ateliers monétaires sous Philippe le Hardi', *Cercle d'études numismatiques, Bulletin trimestriel* VII, 2 (1970), 24–37

P. Cockshaw, 'Mentions d'auteurs, de copistes, d'enlumineurs et de librairies dans les comptes généraux de l'État bourguignon (1384–1419)', *Scriptorium* XXIII (1969), 122–44

M. Debersée, 'Une dépense à la charge du duc de Bourgogne à la fin du XIVe siècle: les travaux et réparations effectués à Lille et dans sa châtellenie', *Revue du Nord* LIII (1971), 409–31

A. Graffart and A. Uyttebrouck, 'Quelques documents inédits concernant l'accession de la maison de Bourgogne au duché de Brabant, 1395–1404', *Bulletin de la Commission royale d'histoire* CXXXVII (1971), 57–137

L. van Hommerich, 'Philippe le Hardi et les États du duché de Limbourg et des autres pays d'Outre-Meuse, 1387–1404', *Revue du Nord* XLIX (1967), 193–4

A. Lemon, 'La politique religieuse de Philippe le Hardi en Flandre', *Annales de la Fédération archéologique et historique de Belgique* XVI (1903), 437–49

M. Marchal-Verdoodt, *Table des noms de personnes et des lieux mentionnés dans les plus anciens comptes de la recette générale de Philippe le Hardi, duc de Bourgogne (1383–1389)*, Commission royale d'histoire, Brussels, 1971

R. de Muynck, 'De Gentse oorlog (1379–1385). Oorzaken en karakter', *Annales de la Société d'histoire et d'archéologie de Gand* (n.s.), V (1951), 305–18

A. van Nieuwenhuysen, 'La comptabilité d'un receveur de Philippe le Hardi', *Hommage au Professeur P. Bonenfant*, Brussels, 1965, pp. 409–19

A. van Nieuwenhuysen, 'L'organisation financière des États du duc de Bourgogne Philippe le Hardi', *Acta historica bruxellensia*, vol. I, *Recherches sur l'histoire des finances publiques en Belgique*, Brussels, 1967, 215–47

Ordonnances de Philippe le Hardi, de Marguerite de Male et de Jean sans Peur, 1381–1419, vol. I, *1381–1393*, ed. P. Bonenfant, J. Bartier and A. van Nieuwenhuysen, Recueil des ordonnances des Pays-Bas, Brussels, 1965

W. Prevenier, 'Financiën en boekhouding in de Bourgondische periode.

Nieuwe bronnen en resultaten', *Tijdschrift voor Geschiedenis* LXXXII (1969), 469–81

W. Prevenier, 'Les perturbations dans les relations commerciales anglo-flamandes entre 1379 et 1407', *Economies et sociétés du Moyen Âge: Mélanges Edouard Perroy*, Paris, 1972, pp. 477–97

H. Proot, 'Filips de Stoute en de stad Kortrijk', *De Leiegouw* XII (1970), 131–9

M. Rey, 'Philippe le Hardi et la Franche-Comté', *Publications du Centre européen d'études burgundo-medianes*, VIII (1966), 55–62

M. Rey, 'La politique financière de Philippe le Hardi en Franche-Comté', *Mémoires de la Société pour l'histoire du droit et des institutions des anciens pays bourguignons, comtois et romands* XXVI (1965), 7–50

F. Salet, 'Histoire et héraldique: La succession de Bourgogne de 1361', *Mélanges offerts à René Crozet*, Poitiers, 1966, pp. 1307–16

J. Stengers, 'Philippe le Hardi et les États de Brabant', *Hommage au Professeur Paul Bonenfant*, Brussels, 1965, pp. 383–408

C. Sterling, 'Œuvres retrouvées de Jean de Beaumetz, peintre de Philippe le Hardi', *Bulletin Musées Royaux des Beaux-Arts: Miscellanea Erwin Panofsky*, Brussels, 1955, pp. 57–82

M. Toth-Ubbens, 'Een dubbelvorstenhuwelijk in het jaar 1385', *Bijdragen voor de Geschiedenis der Nederlanden* XIX (1964), 107–10

F. Vignier, 'Réunion du Charolais au duché de Bourgogne', *Mémoires de la Société pour l'histoire du droit et des institutions des anciens pays bourguignons, comtois et romands* XXII (1961), 191–5

JOHN THE FEARLESS, published 1966

W. P. Blockmans, 'La participation des sujets flamands à la politique monétaire des ducs de Bourgogne, 1384–1500.' *Rev. belge de numismatique*, xix (1973), 103–34.

W. Buntinx, 'De enquête van Oudenburg. Hervorming van de repartitie van de beden in het graafschap Vlaanderen, 1408', *Bulletin de la Commission royale d'histoire* CXXXIV (1968), 75–137

P. Cockshaw, 'Comptes généraux de l'état Bourguignon. A propos d'un livre récent', *Belgisch Tijdschrift voor Filol. en Geschiedenis* XLV (1967), 490–93

P. Cockshaw, 'Les premières monnaies de Jean sans Peur: l'émission de 1407', *Cercle d'études numismatiques. Bulletin trimestriel*, VIII (1971), 41–52

Comptes généraux de l'État bourguignon entre 1416 et 1420, ed. M. Mollat and others, 3 vols. Recueil des historiens de la France. Documents financiers, Paris, 1965–9, vol. V

Y. Grandeau, 'Le dauphin Jean, duc de Touraine, fils de Charles VI (1938–1417)', *Bulletin historique et philologique du Comité des travaux historiques*, 1968, 665–728

C. C. Willard, 'The manuscripts of Jean Petit's Justification. Some Burgundian propaganda methods of the early fifteenth century'. *Studi francesi* XIII (1969), 271–80

H. van der Wee, 'L'échec de la réforme monétaire de 1407 en Flandre vu par les marchands Italiens de Bruges', *Studi in onore di A. Fanfani*, Milan, 1962, vol. III, 579–89

A. Zoete, *De beden in het graafschap Vlaanderen onder Jan zonder Vrees, 1405–1419*, Ghent University, unpublished thesis, 1967

PHILIP THE GOOD, published 1970

H. Baud, *Amédée VIII et la guerre de Cent Ans*, Annecy, 1971

R. Berger, *Nikolas Rolin: Kanzler der Zeitenwende im burgundisch-französischen Konflikt, 1422–1461*, Fribourg, 1971

W. P. Blockmans, 'De Bourgondische Nederlanden: de weg naar een moderne staatsvorm.' *Handelingen van de kon. Kring voor oudheidkunde, letteren en kunst van Mechelen* lxxvii (1973), 7–26.

J. de la C. Bouton, 'Un poème à Philippe le Bon sur la Toison d'Or', *Annales de Bourgogne* XLII (1970), 5–29

P. Cockshaw, 'Fragments d'un compte de la recette générale de Bourgogne conservés à Bruxelles', *Archives et Bibliothèques de Belgique* XXXVII (1966), 241–4

P. Cockshaw, 'Nouveaux suppléments aux itinéraires de Philippe le Bon, comte de Charolais, puis duc de Bourgogne, et de Charles le Téméraire, comte de Charolais', *Archives et Bibliothèques de Belgique* XLI (1970), 209–13

C. Desama, 'Jeanne d'Arc et la diplomatie de Charles VII: l'ambassade française auprès de Philippe le Bon en 1429', *Annales de Bourgogne* XL (1968), 290–99

Dispatches with related documents of Milanese ambassadors in France and Burgundy, 1450–1483, vols. I and II, *1450–1461*, ed. and trans. P. M. Kendall and V. Ilardi, Ohio University Press, Athens, Ohio, 1970–1

A. Gandara, *Isabel filha de D. João I. Prolongamento historico de Joana d'Arc*, Lisbon, 1954

J. L. Kupper, 'Marc de Bade au pays de Liège en 1465', *Liège et Bourgogne, Bibliothèque de la Faculté de Philosophie et Lettres de l'Université de Liège* CCIII (1972), 55–80

Y. Lacaze, 'Contribution à l'histoire économique et politique des pays de "par-deça": trois années de la négociation hanséato-bourguignonne ouverte en 1453', *Le moyen âge* LXXV (1969), 94–119, 219–320

Y. Lacaze, 'Politique méditerranéenne et projets de croisade chez Philippe le Bon de la chute de Byzance à la victoire chrétienne de Belgrade', *Annales de Bourgogne* XLI (1969), 5–42, 81–132

Y. Lacaze, 'Le rôle des traditions dans la genèse d'un sentiment national au XVe siècle. La Bourgogne de Philippe le Bon', *Bibliothèque de l'École des Chartes* CXXIX (1971), 303–85

R Laurent, 'L'inventaire des chartes de Brabant établi par Adrian van der Ee en 1438', *Scriptorium* XXIII (1969), 384–92

J. Lejeune, *Les van Eyck, peintres de Liège et de sa cathédrale*, Liège, 1956

W. Maleczek, 'Österreich-Frankreich-Burgund. Zur Westpolitik Herzog Friedrichs IV in der Zeit von 1430 bis 1439', *Mitteilungen des Instituts für österreichische Geschichtsforschung* LXXIX (1971), 111–55

J. H. Munro, 'An economic aspect of the collapse of the Anglo-Burgundian alliance, 1428–42', *English Historical Review*, LXXXV (1970), 225–44

J. H. Munro, 'The costs of Anglo-Burgundian interdependence', *Revue belge de philologie et d'histoire* XLVI (1968), 1228–38

W. Prevenier, 'Les États de Flandre depuis les origines jusqu'en 1790' *Anciens pays et assemblées d'États* XXXIII (1965), 15–59

J. van Rompaey, 'Het onstaan van de Grote Raad onder Filips de Goede. *Handel. kon. Zuidnederlandsch Maatsch. voor Taal en Lett.* XXV (1971), 297–310.

J. van Rompaey, *De Grote Raad van de hertogen van Boergandië en het Parlement van Mechelen*. Brussels, 1973.

U. Schwarzkopf, 'Zum Höfischen Dienstrecht im 15. Jahrhundert: das burgundische Beispiel', *Festschrift für Hermann Heimpel*, Göttingen, 1972, vol. II, 422–42

M. Sommé, 'Les déplacements d'Isabella de Portugal et la circulation dans les Pays-Bas bourguignons au milieu du XVe siècle', *Revue du Nord* LII (1970), 183–97

P. Spufford, *Monetary Problems and Policies in the Burgundian Netherlands*, Leiden, 1970

H. van der Wee, 'Conjunctuur en economische groei in de Zuidelijke Nederlanden tijdens de 14e, 15e en 16e eeuw', *Mededelingen van de koninklijke Vlaamse Academie voor wetenschappen, letteren en schone kunsten van België. Klasse der Letteren*, Brussels, 1965

CHARLES THE BOLD, published 1973

H. Helbling and others, *Handbuch der Schweizer Geschichte*, Zürich, 1972, vol. I

L. T. Maes and G. Dogaer, 'A propos de l'ordonnance de Thionville promulguée par Charles le Téméraire en 1473', *Annales de Bourgogne* XLV (1973), 45–9

L. T. Maes and G. Dogaer, 'De oudst bekende tekst van de stichtingsacte van het Parlement van Mechelen (1473)', *Handelingen van de koninklijke Kring voor oudheidkunde, letteren en kunst van Mechelen* LXXVI (1972), 41–60

Stad Mechelen. 500 jaar Grote Raad. Tentoonstelling van Karel de Stoute tot Keizer Karel, Malines, 1973.

H. Wiesflecker, *Kaiser Maximilian I: Das Reich, Österreich und Europa an der Wende zur Neuzeit*, vol. I, *1459–93*, Munich, 1971

Index

Aachen (Aix-la-Chapelle), 169, 199
Aalst: *see* Alost
Aare, River, 218
Abbeville, 22, 155; mutiny of garrison, 200; ordinance, 126, 127
Achilles, 138
Adam and Eve, 178
Adorne, Pierre, 89
Agincourt, battle of, 7, 20, 22, 51, 62, 116
Ahasuerus, King, 174
aides, 12, 41, 43, 78–9, 82, 91, 103–4, 106–7, 200
Aigle, 210, 211
Aigues-Mortes, 160
Alarts, Daniel, 89
Alençon, John, duke of, 60
Alexander the Great, 77, 81, 146, 172, 174, 178, 189, 192
Alexandria, 157
Alfonso V, king of Aragon and Naples, 8, 72, 163
Alfonso V, king of Portugal, 73
Aliprandi, Petro, 188
Alkmaar, 132
Alost, 9, 86, 88
Alphen, battle of, 132
Alsace, 23, 34, 69, 199, 202–4, 206–11
ambassadors, 10, 46–7, 74–5, 95, 139, 166, 167, 176, 183–4, 187, 209, 215; *see* Bembo, Panigarola
America, United States of, 190
Amiens, 22, 155, 156
Amont, bailiwick, 110
Amsterdam, 24, 26, 70, 106, 130, 132
Andernach, 135
Andromache, 191
animals, 40, 41, 43, 72, 96, 146, 149, 173, 174, 177, 178, 181, 185, 186
Anjou, house of, 8, 62–3

Anjou, Louis I, duke of, 49
Anjou, René, titular king of Naples and duke of, 62–3, 64
Anthon, battle of, 154
Antwerp, 11, 15, 18, 24, 27, 70, 91, 106, 112, 117; *schout*, 114
Aosta, 211
Aragon, 6–7, 20, 23, 54, 71–2, 73; *see* John II, Martin I, Peter IV
Aragon, Peter of, son of King Martin I, 71
Arc, Joan of, 52
Arches, 222
archives: *see* records
Ardennes, church of St Hubert, 186
Argilly, château, 167
Arles, 199
Arlon, 185
Armagnac, Bernard VII, count of, 51, 153
Armagnacs, 7, 51, 56, 153–4
armies, 12, 16, 25, 28, 39, 81, 92, 123–61, 198, 199, 200, 214–15, 218–19, 220–21, 223–4
arms and armour, 26, 167, 180, 191, 192
Arnaut, Amiot, 86
Arnolfini, Giovanni, 168
Arras, 25, 75, 80, 114, 154, 155, 164, 179, 187; bishopric, 59, 83; bishops: *see* Canard, Menart; Congress/treaty, 52, 151, 195, 197
Arthur, King, 163, 171
artillery, 39, 43, 101, 129, 133, 142, 143–7, 152, 155, 156, 192, 208, 214, 221, 224
Artois, county, 15, 16, 18, 21, 24, 25–6, 27, 29, 36, 59, 76, 78, 93, 103, 111–14, 122, 124, 152, 154, 226; *aides*/Estates, 104, 114, 120
Artois, Margaret, countess of, 15, 16
Artois, Robert, count of, 95

239

Moses, 178; Well, 169–70
Mude, 114
Mulart, Symon, 177
Mulhouse, 202, 206
Murten, 202, 216, 218; battle, 124, 129, 192, 217–19, 220–21; Museum, 192; siege, 216–17
Murtenwald, 218
music, 78, 143, 159, 168–9, 170, 176, 177, 181, 184, 187

Naarden, 132
Namur, 84, 137, 143
Namur, county, 18, 100, 130, 148, 197
Namur, William II, count of, 84, 141
Nancy, 135, 183, 201, 211, 212, 221–4; battle, 4, 128, 192, 194, 224–5, 227
Nani, Alexander, bishop of Forlì, 187
Naples, 163
Naples, kingdom, 8, 23, 72, 73, 128, 160, 183, 187; archives, 47; see Alfonso, Farrante
Narbonne, Aimeri de, 163, 170
Nassau, counts, 68
Nassau, Adolf von, archbishop-elector of Mainz, 73
Nassau, Engelbert II, count of, 68, 84
Nassau, John IV, count of, 68, 84
Neauville, Hervé de, 86
Nesle, 154, 155, 156, 206
Neuchâtel, 214, 202; count: see Hochberg, king of; Lake, 210, 213–14
Neuchâtel, Claude de, lord du Fay, 121, 125
Neychâtel, Henry de, 208
Neuchâtel, Jehan, count of Fribourg and of, 84
Neuss, 135, 146; siege, 57, 68, 73, 81, 123–124, 128, 129, 145–50, 155, 156, 169, 184, 186, 201, 209, 211, 215
Nevers, bishops: see Danguel, Germain
Nevers, county, 14, 18, 78, 109
Nevers, Charles de Bourgogne, count of Rethel and of, 60
Nevers, Jehan de Bourgogne, count of, Étampes and of, 54, 60, 155, 172
Newcastle merchants, 43
New York, Metropolitan Museum, 191

Nicholas V, pope, 6
Nicopolis (Nikopol), crusade of, 9, 72, 78, 105, 125, 157–9, 166
Nijmegen, siege, 133, 147
Nine Worthies, the, 173
Nivelles, 115, 139
Nördlingen, 46
Normandy, 11, 51, 53
North, Council of the, 109
Norway, 5, 7, 73, 186
Norwich, bishop of: see Despenser; merchants, 43
Nozeroy, 215
Nürnberg, 71

Ockham, William of, 6
Ogier of Denmark, 171
Oleye, treaty of, 142, 143
Oom, Godscalc, 120
Orange, princes of: see Chalon
Orbe, 204, 210, 215
ordinance, companies of the, 126–7, 128
Orleans, 156
Orleans, Charles, duke of, 62
Orleans, Louis, duke of, 49–50, 62, 165, 173
Orleans, Mary of Cleves, duchess of, 67, 68
Orsova, 158
Ostend, 41
Othée, 144; battle of, 71, 126, 139–41, 144, 166, 174
Oudenaarde, 112, 172
Oudewater, 130

Padua, Giuliano de, 188
Padua, Marsilio of, 6
painting, 40, 72, 77, 78, 162, 167–8, 176, 191
Panigarola, J. P., 47, 80, 81, 126, 149, 150, 169, 188, 212, 216, 219
Paris, 25, 41, 44, 49, 50–51, 62, 76, 78, 87, 91, 110, 111, 123, 125, 137, 142, 153, 154, 155, 165, 186; Bibliothèque Nationale, 35, 190; chambre des comptes, 55; Hôtel d'Artois, 95, 190; Louvre, 171, 191; Parlement, 100, 108, 138, 195, 196, 199; Place de Grève, 93; University, 165, 196
Passe-Temps Michault, Le, 166

Pastoralet, 165
Pavia, 91, 171
Peñiscola, 20
Péronne, 74, 145, 154, 155; treaty, 54, 198
  Péronne, Roye and Montdidier, 18, 53, 155
Perwez, Henry, lord of, 138–9
Perwez, Thierry de, 138
Petit, Jehan, 165
Petit Jehan de Saintré, 166
Petrarch, F., 4, 10
Pfettisheim, Conrad, 208
Pheasant, Feast of the, 105, 159, 176, 194
Philip II, king of Spain, 190
Picards/Picardy, 84, 93, 132, 136, 139, 144, 148, 152, 153–4, 160, 197, 220
Picquigny, 156
Piedmont, 209; troops, 148
Pisa, 72
Pisan, Christine de, 77, 164
Pius II, pope, 82
Plancher, U., 35
plate, 40, 167, 173, 176, 192
Poeke, 136
poetry/verse, 166–7
Poitiers, battle of, 14
Poitiers, Alienor de, 184
Poitiers, Philippe de, 148
Poland, 7–8, 48, 72, 73; Ladislas, prince of, 72
Poligny, 87, 119; bailiwick, 110
Pompey, 189
Pont-à-Mousson, 222
Pont-de-Norges, church of St Anthony, 185
Pontailler, Guy de, 136
Pontarlier, 211
Ponthieu, county, 22
Poperinge, 152
popes/papacy, 4, 6, 8, 10, 47, 48, 57–9, 69, 73, 92, 160, 170, 185–6, 201; *see* Benedict XIII, Clement VII, Eugenius IV, Gregory XI, Martin V, Nicholas V, Pius II, Urban V
Portinari, Tommaso, 91–2, 188
Portugal/Portuguese, 7, 10, 23, 48, 72, 163, 167, 184; merchants, 43; *see* Alfonso V, John I
Portugal, Henry the Navigator, prince of, 72

Portugal, John of, duke of Coimbra, 72
Poucques, J. de, 87
Prague University, 13
printing, 9, 55, 208
Prise Gaulax, 214
Prophets, the, 170, 173
Provence, 63, 160
Prussia, 158; *see* Teutonic Order
Public Weal, war of the, 28, 54, 60, 107, 142, 155

Ramstein, Bernhart von, 148
ransoms, 14, 63, 159
Rapondi, Dino, 11, 90–91, 171, 187–8
records, 34–47, 90, 96, 101, 119, 177, 186–7
Regensburg, 57, 160
Reiffenberg, F. A. F. T. de, 46
Renaud of Montauban, 172
Renty, lord of: *see* Croy, A. *and* P. de
Repreuves, Jaques de, 148
Rethel, county, 15, 16, 18, 78, 112
Rheims, 52, 53
Rhine, River, 12, 29, 52, 54, 57, 82, 146, 147–9, 160, 201, 223
Rhine, electors-palatine of, 69
Rhine, Frederick I (the Victorious), elector and count palatine of the, 8, 73
Rhine, Ludwig of Zweibrucken, count palatine of the, 64
Rhodes, 157, 159
Rhône, River, 160
Richard II, king of England, 17
Rochefort, Guillaume de, 94, 209
Rolin, Anthoine, lord of Aymeries, 87, 118
Rolin, Guillaume, lord of Beauchamp, 87–8
Rolin, Jehan, bishop of Autun and cardinal, 58, 87
Rolin, Nicolas, chancellor, 58, 83, 87–88, 118, 191, 198
Romance of the Rose, 173–4
Rome, 92; crown, 199
Romont, count: *see* Savoy, Jaques de Savoie
Roosebeke, battle of, 16, 91, 136, 141, 173
Rossano, Troylo da, and sons, 128